TH ADVENTURE GUIDE TO BARBADOS

Harry S. Pariser

MPC
HUNTER
PUBLISHING INC

Hunter Publishing, Inc.
300 Raritan Center Parkway
Edison NJ 08818
(201) 225 1900

ISBN 1-55650-277-X

© 1990 Hunter Publishing, Inc.

All rights reserved. No part of this publication may be reproduced, stored in a retrieval system, or transmitted in any form, or by any means, electronic, mechanical, photocopying, recording or otherwise, without the written permission of the publisher.

Printed in Singapore through Palace Press

Published in the UK by:
Moorland Publishing Co. Ltd.
Moor Farm Road, Airfield Estate
Ashbourne, Derbyshire DE6 1HD
England

ISBN (UK) 086190-420-6

Photo Credits

Sam Lord's Castle: 4, 36, cover. Barbados Tourist Board: 15, 45, 50, 66, 76, 80, 107, 139, 166, 201, 216. Peter Rothholz Associates: 42, 202, 208. Atlantis Submarine: 94. Robin Bainnson: 190. All others by Harry S. Pariser. Cover photo: St. Philip coast.

ACKNOWLEDGMENTS

I would like to thank my publisher Michael Hunter and his staff and my mapmaker Joyce Huber of PhotoGraphics. For their invaluable comments I would like to thank Francis Roman and Dr. John Gilmore as well as Betty Carillo-Shannon and Elombe Mottley. Dave of Jasmine and Junie Tantolo were both of tremendous assistance when my MacIntosh computer and Jasmine hard disk failed. Finally, I would like to express my gratitude for their tolerance to my flatmates—Susie Poulelis, Winnie Lam, and Regina Maher—during the period of writing this manuscript.

CONTENTS

INTRODUCTION	1
THE LAND	2
FLORA AND FAUNA	7
HISTORY	17
ECONOMY	33
THE PEOPLE	38
LANGUAGE	51
RELIGION	56
MUSIC	65
THE ARTS	71
FESTIVALS AND EVENTS	75
FOOD AND DRINK	77
PRACTICALITIES	85
BRIDGETOWN AND ST. MICHAEL'S PARISH	125
THE NORTHERN PARISHES AND THE SCOTLAND DISTRICT	151
SAINT JAMES AND THE PLATINUM COAST	153
ST. THOMAS PARISH	163
ST. JOSEPH PARISH AND BATHSHEBA	167
ST. ANDREW'S PARISH	173

Contents

SAINT PETER'S PARISH AND SPEIGHTSTOWN	179
SAINT LUCY'S PARISH	193
THE SOUTHERN PARISHES	199
SAINT JOHN'S PARISH	205
ST. PHILIP'S PARISH	211
CHRIST CHURCH PARISH AND THE GOLD COAST	221
ISLAND WIDE ACCOMMODATION FINDER	233
GLOSSARY	249
BOOKLIST	255
INDEX	257

ABOUT THE AUTHOR

Harry S. Pariser was born in Pittsburgh and grew up in a small town in southwestern Pennsylvania. After graduating from Boston University with a B.S. in Public Communications in 1975, Harry hitched and camped his way through Europe, traveled down the Nile by steamer, and by train through Sudan. After visiting Uganda, Rwanda, and Tanzania, he traveled by passenger ship from Mombasa to Bombay, and then on through South and Southeast Asia before settling down in Kyoto, Japan, where he studied Japanese and ceramics while supporting himself by teaching English to everyone from tiny tots to Buddhist priests. Using Japan as a base, he returned to other parts of Asia: trekking to the vicinity of Mt. Everest in Nepal, taking tramp steamers to remote Indonesian islands like Adonara, Timor, Sulawesi, and Ternate, and visiting rural areas in China. He returned to the United States in 1984 from Kanazawa, Japan, via the Caribbean where he did research for two travel guides: Guide to Jamaica and Guide to Puerto Rico and the Virgin Islands, the first editions of which were published in 1986. Returning to Japan in 1986, he lived in the city of Kagoshima—a city at the southern tip of Kyushu which lies across the bay from an active volcano. During that year and part of the next, he taught English and wrote numerous articles for *The Japan Times*. He currently lives in San Francisco. Besides traveling and writing, his other pursuits include printmaking, painting, cooking, hiking, photography, reading, and listening to music—especially jazz.

HELP US KEEP THIS GUIDE UP-TO-DATE

In today's world, things change so rapidly that it's impossible for one person to keep up with everything happening in any one place. This is particularly true in the Caribbean, where situations are always in flux. Travel books are like automobiles: they require fine tuning and frequent overhauls to keep in shape. Help us keep this book in shape! We require input from our readers so that we can continue to provide the best, most current information available. Please write to let us know about any inaccuracies, new information, or misleading suggestions. Although we try to make our maps as accurate as possible, errors do occur. If you have any suggestions for improvement or places that should be included, please let us know about it.

We especially appreciate letters from female travelers, visiting expatriates, local residents, and hikers and outdoor enthusiasts. We also like hearing from experts in the field as well as from local hotel owners and individuals wishing to accommodate visitors from abroad.

INTRODUCTION

Barbados: the very name conjures up an aura of mystery. There's an almost rhythmic beat to it. In fact, its name is Portuguese—allegedly after the island's bearded fig trees which indelibly impressed the first explorers. A hybrid blend of Africa and England set in the tropics, this "singular isle" combines British institutions, architecture, and style with open, African-style hospitality. Nowhere in the world have African and British cultures combined in such a remarkable synthesis. Nicknamed "Bimshire" or "Little England" because its land—reforested with green and yellow slopes of sugar cane fields—came to resemble the motherland, the island's shape has been compared to that of a ham, a leg of mutton, a pear-shaped emerald, or a lopsided pear with the stem end pointing north. All of 21 miles long by a "smile" wide, Barbados, an island of dramatic contrasts, offers a variety of picture postcard terrains compacted into one small area. Its gentle west coast—graced with pink and white beaches—contrasts vividly with the rough and ragged eastern-facing Atlantic coast. In addition to a smorgasboard of beaches, there are fantastic panoramas, densely-foliated tropical gullies, and breathtaking stretches of craggy coast. In addition, the intelligent and perceptive visitor has a chance to gain a great deal just by traveling around and interacting. In few places in the world are people as receptive and accepting of strangers. For such a small island, there's an enormous amount to take in. The island's geological history has transformed it into a living laboratory for studying the workings of the earth; the nature-rendered ecological effects of the erosion in the Scotland District and the manmade transformation of a heavily forested island into a vast plain of sugarcane bear witness to the effects on geology and ecology wrought by both man and nature. Finally, the island's greathouses, old churches, and forts bring history to life. For its size, one can envision no place in the world more jam packed with variety and experiences than Barbados.

THE LAND

the big picture: The islands of the Caribbean extend in a 2,800-mile (4,500-km) arc from the western tip of Cuba to the small Dutch island of Aruba. The region is sometimes extended to include the Central and S. American countries of Belize (the former colony of British Honduras), the Yucatan, Surinam, Guiana, and Guyana. The islands of Jamaica, Hispaniola, Puerto Rico, the U.S. and British Virgin Islands, along with Cuba, the Cayman, and Turks and Caicos islands form the Greater Antilles. The name derives from the early geographers, who gave the name "Antilia" to hypothetical islands thought to lie beyond the no less imaginary "Antilades." In general, the land is steep and volcanic in origin. To the S are the lesser Antilles whose islands include the Windward and Leewards, Barbados, Trinidad, Tobago, and Grenada.

Introduction 3

geography: Lying as far east as Nova Scotia and as far south as Senegal, Barbados is the most easterly of the Caribbean islands, lying 200 miles (322 km) NNE of Trinidad and 100 miles (161 km) ESE of St. Lucia. Farther afield to the N are Miami, 1,611 miles (2,592 kms); New York City, 2,000 miles (3,220 kms); and Toronto, 2,429 miles (3,908 kms). On the other side of the ocean lie London, 4,195 miles (6,750 kms) and Luxembourg, 4,500 miles (7,240 kms). With an area of 166 sq mi (430 sq. km) extending 21 miles (34 km) N to S and 14 miles (23 km) E to W, it is one of the Americas' most miniscule nations. Viewed from the S and W, the island appears flat with ridges extending up to about 1,000 feet (300 m) and then falling steeply off to the sea. Unlike the Windward Islands some 100 miles to the W, Barbados has literally pulled itself up by its own bootstraps. Its base originated with the compression, folding and uplifting of the sea floor. During the course of subsequent upliftings and sea level fluctuations, billions of coral polyps willed their skeletal structures so that the island might secure a limestone cap—over 300 feet (90 m) thick in some locations—atop its sedimentary base. Later uplifting and tilting formed the island's terraced landscape which rises toward the Atlantic side. Geologically speaking, the island is young: somewhere between 750,000 and a million years old. By way of contrast, parts of Western Australia are more than three thousand million years old. In places like Hackleton's Cliff and at Cherry Tree Hill in the Scotland District, the land falls away abruptly—having eroded swiftly over time because it lacks the protection of the spongelike coral cap which soaks up erosion-causing rain. The presence of this coral layer elsewhere, in turn, means that the only stable streams are found in the Scotland District. In other locations streams only arise during flash flooding in coral gullies. Most of these gullies are believed to have been the result of cracking in the layer of the coral cap. Another theory is that they were formed by collapsed underground stream channels which once interconnected caverns. But the lack of rivers is compensated for somewhat by the deliciousness of the drinking water. And there's a good reason why Barbados has such delicious water. Because seawater has a higher specific gravity than fresh, it serves as a seal to lock in the enormous reservoirs of fresh

water it surrounds. While the largest of these stores lies under St. George's Valley, the best known of the island's underground channels is Cole's Cave. The highest point is Mt. Hillaby at 1,105 ft. (336 m) near the island's center. To its S, the land descends steeply to the broad St. George Valley. Estimated to be a comparatively youthful 350,000 years old, Christ Church Ridge rises 400 feet between the valley and the sea. Coral reefs encircle the coast.

Climate

The island has a delightful climate. Located within the belt of the steady NE trade winds, its mild, subtropical weather varies little throughout the year. Winter temperatures average from 70-85°; summers (75-87°) are hotter and humid. The island's lowest recorded temperature is 59° (15° C). Few days per year are entirely without sunshine. The E and SE coasts cool down delightfully at night during the winter. Rain, which usually consists of short showers, is most likely to occur from July through the end of November; the driest months are February and March. Although the average rainfall is about 60 inches (1,525 mm), annual precipitation totals actually vary from 40 in. (101.60 cm) on the coasts to 90 inches (228.60 cm) along the central ridge region. Winds prevail from the N during the winter and early spring months and come in from the SE during the rest of the year.

hurricanes: There's always something to spoil a utopia, and the Caribbean as an area is by no means immune. The region as a whole ranks third worldwide in the number of hurricanes per year. These low-pressure zones should not be taken lightly. Where the majority of structures are poorly constructed, a hurricane is serious business, and property damage from them may run in the hundreds of millions of dollars. A hurricane begins as a relatively small tropical storm, known as a cyclone

---

The St. Philip coast

BARBADOS

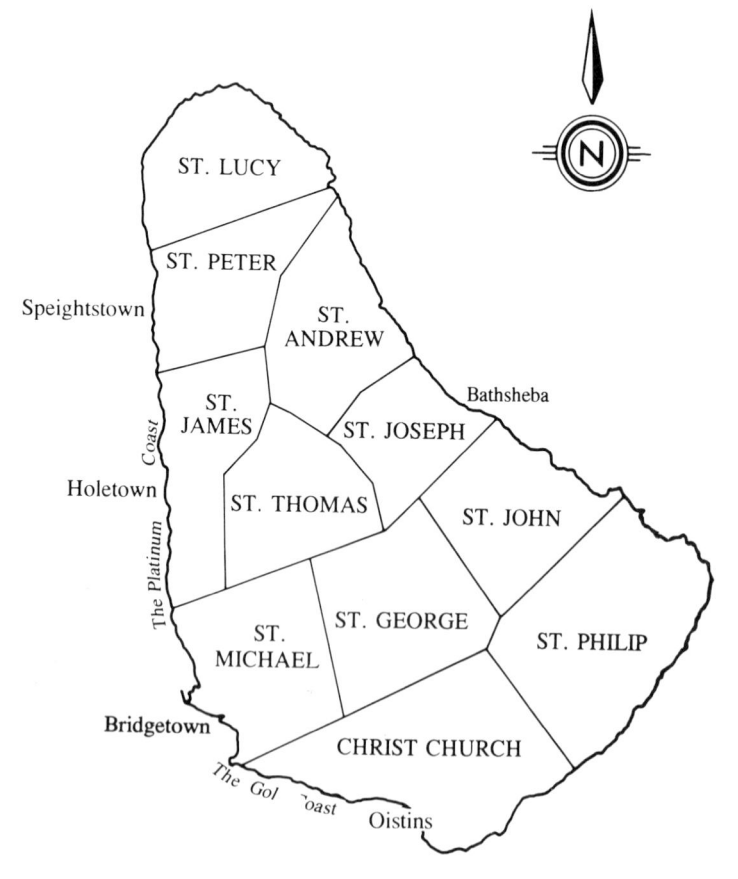

when its winds reach a velocity of 39 mph (62 kph). At 74 mph (118 kph) it is upgraded to hurricane status, with winds of up to 200 mph (320 kph) and ranging in size from 60–1,000 miles (100–1,600 km) in diameter. A small hurricane releases energy equivalent to the explosions of six atomic bombs per second. A hurricane may be compared to an enormous hovering engine that uses the moist air and water of the tropics as fuel, carried hither and thither by prevailing air currents—generally eastern trade winds which intensify as they move across warm ocean waters. When cooler, drier air infiltrates it as it heads N, the hurricane begins to die, cut off from the life-sustaining ocean currents that have nourished it from infancy. Routes and patterns are unpredictable. As for their frequency: "June—too soon; July—stand by; August—it must; September—remember." So goes the old rhyme. Unfortunately, hurricanes are not confined to July and August. Hurricanes forming in Aug. and Sept. typically last for two weeks while those that form in June, July, Oct., and Nov. (many of which originate in the Caribbean and the Gulf of Mexico) generally last only seven days. Approximately 70 percent of all hurricanes (known as Cabo Verde types) originate as embryonic storms coming from the W coast of Africa. Fortunately though, they are comparatively scarce in the area around Barbados. Since record-keeping began, a number of hurricanes have wreaked havoc on the island. The most serious of these have been in 1780, 1831, and 1898. The most recent hurricane to hit was in September 1955—which damaged the S extensively. In recent years it seems as though an invisible shield is protecting the island. Every time one is predicted to hit, it either veers N or S.

FLORA AND FAUNA

Plant Life

In order to appreciate the island's wealth of flora, one must dwell for a moment on what has vanished. The thick forests—

once so close knit that they impeded agricultural cultivation—are a thing of the past. After colonization began, ship after ship bore away tons of felled logwood, fustic, lignum vitae, and West Indian cedar while others of their majestic species ended up used as beams in great houses or as fuel to fire cauldrons in sugar manufacturing plants. As the population and sugar's value climbed so were the island's forests ruthlessly pruned back until the expanses of forest with their thick, twisted tropical undergrowth gave way to smoothly rolling fields of cane. By the 1660s, there was less woodland on Barbados than in most districts of England. A 1671 report noted that "at the Barbadoes all the trees are destroyed, so that wanting wood to boyle their sugar, they are forced to send for coales from England." One particularly fine wood tree, the mastic, was driven into extinction. Today, reminders of the island's virgin verdant past remain only at **Foster Hall Wood** and **Forest Hall Land**, both near Hackleton's Cliff and at **Turner's Hall Woods**, St. Andrew, in the Scotland District. Because Barbados is much drier than neighboring Dominica, St. Vincent, or Trinidad, it lacks their rich profusion of flora. One of the best places to see a sampler of island's trees is in Bridgetown's Queen's Park.

trees: Indigenous to the forests of Honduras, the mahogany tree was introduced sometime between 1780–1800. Surprisingly, it sheds its leaves in April and May. Watch out for its falling fruit which can be dangerous! Native to Indonesia, the majestic, heavily-branched tamarind was imported around 1650 possibly via Mexico. Its branches once provided switches for beating slaves. Nowadays, its pods are exported to Britain where they form one of the key ingredients in Lea and Perrin's Worcestershire Sauce. A common feature on sugar estates where it was planted as a shade tree near houses, the low lying evergreen tree stands with stately dignity—its thick, highly horizontal branches spreading widely. Originally from India, it was introduced around the mid-18th C. It can still be found near the greathouses or dwelling where it provided shade for beasts of burden and a spot for siesta for slaves and indentured servants. One of the taller trees with an average height of 150 ft., the casuarina or "mile tree" waves with majestic grace in the breeze. A native of N Australia where it flourishes in deserts, it was imported to Barbados about 1870. Originally introduced as a windbreak, it soon gained fame as an ornamental; an extensive root system renders it immune from drought. Like the casuarina, the cabbage palm also lines the sides of Bajan roads. Better known internationally as the royal palm, its Bajan name comes from the bud in the center of its palm which can be eaten as a vegetable. Graceful coconut palms frame the island's coastline and its beautiful beaches. The most useful tree on the island, its nut provides food, oil, and soap; its fronds are used in basketmaking, to make brooms, and to cover roofs. Also known as the Lent tree because it blooms during the Lenten season, the devil's tree, African tulip tree, or Judas tree possesses nearly-circular dark green leaves and intricate blood-red flowers.

unique natives: The indigenous bearded fig is found largely along gully walls or inland cliffs where it perches precariously, its aerial roots dangling from its branches. Found chiefly in gardens, the Bajan ebony or shak shak is known as the "mother in law's tongue." This tree's long, straw colored pods clatter on and on in the breeze like a remonstrating mother in law. The tree's wood, along with that of the fustic, has been used to make wheels for the island's donkey carts. Its lovely white or green sweet-scented flowers appear in April or May. The twisted, horizontal branches of the clammy-cherry rise 30 ft. into the air. After blooming in April and May, it produces a semi-transparent orange berry which schoolboys use as glue. Large, symmetrical, strong, and stout, the sandbox tree's name comes from its fruit; the ribbed peel, when de-seeded and flattened, was used to sprinkle sand used for blotting ink spilt on parchment. Its other name, monkey's pistol, comes from its poisonous moon-shaped seeds which fire off into the distance as the pods split open. A local legend insists that when this happens a lizard wedding has just taken place. The tree's acrid, milky sap irritates the skin. Possessing a stout trunk covered with sharp prickles, this tree may rise as high as 100 feet. Possibly native, the calabash is heavily branched, deciduous, and has a flat crown. Its gourd-like fruit can be used as a utensil when dried and emptied. Mangroves grow in swampy areas along the coast. While the white mangrove is widely distributed on the island, the red mangrove is found only in Graeme Hall Swamp. The *ceiba* or silk-cotton tree was once believed by slaves to walk at night. A shade tree, the West Indian almond has an edible but difficult to open fruit.

flowering trees: Introduced to the island in the early 1700s, the white and red frangipanis are closely related species. Better known as the jasmine tree, the white frangipani bears bunches of leaves on forked twigs. At the beginning of the dry season, the leaves fall off to be replaced by the heavily scented flowers. The frangipani's name comes from that of a legendary European perfume whose scent was unparalleled at the time. Unmatched by any other ornamental tree in the tropics, the red flamboyant has distinctive orange-red flowers. While not quite as attractive, another related bloom, the yellow flamboyant, is a close competitor.

fruit trees: These include the mango, tamarind, coconut, guava, and the genip. Prominent deciduous fruit trees include the hog and Chili plum trees, golden apple, sugar apple, pomegranate, and soursop. Fruit trees that flower and fruit irregularly include the dunk, gooseberry, cherry, guava, sapodilla, and star apple.

forbidden fruit: Small, with a short trunk and numerous branches, the machineel grows near the sea. Its elliptical-shaped leaves possess a strange bright green sheen. The machineel secretes an acid which may be deadly. Said to be the original apple in the Garden of Eden, biting into this innocuous-looking yet highly poisonous fruit will cause your mouth to burn and your tongue to swell up. In fact, all parts of this tree are potentially deadly. Cattle, standing under the tree after a torrential tropical downpour, have been known to lose their hides as drops fall from leaves. Other tales tell of locals going blind after a leaf touched an eye. Slaves (in the Virgin Islands to the N) wishing to do away with a particularly despicable master would insert minute quantities of juice into an uncooked potato. Cooked, these small doses were undetectable but always fatal if served to the victim over a long period of time. If you should spot one of these trees—which are not uncommon along the island's beaches—stay well away!

Introduction   11

Machineel trees, St. Peter

others: Other trees include the bead tree or Barbados lilac, the continually-flowering willow, the lavender horse-radish, the bright green wild pine, and the lignum vitae—a hardwood whose name (tree of life) refers to the medicinal qualities attributed to its resinous gum. The trumpet or pop-a-gun tree is easily recognized by its large leaves which are divided into finger-like lobes; they are nearly white underneath. The phallic dildo cactus grows in the drier areas.

vines, plants, and flowers: The bright orange leafless stems of the parasitic love vine are a frequent sight. At one time one could be fined for having the vine on one's property. Another creeper is the clinging creeper golden shower. The climbing crab eye vine has poisonous black-spotted red seeds. Known locally as the maypole, the century plant lives about ten years, not the 100 its name suggests. As the plant blooms for its first and last time in its last year, the canary-yellow bilbils wilt and cast their seed to the wind. Its bouyant stems are used by fishermen when they gather sea urchins. Leaving the stem to float above water, they tie a net bag on to it in which they insert their harvest. Colored a beautiful red with yellow borders and possessing protruding stamen arching up like antennae, "Pride of Barbados" *(Caesalpinia pulcherima)* is the national flower.

Animal Life

As with its flora, Barbados's animal population has been deeply influenced by its human settlement patterns. Unlike mainland Guyana—where gargantuan primeval forests still maintain a universe for wildlife—Bajan fauna features your usual barnyard stuff: cows, pigs, horses, sheep, chickens, dogs, cats, mules, and goats. There are very few indigenous species of any genre. The most spectacular native species, the Bajan parrot, has been driven into extinction.

mammals: On an island that is almost totally cultivated and so heavily populated, it takes such a lot of resourcefulness to survive that only the most intelligent and the smallest of the wild kingdom have been able to adapt. The most notable survivor is the Barbados green monkey *(Cepus Capucinus)*. Widely distributed in West Africa, it measures some 16–18 inches excluding its lengthy tail, and has a black face fringed with white hairs. Probably introduced by sailors manning slave ships who brought them over for pets, Bajans regard the creature as an infernal nuisance—for it ravages both vegetable patches and cane fields—and there is a bounty out for its tail. One popular use for them is in medical research. In one particular, the modern era has actually assisted their continued survival. Because Bajans now cook on gas, the gullies are now thick with brush—allowing the monkeys to thrive. Other introduced animals include the hare and raccoon. Mongooses, imported from Jamaica (which had, in turn, imported them from India) to combat rats and now-extinct poisonous reptiles, have propogated to the point where they too have now become an agricultural pest—attacking lambs, calves, and baby pigs as well as the reptile and bird population. Although the Barbados

Legislature ordered their extermination in 1904, they can still be seen today darting among the bushes.

birds: There are over 18 species of resident birds, including brightly colored wild parakeets, pelicans, and egrets. One of the most common and most prolific is the yellow-breasted bananaquit also known as the sugar bird or yellow breast. Addicted to fruit juices and flower nectar, this small, sooty grey-and-yellow breasted creature is often seen around flowers and fruit trees. Its white eyestripe and the coral-red patch on its bill make it even more conspicuous. Another very attractive but rarely sighted bird is the golden warbler whose yellow mass is laced with streaks of dark chestnut. It may also have a green or golden tint. Creatively colored in orange, black, and yellow, the Christmas bird winters in the island. Larger than the ground dove, the thick-set wood (or Zenaida) dove combines a grey body with sprinklings of black, white, and cinnamon brown. Its soft cooing cry so much resembles a chant of praise that Bajans have long maintained that it is uttering "Moses spake God's word." Making its debut on the local scene only this century when it arrived from South America, the yellow-breasted brown colored grass finch resides in fields and savannahs. Often confused with the blackbird because the male of the species is the same color, the cow bird or cattle egret arrived from South America in 1899. Its residency threatens the other species because it lays its eggs in other bird's nests, thus posing difficulties for the survival of their young. Also known as the cobbler or the man-o'-war bird, the nearly jet black frigate bird swoops ominously overhead, occasionally veering down to the water to make a capture. The rarely-visiting brown pelicans fly in small flocks. Atlantic birds that winter on Barbados include the wood sandpiper, the Greenland wheatear, the alpine swift, the black-headed gull, and the ruff. There are two varieties of hummingbirds: the smaller, straight-billed Antillean crested hummer and the larger, curve-billed emerald-throat hummer. The island's other species include hawks, grey plover, snipes, sandpipers, doves, sparrows (finches), thrushes, parakeets, blackbirds (grackles), yellow breasted moustache birds, West Indian crows, wild pigeons, and canaries.

reptiles and amphibians: The two species of snakes are harmless. There are seven varieties of lizards. The giant toad or "bull frog" immigrated from South America and made itself right at home. Known locally as crapauds, they were traditionally used in *obeah* (magic). One practice by an *obeah* man in Speightstown was to take a police summons, fold and stuff it into an unfortunate frog's mouth, and then sew the mouth shut. After the frog was dumped from a boat in the ocean, the petitioner would be assured that his or her case would be set aside. Most notable (some might say infamous) among the island's cold blooded critters is the "whistling frog" which frequently keeps visitors awake at nights with its piercing hum. The brown and yellow adult is one inch long, and the female is the larger of the two. It has no tadpole stage. Instead, ten days after deposition, offspring emerge from their formative jelly ready to pump their lungs out.

insects and spiders: These include the common house fly, the destructive cabbage white butterfly, bees, wood ants, three different varieties of mosquitoes, and grasshoppers. The local centipede is known as a "fortyleg." One of the biggest miseries to visitors is the merrywing, the local biting sandfly. But one consolation is that Barbados has fewer of them than other islands; they generally are found only in "dead sand" areas which the tide does not cover. Butterflies here are called "bats;" and what the Western English speaking world calls bats are known as "leather bats."

sealife: Divers and snorkelers will find a dazzling array of coral, fish, and sponges of all colors of the rainbow. Delicate in appearance only, yellow or purple (depending on diet) sea fan, a coral with fanlike branches, is so strong that it will support a man's weight without tearing. Normally the size of a pinhead, the sea jewel *(valonia)* is the largest single-cell animal in existence. Saclike and round in appearance, it reflects the colors of whatever's nearby. A kaleidoscope of fish include the doctorfish, grouper, cavalla, old wife (ale wife), one-eye, silver angelfish, sergeant fish, marine jewel, and trunkfish. Other species of fish include the leather jacket, barracuda, sawfish, parrotfish, weakfish, lionfish, big-eye fish, bananafish, lady-

Barbados coral

fish, puffer, sea-bat, sardine, mullet, grouper, king fish (wahoo), albacore (yellow-finned tuna), Spanish and frigate mackerels, red snapper, eel, barracuda, and a variety of sharks. But, if one were to pick a "national" fish, it undoubtedly would be the flying fish which forms the national dish when served with *coo coo*. Attracted by the plankton-rich waters surrounding the island and brought in by the warm water currents, their presence has given the island its nickname, "Land of the Flying Fish." Their season generally runs from October through July. Year by year, however, their numbers have been decreasing. Another delicacy, the spiny lobster, resides 20–30 ft. down in homes dug out under the reefs. Avoid trampling on that armed knight of the underwater sand dunes, the sea urchin. Another marine creature to keep away from is the floating Portuguese Man-of-War which is mainly found on the Atlantic side. Actually a colony of marine organisms, its stinging tentacles can be extended or retracted; worldwide, there have been reports of trailing tentacles reaching 50 feet! Unlike other islands, there are no jellyfish.

coral reefs: Indisputably the most important living organisms in the island's history, corals produce the calcium carbonate responsible for the buildup of most of the island's offlying cays and islets as well as most of the sand on the beaches. Bearing the brunt of waves, they also conserve the shoreline. Although reefs were formed milleniums ago, they are in a constant state of flux. Seemingly solid, they actually depend upon a delicate ecological balance to survive. Deforestation, dredging, temperature change, an increase or decrease in salinity, or sewage discharge may kill them. Because temperature ranges must remain between 68° and 95°, they are only found in the tropics. Acting more like plants than animals, they survive through photosynthesis: the algae inside the coral polyps do the work while the polyps themselves secrete calcium carbonate and stick together for protection from waves and boring sponges. Reefs originate as the polyps die, forming a base for the next generation.

corals: Closely related to the sea anenomes, they may be divided into three groups. The hard or stony corals (such as staghorn, brain, star, or rose) secrete a limey skeleton. The horny corals (for example sea plumes, sea whips, sea fans, and gorgonians) have a supporting skeleton-like structure known as a gorgonin (after the head of Medusa). The last category consists of the soft corals. Nocturnal, corals snack at night by steering plankton into their mouths with their tentacles. The coral appear to be able to survive in such packed surroundings through their symbiotic relationship with the algae present in their tissues: Coral exhale carbon dioxide and the algae consume it, producing needed oxygen. Not prone to celibacy or sexual prudery, corals reproduce sexually and asexually through budding.

Barbadian reefs: The island's offshore reefs have played an important role in its history, acting as a natural barrier against conquest. Most common are fringing reefs which occur close to shore, perhaps separated by a small lagoon. Elongated and narrow bank or ribbon reefs are offshore in deep water. Atolls and barrier reefs are absent.

Introduction 17

Archer's Bay, St. Lucy

HISTORY

the start: Barbados's beginnings differ from those of other Caribbean islands in at least one respect: Columbus never arrived to "discover" the island. Nor did he name it. Some unknown Portuguese or Spanish explorer did. The island may have been named for its "bearded" fig trees which send down aerial roots from their branches. Another theory is that the island is named after a tribe of bearded Indians whose blood had mixed with that of ancient African explorers. Sixteenth C. variants of its name appearing on Spanish charts include St. Barbado, Barbudos, Bernardo, and even Barnodo. It is believed that those first to settle were members of the Saladoid/ Barrancoid culture—named after the Venezuelan spot on the Orinoco River where their pottery was first unearthed. They may have arrived in Barbados as early as 2,000 years ago. Although little archaeological evidence remains, it *is* known that they were predominantly farmers and fishermen. Seven hundred or so years later these placid farmers and fisherfolk are thought to have already been supplanted by the Arawaks. Also hailing from the NE sector of the enormous continent to the S, the Arawaks brought along their crafts, including a simple but stylistic pottery style. Lacking the implements and beasts of burden that would have made large scale agriculture feasible, their cultivation consisted of literally "scraping by"— carving out meager plots in the bush. Utilizing tools fabricated from conch shells, they congregated near the ocean where they supplemented their limited diet (of cassava, maize, peanuts, squash, and papaya) with fish. The Arawaks lived on Barbados until the 1200s when the fiercer, more nomadic Caribs are believed to have arrived. The Caribs—after whom the Caribbean is named—may have lived on the island for up to 300 years. While the Caribs lacked the artisan skills of the Arawaks, they were master canoe builders. Their name comes from *caribal* which is the Spanish word for cannibal—although it remains uncertain whether the Caribs actually ate human flesh. Indeed, little is known about all of these earlier inhabitants; their differentiation has been based on their differing pottery styles, something which may have evolved naturally over the course of time.

English settlement: Arriving to settle in 1627, the English found an uninhabited paradisical island of spectacular beauty. Where were the Caribs? While there are no historical records, it seems fairly certain that the usual scenario had taken place. In the best dog-eat-dog tradition of the Americas, they had been carted off to work Spanish and Portuguese mines and plantations. The ones who had been left behind succumbed to the White Man's dreadful diseases. This massive genocide happened between the first visits in the early 1500s by Spanish or Portuguese ships and the 1536 visit of Portuguese navigator Pedro A Campos. What happened in Barbados was replicated with variations all over the Caribbean. Today, the only surviving Caribbean Caribs live in a small reservation on Dominica. The major artifact left by the Indians on Barbados was a bridge over the arm of the sea at what is now Bridgetown. In July 1625, the *Olive,* the first English ship to dock, stumbled onto the island by mistake. The ship's captain, John

Powell, reported the discovery to Sir William Courteen, his employer, who in turn ordered him to go back to the island and start a settlement forthwith. After capturing a Spanish ship enroute, Powell decided to return to England and abandon the expedition. Bent on having his own Caribbean island together with its profitable export crops, Sir William Courteen sent out the *William and John* which arrived at Holetown on 17 Feb. 1627. In a complicated series of crafty maneuvers popularly known as the "Great Barbados Robbery," the unscrupulous Earl of Carlisle stole Barbados from Courteen in 1629. Feuding between Carlisle and Courteen factions sapped the island's economic vitality, and the mid-1630s were dubbed "the starving time." In 1639, the nation's Parliament began when the House of Assembly was instituted by the infamously corrupt Gov. Henry Hawley as a representative rubber stamp. A new, more genteel rush of settlers arrived in the 1640s as the English Civil War progressed. Both factions, Cavaliers and Roundheads, peacefully coexisted through a system known as the "Treaty of Turkey and Roast Pork." Anyone who mentioned either "Cavalier" or "Roundhead" would have to provide a young hog and turkey for consumption at his house by all who heard him pronounce the forbidden words. However, the island's Cavaliers gained ascendency, and they proclaimed their loyalty to the Royalist cause on 3 May 1650. In February 1651, a fleet was dispatched to put down this insurgency. This "Barbados Fleet" arrived in October of 1651. Even with the help of the "Virginia Fleet," which arrived subsequently, the English failed to occupy the island. However, a compromise emerged, and the 23-clause Articles of Agreement (also known as The Charter of Barbados) were ratified by the British Parliament in 1652. They allowed for freedom of religion, no taxation without representation, a system of open ports, and a freeholder-elected Assembly. The controversial 4.5 percent duty on all exports was instituted by the Brits in 1663. Over the years this tax provoked frequent conflicts between the plantocracy and the British government.

slaves and sugar: Meanwhile, the colonists had wasted no time beating down the bush and planting cotton and tobacco. Their tobacco, however, paled in the face of Virginia's aromatic blend, and cotton could only be grown near the coast. At a loss for what to do, the colonists were saved by the introduction of sugarcane. This hardy, toothache-fostering weed was soon solely responsible for the deforestation of the entire island. By the 1640s the vast majority of the population consisted of indentured servants and English yeoman farmers. The mix included 10-15 percent African slaves. Slavery was nothing new: it had come with the British. When the *William and John* arrived in 1627, she brought with her 10 slaves, taken from a Portuguese ship captured enroute. Arawak Indians, brought as agricultural consultants from Guyana, were later treacherously doublecrossed and enslaved. Even the whites were not immune: Indentured servants, in some cases political opponents of Oliver Cromwell, were shipped off to the island where they subsisted under oppressive conditions. Some of them had been "barbadosed"—the 17th C equivalent of being "shanghaied." One charming Barbadian method of punishment was to string servants up by their hands and light matches between their fingers! They revolted twice: once in 1634 and once in 1639. But the numbers of indentured servants proved insufficient so the slave trade evolved and flourished. By the early 1650s, slaves outnumbered whites two to one. The immensely increased profitability of the land under sugar cane cultivation was directly responsible for this remarkable socio-economic transformation; this made the importation of slaves—despite the heavy initial investment—financially viable. Sugar had first been brought to the island by Dutchman Pieter Blower in 1637. He brought Brazilian cane with him, and the first vats of rum were brewed. Going down to study in Brazil, the planters learned the ropes of cane growing. Underwriting this effort were the Dutch who provided commodities; supplied cheap loans, insurance, and equipment; and introduced the Bajans to the horrific wonders of the West African slave trade. By 1684, the 60,000 slaves now outnumbered the whites by four to one and white indentured servants by 30 to one! The first planned uprising had taken place in 1675, but it failed because a female slave informed on the conspirators. In retribution, the 17 ringleaders were executed: 11 were beheaded and six were burnt alive. Then, their beheaded bodies were dragged through the streets. Other scares and plots were uncovered in 1683, 1686, 1692, and 1702 and similarly suppressed. On such a small, crowded and deforested island—with a majority of slaves kept in superstitious awe of the powers of their owners—it was nearly impossible for a rebellion to succeed. A dark cloud of misfortune cast its shadow over the last two decades of the 1600s. A fall in the price of sugar was coupled with a smallpox epidemic which decimated the population.

England in the Caribbean: Ironically, the cultivation of sugarcane brought about a remarkable transformation in appearance: the island came to resemble a "Little England"— one with superior weather of course! As the decades wore on, the island became the wealthiest and most profitable of the British Empire's New World possessions. Up until about 1700, Barbados was second only to Massachusetts in population among the colonies and settlements. Unlike the other British islands, whose planters lived in splendid comfort back in jolly old England, the majority of Barbadian planters chose to make the island their home. Holding down the easternmost upwind position, the island was of strategic military importance. From the time of its founding, the island had a militia, the presence of which was largely responsible for the fact that the island never changed hands. It also sheltered imperial forces that were sent out from time to time to fight in the region. As the decades progressed the island became more "civilized" in the British sense of the word. A monthly packet ship carrying cards and letters began arriving in 1703. Codrington College was founded in 1710, and construction of St. Anne's Castle was begun that same year. The *Barbados Gazette*, the island's first newspaper, began publication in 1731. Its editor, Samuel Keimer from Philadelphia, had taught Benjamin Franklin how to use a press. Nevertheless, misfortunes continued to plague the island. Swarms of sugar ants decimated the cane crop in 1760. Two incendiary fires razed Bridgetown in both 1776 and 1777. Killing 4,000 and razing all but four of the churches, the hurricane of 1780 was the worst in the island's history; damage was estimated to be £1,250,000.

the end of slavery: The slave trade was abolished by the British Parliament in 1807. Under the sponsorship of the African Institution, a Slave Registry Bill was introduced in the British Parliament in June of 1815. The lively, antagonistic debate among the planters was picked up by the slaves who—misinterpreting the exchange of dialog—imagined that the bill would emancipate them. On Easter Sunday, 14 April, 1816, cane fields and various trash heaps were set ablaze signalling the beginning of the insurrection. At 1:30 AM on Easter Monday, 15 April, the firing of a cannon in Bridgetown sounded the planters' response. Before the revolt was suppressed a great deal of damage was done. Plantations were burned and sacked and 20 percent of the island's sugar crop was destroyed. Property loss was estimated at £179,000. While only one white was killed, 176 blacks died. Another 214 were executed after a court martial. In 1823, the African Institution was absorbed by the Society for the Mitigation and Gradual Abolition of Slavery which declared that slavery was "opposed to the spirit and precepts of Christianity as well as repugnant to every dictate of natural humanity and justice." A ten point program of reform was circulated in the West Indies by the Secretary of State for the colonies. It met with a tepid response. The planters' love affair with authoritarian power was such that they could not see the light of day, and conditions failed to improve. In 1831, the Great Hurricane struck the island killing 1,591 and causing more than £1,600,000 worth of damage. Passed into law on August 28, 1833, the Emancipation Act took effect on August 1, 1834. The slaves, however, were not to be freed immediately but after a "period of apprenticeship" which was intended to last six years. In 1838, the 4 1/2 percent export duty—long viewed as onerous by the plantocracy—was repealed and replaced with a tax on essential imports. That same year, on August 1, the slaves were finally emancipated, two years ahead of schedule.

post-abolition Barbados: Despite the problems caused by competition with places like Brazil, Louisiana, and Cuba (where slave labor was still in use), the cultivation of the sugar beet in Europe, and fluctuations in the worldwide demand, the planters managed to stay afloat and even prosper. Indeed with wages at 1 shilling per day during the harvest and 10 pence during the rest of the year, the laborers were little more than salaried slaves! The Masters and Servants Act of 1840 established the system of "Located Labor" which bound the ex-slaves as tenants on their former master's estate! In 1843, another milestone was reached, however, when Samuel Jackman Prescod—the son of a white father and a black mother—became the first non-white member of Parliament. After helping to establish the Liberal Party, he retired in 1863. In 1871 there were 161,594 inhabitants including 16,560 whites, 39,578 "coloured," and 105,904 blacks. In early 1876, Governor John Pope-Hennessy attempted to implement a Colonial Office Plan which Bajans feared might pave the way for introducing the Crown Colony system of government and the end of the elected Assembly. Irish to the core, Pope-Hennessy sympathised with the lower classes and let them know how the plan would benefit them. The plantocracy, however, remained virulently intractable. Riots broke out in support of the plan from April 20-22. After 89 estates were attacked by about 1,000 people, eight people were killed in the ensuing suppression. The uprising's most startling feature was that the rioters believed that they had the Governor's blessing. Therefore, they had largely destroyed property rather than person. The affair's aftermath culminated with Pope-Hennessy's transfer to Hong Kong. Judged to be the worst disaster in the island's history, a major cholera epidemic in 1854 killed at least 20,000. The late 1800s were marked by a decline in the sugar industry sparked by high European tariffs and irregular rainfall. The Franchise Act of 1884 opened up suffrage to a slightly wider segment of the population while still excluding the impoverished and landless majority. Considered to be almost singlehandedly responsible for having rescued Barbados from the dreaded clutches of the Crown Colony system and with having pushed through the Franchise Act, mulatto William Conrad Reeves was knighted and served as Chief Justice from 1886–1902. The hurricane of 10 September 1898 devastated 18,000 houses and killed 80.

the 20th Century: The new century had a very unpromising start: an epidemic of smallpox in 1902 was followed by one of yellow fever in 1908. Bajans began to emigrate in record numbers. About 20,000 males went to work on the Panama Canal and remitted "Panama Money" home. Some of this new-found wealth enabled the descendants of slaves to purchase land from indebted planters. Molasses exports to Canada helped compensate for the downturn in the sugar industry. Found to be a suitable crop for the drier areas of the island, cotton became a substantial industry until WWI arrived. The war devastated Europe's beet sugar fields—thus bringing the planters back to sugar. The boom, however, did not last long. In 1920, the market crashed, and sugar plunged from 146 shillings per hundredweight to 18 shillings per hundredweight. The market rebounded in 1923. The 20s saw the passage of a great deal of progressive legislation as well as the establishment of governmental departments dealing with public health, agriculture, and roads. Liberal crusader C. P. Clarke pushed through an Income Tax measure in 1921. Another prominent social crusader was *Herald* columnist Clennell Wilsden Wickham. Yet another was Charles Duncan O'Neal, a doctor who, following in Prescod's footsteps, founded both the Democratic League and the Workingman's Association. C. A. Brathwaite, the League's first candidate, secured a house seat in December 1924. Although other League candidates scored victories, O'Neal himself only secured a seat in 1932—after his health and spirit had deteriorated. Originally modeled on the British Labour party, the Democratic League promulgated the pioneering gospel of such progressive goals as universal suffrage, compulsory education, health and unemployment benefits, and workmen's compensation—ideals which took decades to bear fruit. The 1929 depression hit the Caribbean hard, but the sugar industry was one of those least affected. Preferential assistance by Britain and Canada helped the industry, but the International Sugar Agreement of 1937 restricted the growth of the industry. The number of unemployed swelled as the population grew and emigration outlets were cut off after 1929. Between 1928 and 1935, the world price of sugar was cut in half. As part of the general upheaval affecting the Caribbean in the mid-1930s, riots broke out in 1937. These were blamed on Trinidadian expatriate unionist Clement Payne because they began after a rally protesting his deportation. (Payne's parents, brothers, and sisters were all Bajan-born). Investigating the riots, the Deane Commission found that the Payne incident was merely a "detonator" and that the underlying explosive tension resulted from the desperately harsh economic realities of day-to-day existence. With a mere two percent of the population controlling 30 percent of the national income, combined with a church that appeared still locked in the Middle Ages, the average Bajan had ample reason for discontent. Things just had to change! Given the breath of life as the Barbados Labour party—a name to which it later reverted—the Barbados Progressive League was launched in October 1938. Its first policy statement, released towards the end of the following year, delineated a policy of combining both socialist and democratic principles. The League advocated equal distribution of wealth and material resources in tandem with governmental control of production. While the League's first political triumph came with the passage of the Trade Union Act in 1939, its first political victory came in 1940 when it secured five House of Assembly seats. The Barbados Workers Union was formed in 1941 with G. H. Adams and H. W. Springer from the League serving as President General and Secretary respectively. However, the League was hampered by the island's archaic representative system which still limited voting rights and access to public office to a tiny elite. Taking careful note of the failure of O'Neal's now defunct Democratic League, the Progressive League leadership realized that it must widen its base of supporters if the party was to have any hope of achieving its goals. In order to do this, they introduced a bill that would have provided for complete suffrage as well as the ending of property qualifications which were *de rigueur* for admission to the House. Although the bill failed to pass, the League was successful in enacting both a minimum wage bill and one securing the collection of Death Duties (inheritance taxes). In a 1942 compromise, the income qualification for voters was reduced to an annual income of £20, and women were granted the right to vote and be elected to the House. However, the League failed to eliminate the property requirements required for entry to the House. And, the Legislative Council succeeded in introducing an amendment which made it obligatory for all election candidates to deposit £30 which would go to the Public Treasury should the candidate fail to win a certain proportion of the vote. One notable triumph that year, however, was the passage of the Workmen's Compensation Act. After the election of 1944, the League's representation doubled—from four to eight. Led by W. A. Crawford, the newly formed West Indian Congress Party, whose platform was similar to the Progressive League's, also gained eight seats. In the 1946 elections—because neither party gained a clear majority—the West Indian National Congress Party and the Barbados Labour party (formerly the Progressive League) joined in a coalition government which lasted until 1947. Adams was elected President of the Caribbean Labour Congress in 1947 and, in 1948 his party swept the general elections, capturing half of the 24 seats. The end of the 40s was marked by continued conflict between the more liberal Assembly and the reactionary Legislative Council controlled by the white conservative interests. Finally, the powers of the Council were reined in and those of the Assembly predominated. All Bajans became eligible to vote and property requirements for Assembly membership were eliminated in

Grantley Adams bust, Government Headquarters

time for the General Election of 1951, which the Labour Party also swept. One freshman Assemblyman was Errol Walton Barrow. The more conservative Walcott quarreled continually with leading leftist Barrow and the BWU. When the new ministerial system of government was introduced without including any BWU or left wing BLP members, a major schism occurred. Barrow quit, and the "Siamese twin relationship" between the two parties also came to an end. The Democratic Labour Party (DLP) was formed in 1955. In the 1956 election, the BLP won 15 seats, the DLP four, the PCP (Progressive Conservative Party) four, and Barrow lost his Assembly seat. The cabinet system of government was inaugurated in 1958 with G. H. (later Sir Grantley) Adams as Premier. When Adams was selected as the Prime Minister of the West Indies Federation later that year, his place was taken by Dr. Cummins.

the West Indies Federation: Although Barbados had been represented at the 1932 Dominica Conference on West Indian Federation, Barbadians were not passionate about the concept of federalism. The concept gained steam only in 1938 when Barbadians began to comprehend that only by joining together could the small islands of the British West Indies achieve independence and worldwide recognition. Negotiations began in earnest in Montego Bay in 1947, and the final decision was implemented in London in 1956. Initially, the concept was received with a bang. All of the British West Indian islands' political leaders were strongly in favor, and Grantley Adams led a torch-light procession of 30,000 supporters through the streets of Kingston. However, as time elapsed, spirits cooled and differences emerged. Jamaica's Norman Manley stressed the need for an independent role for his island while Trinidad's Eric Williams preached the gospel of a strong federal government. Although the two leaders' diametrically opposed positions were one major factor in the Federation's demise, it was further weakened right from the start by the failure of the leaders' parties in the 1958 federal elections! The Federation also had aspects of a puppet show. The Queen could legislate on behalf of the Federation in the realms of defense, finance, and external affairs. The Governor General also had the right to veto any legislation he disapproved of. Manley met with

Williams and resolved their difficulties. The truce, however, was only temporary and the negotiations' secrecy had aroused the other island leaders' suspicions. By the time the curtain fell at the end of the Federation's final conference, held at London's Lancaster House in June of 1960, hardly any of the major participants were still on speaking terms. Jamaica seceded in Sept. 1961; Trinidad followed suit in Jan. 1962. After the rest of the "Little Eight" fell down to five and then none, the capsized Federation was dissolved on 31 May 1962.

Barrow on top: Having lost his seat in St. George in 1956, Barrow won a by-election in St. John in 1958. The DLP gained the support of the BWU; Barrow became the Chairman of the DLP; and the DLP swept the 1961 elections. Loaded with dynamism, the new government began a crash program of public works in order to supply work to the nation's unemployed; instituted tuition-free education at all government-aided secondary schools; and inaugurated a system of school meals. The College of Arts and Sciences of the University of the West Indies (UWI) opened its doors in Oct. 1963. Additionally, tourism was expanded, 45 factories were built, civil servants' salaries were increased, and a system of national health insurance was introduced.

independence: The next election was held on 3 Nov. 1966 just a few weeks before independence on November 30th. The DLP won 14 seats, the BLP eight, and the BNP two. Independence Day passed as a matter of course. Barrow's DLP won an overwhelming victory in 1971 only to suffer defeat in 1976 when J.M.G.M. (Tom) Adams, Grantley Adam's son, grasped the reins of leadership.

IMPORTANT DATES IN BARBADOS HISTORY

Before 1600: Various Indian tribes settle.

1518—early 17th C: Portuguese and Spanish ships visit.

1529: Barbados makes its first appearance on map of the world.

1536: Arriving Portuguese captain finds Carib population has vanished.

1625: *Olive Blossom*, first English ship, arrives by accident. Its report results in the formation of a colonizing expedition.

1627: The *William and John* arrives at Holetown.

1637–40: Sugar cane introduced from Brazil.

1639: Elected House of Assembly (House of Burgesses) convened.

1652: Charter of Barbados (Articles of Agreement) signed at Oistins. In exchange for guarantees of certain rights, the Bajans agree to recognize Oliver Cromwell's Commonwealth.

1663: End of the proprietary system under which Barbados had been the property of and controlled by a private patentee. The island is now directly ruled by the British Crown. First postal agency is established.

1665: Dutch Admiral De Ruyter destroys buildings in Barbados during attack.

1668: Over 100 Bridgetown houses burn causing an estimated £30,000 in damage. Drought ruins crops. House of Assembly petitions for "dominion status" for Barbados.

1675: Hurricane hits.

1722: Bishop of London extends his jurisdiction to include colonies.

1731: The *Barbados Gazette*, first newspaper, published.

1766: Fires destroy Bridgetown twice.

1780: Another hurricane hits. Bridgetown reduced to ruins.

1807: British Parliament abolishes slave trade.

1816: Major slave rebellion led by slave Bussa and free mulatto Washington Franklin.

1818: Gun Hill Signal Station erected.

1827: First steamship arrives.

1831: Right to vote extended to include "free coloured men." However, the property ownership requirement remains in effect. Another "Great Hurricane" hits; over 2,000 are killed.

1835: British Parliament abolishes slavery.

1838: Slaves are finally freed.

1843: Samuel Jackman Prescod, first "coloured" man, elected to House of Assembly.

1845: Ten acres of Bridgetown destroyed by fire.

1852: First lighthouse erected at South Point. First postage stamps issued.

1854: Cholera epidemic kills 20,000.

1875: Bridgetown first illuminated by gas.

1924: Founding of Democratic League by Charles Duncan O'Neal, an organization fighting for social reform and widening political participation.

1934: Grantley Adams elected to House of Assembly.

1937: Rioting in Barbados and throughout the British West Indies spurs foundation of Barbados Progressive League which carries on the struggle begun by the Democratic League.

1950: Universal adult suffrage instated.

1954: Sir Grantley Adams becomes the first Premier under a system of ministerial government.

1955: The Democratic Labour Party (DLP) formed.

1958: Foundation of the West Indies Federation, a nation composed of five Caribbean territories including Barbados. Sir Grantley Adams becomes its first Prime Minister.

1962: West Indies Federation dissolved.

1966: Barbados becomes an independent nation within the British Commonwealth (Nov. 30). Errol W. Barrow becomes the first Prime Minister.

1969: National government establishes control over local parish administrations.

1971: Ernest Barrow becomes Prime Minister after the DLP wins a two-thirds majority in the election.

1973: The Barbados dollar replaces the East Caribbean dollar as the official currency.

1976: In upset victory, the BLP gains 17 seats in House of Assembly; J.M.G. Adams becomes Prime Minister.

1978: Exposure of group of mercenaries led by Robert Denard who were plotting takeover of the island. Establishment of the Barbados Defence Force.

1979: Grantley Adams International Airport opened.

1983: Barbados throws government support behind U.S. invasion of Grenada. Oistins Fish Terminal is opened.

1984: Sir Hugh Springer replaces Sir Deighton Lisle as Governor General after the latter's death.

1985: H. Bernard St. John takes office as Prime Minister after J.M.G. (Tom) Adams dies. General Post Office opened.

1986: The DLP sweeps the elections, securing 24 of the 27 seats.

1987: Prime Minister Barrow passes on; he is succeeded in office by Mr. Lloyd Erskine Sandiford.

GOVERNMENT

One of the oldest and strongest democracies in the Caribbean, Barbados—in keeping with the character of its people—is also one of the least contentious. Despite the short time during which universal suffrage has been in effect, democracy and politics have become imbued in the island's psyche. Unlike other Caribbean nations such as Trinidad, Jamaica, and Guyana, Barbados was never controlled by the Crown colony colonial system. It has the third oldest continuously functioning legislature in the Commonwealth (ranking after Britain and Bermuda) and it is not uncommon to hear Assembly members cite 17th C. parliamentary precedents when defending their stand!

political structure: The 1966 constitution set up a British parliamentary-style system. The Queen is the titular Head of State, and her interests are represented by an appointed Governor General. He, in turn, selects the Prime Minister, a minority of the Senate, and an advisory Privy Council. The Council's functions are to hear appeals from civil servants; consider appeals for remission from convicted felons; and to listen to appeals from criminals on death row. The Governor General acts upon its recommendations. Executive authority is vested in the Prime Minister and his cabinet, which must contain at least five ministers. The leader of the opposition receives a salary from the Crown. The bicameral legislature consists of an appointed Senate and an elected House of Assembly. Of the 21 members of the Senate, 12 come from the majority party, two are from the opposition, and seven appointees represent economic, religious, and social interests. In line with the practice in other Commonwealth countries, the Senate's primary tasks are representation and debate; while it does vote on bills, introduction of legislation is left to the House. All Bajans older than 18 may vote. Since 1981, the island has been divided into 27 single-member constituencies. Elections for the House of Assembly are held every five years, but early elections may be called by the government or if the majority party should fail in a "no confidence" parliamentary vote.

the courts: Headed by a Supreme Court, the judicial system also includes a Court of Appeals and a High Court. The lower magistrates are appointed by the Governor General who follows the advice of the Legal Service Commission. He also appoints the Chief Justice after consulting with the current Prime Minister and the opposition leader. Barbados's judiciary system is among the most impartial and nonpartisan in the entire world. In a celebrated case during the 1970s, the Supreme Court decided against *The Democrat,* the official paper of the DLP, which resulted in the publication's termination and in the removal from office of the Speaker of the House of Assembly.

the parish system: Along with the Municipality of Bridgetown, the island's 11 parishes, modeled after those once controlled by the clergy, are now controlled by the central government. Two years after the arrival of the English settlers, the island was divided into six parishes. Then, under the revision of 1645, eleven parishes were established: St. Michael, St. George, Christ Church, St. Philip, St. John, St. Joseph, St. Thomas, St. James, St. Andrew, St. Peter, and St. Lucy. Each of these parishes was governed by a Vestry, composed of local property owners, whose chairman was the church rector (except in St. Michael whose chairman was the Dean of the Cathedral.) Responsible for welfare for the poor and maintenance of the churches and roads, the Vestries levied property taxes to pay the cost. After the 1956 elections, the disestablishment of the church began—a process completed only on 31 March 1969. In 1959, the island was re-divided into three areas: the City of Bridgetown, the Northern District, and the Southern District. Bridgetown was governed by Mayor and City Council; the other areas were governed by the Northern District Council and the Southern District Council. Council members were to be elected under universal suffrage for three year terms. Although the Vestry system endured for three centuries, the Council's couldn't even hold up for a decade. In a complicated system of manuevers, the Councils were abolished in 1967, and, by 1969, their services had been transferred to the Central Government or to statutory boards controlled by the Central Government.

political parties: The moderate centrist Democratic Labour Party (DLP), allied with the Barbados Workers Union (BWU), holds power at present. Main opposition is the slightly left-of-center Barbados Labour Party (BLP). Although there traditionally have been few substantive differences between the two, the BLP has adopted some right-of-center policies in recent years. The new opposition leader, Henry Forde, has announced that the Barbados Labour Party must be restructured into a "highly decentralized" organization featuring "mass democracy in the formation of policy." There are also three minor parties. The People's Progressive Movement (PPM), founded in 1979, is led by Eric Sealy. The left wing Workers Party of Barbados (WPB), run by founder Doctor George Belle, dates from 1985. Farthest to the left is Bobby Clarke's Movement for National Liberation (Monali) which became the center of a controversy in 1982 when it was offered distribution rights to three Barbadian student scholarships (in agronomy and audio-visual technology) granted by the Cuban government. Although Monali accepted, the Cubans retracted the offer after the government protested.

post-independence politics: The island's support for the 1983 U.S.-led invasion of Grenada—for which Barbados supplied troops—strained its relationship with Britain and Trinidad. The latter claimed that the invasion was undertaken without proper consultation all around. Tom Adams died in March 1985 leaving H. Bernard "Bree" St. John to carry on. While said to be charismatically-deficient, he was competent nevertheless. After Adam's death, the government tilted briefly even more towards the US. In 1985 it was designated as the Center of the US-created Regional Security System (RSS); Barbados coordinated Eastern Caribbean military maneuvers that September.

the 1986 election: The May 1986 elections saw the return of the sometimes bombastic Errol Barrow. Barrow zeroed in on the economy's stagnation and the limited employment possibilities it presented. Other issues debated included high prices, governmental corruption, US foreign policy, and racism. Don Blackman, a prominent cabinet minister quit the BLP and joined the opposition claiming that the BLP was not doing enough to stem white racism, possibly because of white influence in the party. The DLP's promise to lower energy rates and to lower taxes proved popular. The election itself was quite a stunning upset. For the first time, one Barbadian political party thoroughly trounced another: the DLP netted 24 out of 27 seats! Independent and strong-spirited, Barrow was determined to keep the Caribbean free of superpower political maneuvering. His political positions put him at odds with the US, and he criticized the US-sponsored Regional Security System (better known as RSS). It is maintained that he inherited enormous problems: a national debt of over US$1 billion towering over the island, strained relations with Caricom (the Caribbean trading community), an official unemployment figure of 19 percent, a heavy burden of taxes, and a developing drug problem. Barrow moved to abolish income tax on the first B$15,000 of earned income in order to spur consumer spending. On June 1, 1987, however, Barrow died of a heart attack, outliving opposing BLP party leader Tom Adams by just two years. He was succeeded in office by the more conservative and less flamboyant Lloyd Erskine Sandiford, the 50-year-old deputy Prime Minister.

ECONOMY

As is the case with other Caribbean mini-state economies, Barbados has always had a rough time. Small fish in a big sea, these small states are treated by the large economies as if they are so much krill for consumption. Once one of the most profitable and prosperous of Britain's possessions, the West Indies had become the Empire's poorhouse by the late 1930s. A British government panel investigating the riots resulting from the economic hardships of the 30s had to withhold its report for fear that release would have damaged the Allied war effort. At the end of WWII, per capita income in Barbados was still well below US$200 per year, and emigration was encouraged just to keep unemployment below double digits. The economy was still totally enslaved by sugar. Things improved tremendously from the period between 1965–1979, but the 80s were depressed. Developing one of the most advanced infrastructures of any Caribbean nation, Barbados during the period stretching from 1957 to 1980 moved up from eleventh to third place among Caribbean Basin countries. But since 1980 it has become the fastest borrowing nation in the Americas. Its external debt now stands at over US$600 million; scanty compared to the US$3.5 billion owed by Jamaica at the end of 1987 but still enormous for a nation of such small size and limited resources. In 1987 unemployment stood at 17.9 percent and per capita income was B$9,850. Over the years since independence, Barbados has attempted to woo investment from abroad. However, as the island is learning, outside investment can be as fickle as tourism.

Caribbean Basin Initiative: The CBI, much touted by former American President Reagan, has been perceived as a failure. Under this three-part aid-investment-trade agreement, originally touted as a neo-Marhsall Plan, nonmilitary aid has been minimal, and few businesses have relocated or opened up subsidiaries. Although Barbados has invested substantial manpower and effort in promoting the plan and adopted its investment incentives, labor unions and political parties have resisted attempts to turn the island into a sweatshop on the East Asian model. Although the CBI was supposed to promote duty-free trade, it excluded goods such as automobile accessories and clothing while permitting rum and tobacco into the US only under modified duties. Meanwhile, reductions in US sugar imports have nullified the program's benefits. And, despite pledges to the Industrial Development Corporation, there has been little or no transfer of technology.

light industry: Although it has the third highest per capita income in the Caribbean, Barbados offers comparatively low salaries which have attracted export-oriented assembly and subassembly plants. Over 150 factories produce such items as soft drinks, biscuits, bread, ice cream, furniture, cement, and textiles for local consumption. A joint venture with Trinidad that is a fiscal disaster, the Arawak Cement Plant, dominates Checker Hall, St. Lucy. Another industry which takes advantage of the island's relatively cheap but English-literate work force is data processing in which Barbadians receive data, process it, and transmit it back to the US. Recently, however, this too is in decline as operations here have closed. The island also produces more than half of its own oil needs.

tourism: The construction of the Deep Water harbour during the 60s made it possible for cruise ships to dock, and the steady improvement in air service—the arrival of the jet airplane slashed the travel time from NYC down to four hours from eight—has increased tourism. Although tourism is seen as superceding the sugarcane industry, this "new sugar" depends upon the whims of the tourists as much as the original depended upon supply and demand.

other sectors: Although tourism, manufacturing, and sugar bring in the bulk of foreign exchange, they only provide employment for about a third of the work force. Others are employed in retail and government service. The retail workforce is employed by shops, banks, and insurance companies. The government civil service, said to be overmanned and underproductive, was once called an "army of occupation" by the late Prime Minister Errol Barrow. Offshore banking, Foreign Sales Corporations (FSC), International Business Companies (IBC), and insurance are also significant sources of income; these businesses come in order to take advantage of tax exemptions extended in return for setting up here. Although it is now much more difficult to emigrate to Britain and the US, the innovative Canadian Farm Labour Programme ships farm labor to Nova Scotia; negotiations to broaden this program to include waiters, waitresses, and bus boys are now underway.

Agriculture

area: Out of a total land area of 106,253 acres, nearly 60 percent is used for agriculture; farmers and agricultural workers constitute 7 percent of the workforce. Sugarcane consumes over half the acreage; about 20 percent of the cane fields are rotated with other crops. The coral limestone has become fertile and loamy through the process of decay. Adding to this has been the infrequent but agriculturally significant deposits of volcanic ash which have come wafting in from other islands. Sufficient rainfall also contributes to the island's fecundity, and a gently rising terrain makes transporting crops a breeze. Up to 80 percent of the surface area is planted in crops ranging from sugar cane to the "sour grass" that provides fodder for cattle. Agriculture is of such importance that buildings are seldom constructed on fertile land. Major export crops include cotton, sugar cane, and coconuts; bananas have also been introduced. Food crops are grown mainly by smallholders of whose farms only a miniscule percentage are over 10 acres; mechanization is practiced only on the large plantations which control the bulk of the land.

sugarcane: The island is so tied up with sugar growing that Barbados has been called a city state in which sugarcane grows in the suburbs. While King Sugar's role has diminished over the century, it still plays a major role in sweetening the economic pot. Planted in every area where soil is more than a foot deep, it requires 16 months for a cane crop to mature. Fertilizers such as ammonia and potash are used to improve

Sugar harvesting

the annual yield, which stands at about 30 tons per acre. Of the approximately 30,000 farmers who own their own land, the average property owned is less than half an acre; most of the cane is still being grown on large estates. Crops are usually grown for four consecutive years, after which other crops (sweet potatoes, yams and taro) are rotated for one year. Although less important than in the past, the sugar industry is still a major employer. Sugarcane harvesting is one of the filthiest and most exhausting jobs available anywhere, and the young pursue it only as a last resort. Consequently, despite the island's double-digit employment rate, it's been necessary to import labor from other islands. It takes 8.5 tons of this cane to produce one ton of sugar, and the island's factories continue to be consolidated; Portvale is the largest remaining one. Sugarcane production has continued to decrease in recent years; while 1988 saw a harvest of 80,000 tons, 1989 brought only 66,000, and the 1990 harvest is expected to decrease further. Presently, the government, which effectively controls 15,000 acres of land and the four operating sugar factories through the Barbados National Bank, is considering forming a company to assume control of the industry and introducing foreign management—suggestions which have brought scorn from the sugar industry. Currently, sugar contributes about 7 percent of the Gross Domestic Product (GDP) and earns over B$80 million in foreign exchange annually.

other crops: Law provides that each sugar "estate" (defined as a farm of more than 25 acres) must devote 12 1/2 percent of its land to "ground provisions." Much of the food is grown by women. The lime in the island's soil, combined with inadequate rainfall and its exposed terrain, make fruit a scarce but nonetheless significant crop. Currently, 60 percent of the island's requirements are produced locally. Cotton has been unsuccessfully attempted as a major crop in the past; another attempt is currently underway. Japanese textile company Nitto Boseki's Barbados factory is scheduled to begin spinning yarn from locally grown Sea Island cotton in 1991. Corn is grown for local consumption and as cattle fodder. Other vegetables include peas, beans, beets, cabbage, carrots, cucumbers, lettuce, eggplant, pumpkins, peppers, squash, yams, sweet potatoes, shallots, onions, spinach, okra, and tomatoes. Finally, cut flowers are becoming another significant export crop.

animal husbandry: Barbados produces three million pounds of pork annually, and chicken and egg supplies are nearly sufficient for the island's needs. Beef, mutton, and veal are also produced. Although there are a few dairy farms, small farmers own the bulk of the island's livestock: cattle, pigs, sheep, and goats.

THE PEOPLE

Caribbean culture is truly creole culture. The word "creole" comes from *criar* (Spanish for "to bring up" or "rear"). In the New World, this term came to refer to children born in this hemisphere, implying that they were not quite authentic or pure. Later creole came to connote "mixed blood," but not just blood has been mixed here—cultures have been jumbled as well. Because of this extreme mixture, the Caribbean is a cultural goldmine. The culture of a specific island or nation depends upon its racial mix and historical circumstances. Brought over on slave ships—where differences of status were lost and cultural institutions shattered—the slaves had to begin anew from square one. In a similar fashion, but not nearly to so severe a degree, the European, indentured or otherwise, could not bring all of Europe with him. Beliefs were merged in a new synthesis born of the interaction between different cultures—African and European. Today, a new blend has arisen in language, society, crafts, and religion: one which has been shaped by and which reflects historical circumstance.

native Indian influence: Although the Indians have long since vanished, their spirit lives on—in folklore, in the feeling of dramatic sunsets, and in the wafting of the cool breeze. Remaining cultural legacies on many islands include foods, place names, and words. On Barbados, names like Indian Pond, Indian River, and Indian Bridge remind the visitor of their one-time residence.

African influence: This was the strongest of all outside influences on those islands with large black populations. Arriving slaves had been torn away from both tribe and culture, and this is reflected in everything from the primitive agricultural system to food preparation to the African influence on religious sects and cults, mirroring the dynamic diversity of W. African culture.

Spanish influence: Spain was the original intruder in the area. The Spaniards exited Puerto Rico in 1898, after 400 years of influence; other islands with a heavily Spanish-influenced culture include Cuba and the Dominican Republic. Most Caribbean islands, whether the Spaniards ever settled there or not, still bear the names Columbus bestowed on them 500 years ago. (Barbados is a notable exception). And, although other European influences have had a powerful effect, Spanish continues to be the predominant language in the islands once controlled by Spain.

American influence: The history of the US is inextricably linked with the Caribbean in general, and Barbados is no exception to the rule. American institutions such as television and fast food continue to have their effect as have other cultural influences such as tourism and the impact of Bajans who have returned home from North America.

The Bajans

Probably no inhabitants of such a small nation have ever had so many individual qualities and traits commonly ascribed to them. It is said that Barbadians do not take offense easily; that they are down to earth, self confident, and self disciplined; and that they are always ready to oblige but do not leave a feeling of obligation behind them. Their fellow West Indians find the Bajans peculiar, accusing them of being unruffled, reserved—seemingly know-it-all in their behavior, and of being smart-assed. Bajans have a firm sense of identity, one which might be envied by many coming from larger, more diverse countries that have also gained independence in recent

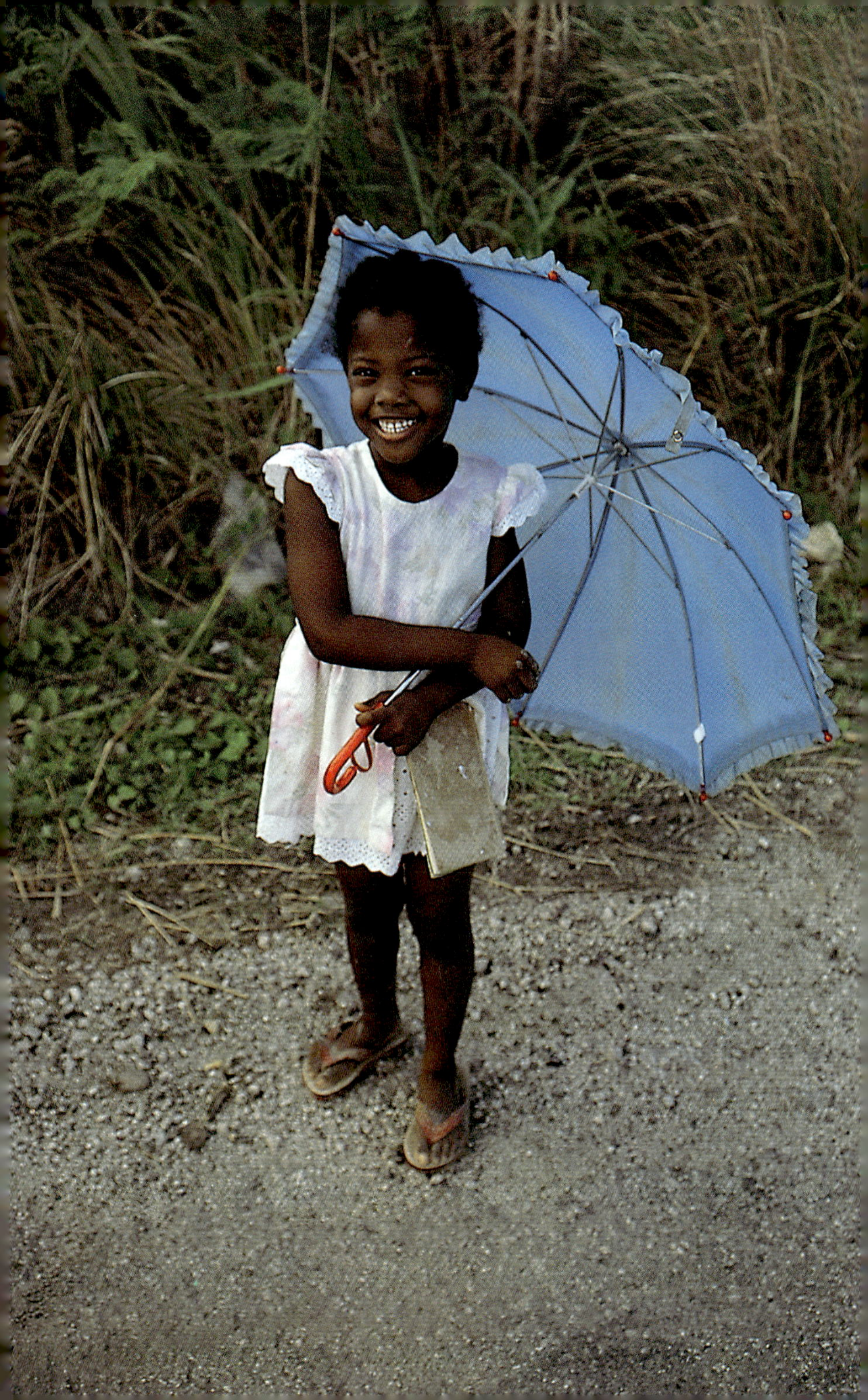

decades. A number of factors have contributed to the development of this national consciousness. Among these are the island's compact size, its relative geographical isolation, its high literacy level, and its long tradition of legislative, judicial, and bureaucratic institutions. Acceptance of the latter has been spurred by the ongoing adaptation or "Creolization" of the society. Black and mulatto leaders from the early and mid-19th C. set role models, and the island's mass political parties and labor unions date from the 30s. One explanation for the extraordinary reserve possessed by Bajans may lie in the pattern of slave movements. Barbados was the first stop for the slave ships, and the planters here were given the first pick of the lot. Naturally, the ones whom they believed least likely to cause trouble were preferred. Thus, the spiritually oriented Ibos—who had a reputation for being more peaceable than some of the other tribes—came to form the bulk of the slave population. However, it is getting more and more difficult to either characterize or stereotype the Barbadian of today for, since gaining independence over two decades ago, Barbados has been in the process of forging a new society. Racial bars are crumbling, and the once isolated island is being influenced by expatriate returnees, tourists, and TV and cinema.

population: Estimated to have about 260,000 people, Barbados boasts one of the lowest (0.4 percent based on annual birthrate of 16.1 per thousand) growth rates in the world. With an overall density of 1,526 people per sq mile (588 per sq km), Barbados ranks fourth in the world in terms of population density and twelfth in the world in terms of agricultural population density—1,745 per sq mile (673.8 per sq km). There are few uninhabited or sparsely populated areas. In order to keep the growth rate down, condoms and oral contraceptives are widely distributed, and abortions and sterilization operations are both legal (although abortion is technically restricted) and commonly performed in public hospitals. Still, the population is forecast to rise to 300,000 by the end of the century. One reason for this is that emigration routes have been blocked.

Girl, St. Lucy's Parish

And, without past emigration, Barbados would be substantially more populated than it is today. From 1950-70, 25 percent of Barbadians migrated. This represents half of all the males and nearly half of all the females born between 1931-1945. If they had not left, the current population would be over 370,000! The average Bajan male can expect to live to 70 years; females live to the ripe old age of 75.4 on average. Since the mid-70s, the infant mortality rate has plummeted dramatically—from 45 per 1,000 live births to around 10 today.

ethnic diversity: Over 70 percent of the island's population is black—direct descendants of those who survived the African diaspora. Another 7 percent are white—either "overseas" (pure) white or "Bajan" (mixed) white. A sizeable 20 percent chunk are varyingly described as "mulatto," "brown-skin," "light-skin," "fair-skin," "high-brown," or "red." The remaining three percent includes North and South American expatriate groups, Syrians, Lebanese, East Indians, and a smattering of Chinese.

Crop Over Festival

"redlegs:" The descendants of Scots, Irish, and Welsh who served as indentured servants are known as "red legs." The name comes from the sunburned skin on their kilt-exposed legs. These immigrants stayed at the bottom of the social ladder until the beginning of this century. Intermarriage kept their bloodlines pure while having the deleterious effect of passing on inherited diseases. Today, they are increasingly becoming subsumed in the evolving societal mass and will soon be indistinguishable from their fellow countrymen.

the upper class: The descendants of the approximately 200 families who dominated the island's economy for centuries are known as "high whites." Today, their monopoly on wealth has ended along with the tradition of racial exclusivity; many families have left the island completely. The stereotypical "high white" may become a thing of the past. In myth, he has a pure West country Bajan dialect which is tempered with a rich West Country brogue. He is passionately possessed with watching and/or participating in such sports as cricket, polo, golf, rugby, soccer, horseracing, and tennis. An avid Anglophile without necessarily ever having set foot in the ancestral homeland, he is intensively supportive of the monarchy and the Anglican Church. His mark is evident on the linguistic landscape. Many of the island's houses, plantations, and villages are named after ones in England. In fact, up until Independence, "high whites" were notorious for supporting visiting English cricket teams over the local ones!

racial stratification: One cannot say that the color bar or class distinctions have disappeared. Only a relatively short space of time has elapsed since the effort to expunge racism began. Although the legislature is 350 years old, the island has only enjoyed majority rule and universal suffrage for a tenth of that time. And although 150 years have passed since Emancipation, it is still only recently that other jobs have begun to open up to blacks. Racial discrimination was openly practiced until comparatively recently in business, the civil service, and in sports. Until the 1930s, blacks were relegated to the back of the Anglican Church. White-only clubs offering cricket, soccer, tennis, and bridge existed openly until 1970 which is when the last school was desegregated. Interracial marriage is still uncommon; although the visitor may notice a number of mixed race couples, most interracial marriages involve foreigners. In 1989 a confrontation took place between the largely white board of directors of Barbados Mutual, the nation's largest insurance company, and its black policy holders when 2,000 of the latter converged on a meeting which had been scheduled to elect two new directors and to change its deed of settlement. Whites, now the less-powerful minority, feel themselves to be besieged at times; blacks sometimes feel that the true power due them has not yet been handed over.

male and female relationships: Barbados's matriarchal society has its roots planted in tradition. In some African societies, matrilineal by custom or otherwise, the sexes are independent of one another. African women and their children spend their lives separate from their husbands and fathers. Wives have their own hut or room and may own property individually. The effects of hundreds of years of slavery have helped bring the present system of social relationships into effect. During the slavery era, male slaves were allowed relationships with females only for the purposes of procreation. Prohibited from establishing long-term relationships, a male might be sold away without ever even casting eyes on the child he'd fathered. As a consequence, children were largely raised by their mothers. This system of casual alignments continues to this day. The grandmother plays a vital role in the family. The custom of the grandmother helping out came about during the days of slavery, when a mother might be sold without her children; the grandmother would then take over their care. Today, a grandmother may look after her daughter's children or even those of her son. If a daughter does not wish to be burdened with the children from a previous relationship, she may ask her mother to take care of them. After a time, she may come to retrieve them. Sometimes the mother goes out to work so that the grandmother may remain home with the children. This type of family pattern exists not only in Barbados, but wherever slavery has been in existence in the New World.

families: The average Bajan lower-class couple lives together for a long time before they get married, if in fact they get

Barbados schoolchildren

married at all. Contributing to this situation is the high cost of a wedding ceremony coupled with a lack of a tradition of formal marriage ceremonies. As a consequence, approximately 78 percent of all births occur out of wedlock. And 35 percent of all marriages end in divorce. Sex is considered to be a natural function which should not be repressed. Male potency and female fertility are viewed as status symbols. Thus, a large percentage of the live births in Barbados occur among unwed teenage mothers, and the island population continues to grow. Having a child may be a way to insure a steady income, and, in many cases, a woman's sole income may come from child support. While in the "visiting union" a man will visit the woman at her house, in the so called "keeper family" a man and a woman will live together. Thrown largely on his own resources, the Bajan male has had to use a combination of his own wits and trickery to survive. Under the "twin household" plan, a man may set up a second household with another woman at the location where he is working.

child rearing and socialization: Children are raised by the mother and her female friends and relatives. Sometimes male relatives may serve as substitute fathers if the paternal father is absent. If a woman has too many children for her to handle, it is not uncommon for children to be farmed out to friends or relatives. Indeed—because friends may address each other as "sis" or "bro"—it may at times be difficult for the outsider to establish exactly who is really related by blood to whom. Raised in a matriarchal society, the young male Bajan views male absenteeism and multiple sexual partners as normal. And he learns that he can expect to "settle down" in his 30s if at all. Children frequently share a bedroom—often with more than one sibling and even with their parents. Schools socialize men for jobs and girls for housewifery or lower paying positions of drudgery. Men occupy 85 percent of the top positions. While the male is brought up to be worldly, the female has traditionally been taught to find her place at home. When they are not at church, women have been expected to be found at home—cooking meals, bearing children, and, above all, obeying orders. Today, women are making great strides and are playing an increasingly vital role in society. Men are made for "movin' around," "stepping outside," "limin'," "firing" a shot of rum, and "slamming" dominoes. Although it is a fact of life, homosexuality is viewed with disdain—and often as a demonic sin—by both sexes. Abortion has been legal only since 1983, and attitudes towards it are ambivalent.

Social Organizations

Friendly Societies: One of the more intriguing of the island's traditions that are on the wane is the Friendly Society. The roots of this organization lie—as do so many other island institutions—back in jolly old England. In the Middle Ages, they were called guilds, and they acted as both trade union and insurance company. In Great Britain, a Friendly Society was legally defined around the turn of the century as one whose purpose is to provide for the relief or maintenance of the members and their immediate families through a voluntary subscription and with or without the use of donations. Additional provisions covered loss of tools, loss by shipwreck, etc. Today in Britain these societies have evolved into high powered insurance companies. On Barbados, from a peak of 161 societies with around 100,000 members, the numbers have plummeted. In the past, many of these societies were led by local schoolteachers. With a community standard bearer running it, a society's success would be assured. Customarily, the teacher would not occupy the position of president but that of secretary, because this gave the impoverished fellow fiscal control. A society's appeal lay in its inexpensive insurance rates, the "sick-relief," and the Christmas "bonus." Every society had its "Sick Visitor" whose task it was to insure that illnesses were legitimate. One reason for the demise of many of the societies was the competition among organizations with competing societies offering higher and higher bonuses until they went under. Another was the increase in transport which made Bridgetown the financial center of the island. Today, the largest societies—such as the Unique Progressive and the Civic—are based there. And the exclusively Bajan verb "to societ," meaning to associate on friendly terms, stands in danger of extinction.

The Landship: Another sadly deteriorating but extremely colorful institution is the Landship. Of obscure origins, the Landship was the lower class equivalent of the fraternal organizations (Elks, Masons, etc.) that the upper classes are so fond of. Ignoring this similarity, the Bajan white upper classes once tended to scorn the landships as stemming from a racial love for mimicry, pageantry, and a love for pet phrases. Of the main functions of the society, the most important were the social heirarchy it created and its function a a mutual aid society. The heirarchy's structure provided order as well as incentive. With each new rise in the ranks, access to new information was provided along with a new medal and ribbon. Crews and officers paid a small weekly fee which partially indemnified them against the expenses of unemployment, sickness, and death. The payments encouraged thrift, and the organization's strictly serious structure taught discipline. Landships usually met in a small house with two "masts" (i.e. poles) on top. Ceremonial visits were often made between landships with each Admiral meeting each other with sword poised in hand. Funerals occasioned major turnouts with a squad of "blues" preceding the hearse followed by a flock of "nurses," each of which had a pair of scissors hanging from her waist. The Lord High Admiral followed behind, walking alone, with the other officers following immediately behind in formation. Today, the remaining landships are best known for their public performances which, although dead serious, are often found comic by onlookers. "Wangle low" consists of a limbo executed while marching in formation; their "center march" proceeds to the beat of an African rhythm. Tuk band music accompanies performances which have titles such as "Changing of the Guard," "Sinking Ship," "Admiral's Inspection," and "Rough Seas."

The Beach Boys

No two ways about it. No visitor save the visually impaired can fail to notice the beach boys. Their local equivalent is found all over the Caribbean—indeed all over the world! Beach boys often hold the same jobs as their social equivalent on a much more prosperous island like Maui: water ski instructor, beach chair attendant, or surfing instructor.

modus operandi: Like the hunter looking for traces of fur in the bush and rapidly scanning the sky for prey, the beach boy cruises the beach scouting his quarry. The beach is a large territory, and, in Barbados, access is legally guaranteed to all. A typical method is to go over to a lone female, strike up a conversation by asking for a cigarette or just sitting down and moving in. Nationality provides the first crucial clue. While *Quebecquoises* are considered to be particularly loose, American women may end an evening very frustratingly with a sweet but curt "thank you" issued by her at the hotel room lobby—a lot of money blown on nothing. If she is lying on a towel marked with the name of an apartment hotel, it means that she is a better prospect than if she is staying in a hotel— which may have strict admission rules! Other clues, learned through past experiences, are to judge by suntan lotion, cosmetics, and reading material. Marital status is of no concern. The typical beach boy thinks nothing of brazenly asking a married woman "Is your husband satisfying you sexually?" Since single women are a small minority of visitors, age or attractiveness are not necessarily of great concern. But being attractive is an added bonus. Because the beach is too public a stage for an erotic encounter, one typical move is to ask her to meet him later at her hotel. Several drinks later—which she may have treated him to—she will be feeling less defensive. In order to defuse the racial barrier, he may ask her straight out if his color bothers her—especially if she appears to be rejecting his friendship. By buying drinks and paying for admission fee to a club (frequented by other beach boys), he molds his image as a companion. By having her pay for some things, he ensures that she will not feel in a subordinate position, and accepting his payment for others ensures a feeling of obligation on her part. If she has fears about the acceptability of a fling, he will point out the other dancing interracial couples—all of whom are also beach boys, thus creating the ideologically acceptable but factually spurious line that there is no racial barrier in Barbados. The goal is always to prevent her catching on that he is "for sale." Unlike the female prostitute for whom it is socially acceptable to prowl for customers, he cannot be overt: to be forthright would blow the scene. He can't let on that he works as a farmer off season for example. His target is likely accustomed to being treated by dates at home, and this may be her first contact with a less "developed" society. Naive, the concept of "paying" may be foreign to her.

psychology: The first-time tourist accepts the greetings of locals as a matter of course—as part of the mythical "welcoming society" that exists to serve his needs. The single woman may be looking for adventure. Feeling temporarily unclosetted from her society's stifling sexual straight jacket, she wants to have an "exotic" experience, and she may be already replaying in her head the tale she'll have to tell her friends back home. The myth of black prowess is firmly established in White Camelot abroad and, from her viewpoint, it may seem to be a particularly physically and psychologically fulfilling form of social interchange. From the beach boy's vantage point, he is entering another world: one in which he is accepted by whites, thus enhancing his self worth. For many years Barbados clubs were the exclusive domain of the whites, and his conquest represents a dramatic and ironic historical aboutface. Even today the color bar is strong for both races; intermarriage and social contact between black and white are voluntarily restrained.

Chattel house

LANGUAGE

origins: But Barbadians speak English, don't they? Yes, but it's not quite as simple as all that! Populated by African slaves from many tribes who had to learn to speak English in order to communicate among themselves and with their overseers, Barbados has developed its own uniquely colorful dialect. In contrast to St. Lucia, where there are strong French influences in the native Creole, or Trinidad which has Spanish as well as French influences, Bajan English has been influenced predominately by W. African languages.

grammatical structure and language content: Both have been affected and shaped by the whims of historical circumstance. As no formal schooling was allowed under the slave system, Africans learned English in the field directly from their overseers, thus creating a unique blend of African and British grammatical structures, language content and intonation. As an example, "d" is substituted for "th" as in "dat" for "that," and "de" for "the." Some aspects of intonation appear to be connected with Welsh as well, as in the dropping of the "w" sound in "woman" (pronounced "ooman"), the enunciation of "turtle" as "turkle," or the pronunciation of little as "likkle." Because of the immense distance from Britain, many words from Elizabethan English remain: jugs are still called goblets, small bottles are vials, and married women are still referred to as "Mistress" instead of "Missus." "Onliest," meaning "only," derives from Cheshire, England. Some words have become so transformed over time as to become virtually unrecognizable. The word virago (meaning "turbulent woman, vixen," or "a woman of extraordinary size and courage") was spelled "firago" in Shakespearean English. It survives today in the form of "fire-rage" meaning one side of a dispute and is frequently used in the query "You going tek up she fire rage now?" ("Are you going to support her in this dispute?"). The double negative, so dear to those living in Shakespeare's England, still finds a welcome home in the Barbadian dialect. When something is running out, a Bajan will cry out "Somebody ain't going get none." Some words are simply mispronounced: "hue and cry" has become "human cry," "spray" is now "spry," and "shrivelled" has been transformed into "swivelled." In other cases, the meaning of words has expanded—as in the case of "bare" which on Barbados also means "raw." African influence is clear in the grammatical practice of reduplication: "Fowl-cock" denotes the common rooster; and "sow-pig" refers to the female swine. Other like terms include "Bull-cows," "boar-pigs," "ram-goats," "ram-sheep," and "hare-rabbits!" Fences have "gate-doors" and houses have "door-mounts." "Play-play" translates as pretence. Numerous words are of African origin. *Duppy* (or *dopie, duppe*), the word for ghost, derives from the Twi term *dupon* which means the roots of a large tree. *Nyam* means "to eat." Probably also African in origin, "unna" or "wunna" is a personal pronoun meaning "all of you." The Bajan imagination has added many new colorful words and expressions to the language. For example the wonderfully expressive "tie-goat" serves to describe a married person. "Own-way" means stubborn. "Stomach-bone" refers to one's chest. "Push breadcart" denotes pregnancy. Other terms are "goat-heaven," "kiddie kingdom," and "heavy-bread." One of the more popular words is "lick." It finds new expression in such colorful terms as "lick away," "lick down," "lick out," "lick up," and "lick cork." One who kisses and tells is a "lick mouth." The phrase "to bite someone's hand" means to cuckold a close friend. There are also numerous types of pots: "coal-pot," "fish-pot," "pepper-pot," "co-hobble-pot," and "buck-pot" number among them. Even food items are imaginatively rendered with relish. Octopus are known as "sea cats;" sea urchins as "sea eggs;" and squid and cuttlefish as "ink fish." The island's language has also been adjusted to reflect social realities. The phrase "outside child" reflects the status of the illegitimate child in society—one which is less pejorative than the harsher term "bastard." The phrase "a certain way" is a vague filler used in conversation when a delicate situation is alluded to. A woman may be getting along with her boyfriend in "a certain way"; a man may be "in a certain way" after stuffing himself at the dinner table; and one's pockets may be "in a certain way" after overspending. The "chupse," a sound formed by sucking in the air between one's teeth, may convey disgust, boredom, frustration, or a combination of all three. Some words even have biblical connotations. The cry "bassa-

bassa" meaning "confused skirmish" in Bajan possibly comes from the Bassa mentioned in the first book of Esdras in the Apocrypha. He had 323 sons and, thus, a wildly prolific social life! Another, more likely, explanation is that it is the same word which in Yoruba means "nonsense."

verb usage: Questions often appear as statements—that is without inverting the subject and the verb. The raising of the voice at the end of the sentence indicates that it is a question. Even though they may be used as adjectives, verbs have no participle endings such as -ed. The verb system also differs in that the present tense of a verb may be used to indicate past action. Instead of using simple present tense, Bajans usually speak of present actions as ongoing activity. Subject-verb agreements are also not of consequence in habitual action statements. "Got" is frequently used instead of "there is" or "there are." (For example they got a lot of boar-pigs on that farm.) Finally, expect to hear unusual patterns such as "must be can" and "must be could."

other linguistic features: The sound "th" does not exist so either "k," "f", "v," "z," "t," or "d" will be substituted. Only one form of a pronoun may be used as subject, object and possessive. For example, "we know," "tell we," and "it is we house." If numbers are used as adjectives before a noun, the plural "s" ending may be dropped (for example "two hill"). The ending for words with two consonant endings is also frequently dropped (for example swimmin', dumplin', hangin'). Instead of using "very," as in "very fast," Bajans will reduplicate the adjective repeatedly—"fast, fast, fast"—or emphasize the word: "f-a-s-t-."

Bajan Dialect: A Capsule Vocabulary

Words

above: on the right
acid: rum

across: means "along" when used in directions
again: now
all two: both
backra: white man
bad: super good
bare: raw, plain
bat: small moth or candle fly
beforetime: formerly, once upon a time
below: on the left
bite: to itch
black lead: pencil
bubbies: female breasts
bush: plant or shrub
caffuffle: confusion, to confuse
change: money
chat down: flirt with a girl
chupse: disgust, boredom, frustration
closet: privy
cool out: relax
de: the
duppy umbrella: mushroom
ever since: a long time ago (pronounced "every sence")
fast-fast-fast: very fast
fig: miniature banana or segment of an orange
fingersmith: thief
fire rage: quarrel
flash: fast
freeness: a giveaway (as at an opening celebration)
fresh: smelly
fuh: for
funny up: contorted, queer, odd, deformed
gap: entrance to a road, driveway, or short road
grabble: to seize
hag: bother
hail: support
jook: stick or punch
jump up: dance
limin': to hang out
malicious: inquisitive or nosy
mind: be careful, move or ignore

mistress: head of a household or superior
nyam, yam: to eat
onliest: only
pass by: to visit
put on some size: gained weight
rice: support, feed, maintain
sand side: beach
sea cat: octopus
sea egg: sea urchin
sea-bath: swim
shagger: sea crab
sih: see
swing round: turn
swizzle: cocktail
t'ink: think
tie-goat: married person
unna: all of you
weather: bad weather
worm: pimple
yuh: you

Phrases and Expressions

break fives: shake hands
c'dear: exclamation expressing impatience, an appeal, sympathy, or delight
can I borrow the phone? may I use your phone?
de body is I.: It's me!
dog dead: expression of finality
don't hag me!: don't bother me!
goat heaven: a state of bliss
gone cross: become pregnant
hold strain: take it easy
horn: to cuckold
huckum, hukkum: how come? why?
indifferent: worthless, good for nothing
push breadcart: to be pregnant
pushing bread cart: become pregnant
who de body is?: who is it?

proverbial Bajan: Perhaps because of the importance of its agricultural roots; possibly because of its unique synthesis of Anglo and African; perhaps because the high population density lends transparency to human motives and foibles; and per chance for all of the above reasons, Barbadians have a tremendous number of proverbs which are well grounded in common sense. A few of the more astute follow.

"De higher de monkey climb, de more'e show 'e tail."
  A rise in social status accords with greater scrutiny (and therefore disclosure) of one's faults and shortcomings.

"Coconut don't grow upon pumpkin vine."
  Children will inherit their parents' characteristics.

"One smart-dead at two-smart door."
  The smarter one thinks one is, the more likely that one can be deceived by someone smarter.

"Pretty-pretty t'ings does fool l'il children."
  The gullible and shallow are deceived by a show of style.

RELIGION

For many Bajans, religion is much more than just lip service to vague ideals; it represents a total involvement, a way of life. Some Bajans may literally eat, drink, sleep, and dream religion. As is true in poorer Third World countries throughout the world, religion is very important because only religion provides respite from the constant difficulties and struggles of everyday life. For people living in acute poverty, anything which gives comfort or some small hope of rising from the surrounding squalor is welcome. Although Christianity forms the model for society, many African elements have crept in. The planters—concerned more with material than spiritual beliefs—saw little incentive to introduce the slaves to the wonders of the Christian God. Although they were nearly all Anglican, the planters defied criticism from clerics by maintaining that Christians could not hold other Christians as slaves. In keeping them out of church, they argued that they would have the moral justification which could continue to keep them slaving away in the fields.

African roots: Although, owing to the mixture of African cultures, no single African religion was transported intact, the slaves nevertheless developed their own hybrid religious system in the absence of formal European proselytizing—one which incorporated both disparate African elements and those copied through observation of Christian rites. The slaves' perception that the English were practicing a powerful form of witchcraft helped keep them in a state of fearful subjugation. Although they are now dying out, some African practices and beliefs have survived. For example, a common practice up until recent years was to plant the umbilical cord of newborn infants near their birthplace in order to link the child's spirit with its new home. A custom having its roots in both Anglo Saxon and African practice is that of the wake. However, the rationale for the practice is different in both cultures. While the British custom has its roots in the desire to protect the deceased from evil spirits, the African version, accompanied by an ostentatious funeral, was designed to make sure that the *duppy* (ghost) would not return to haunt relatives. This fear of *duppies* is still widespread, and it is common to splatter a few drops from a newly opened rum bottle on the ground in order to placate the spirits. One way to prevent a *duppy* from entering a dwelling is to suspend various herbs from the windows and doorsill; another is to leave one's shoes at the door. Scattering sand around the house compels the wandering soul to halt and count each grain—a task impossible to complete as *duppies* can only count up to three and then must begin again. *Duppies* may take various forms. The most notorious of these is the *hag.* Customarily the wife of a planter, she would shed her skin nightly, transforming herself into a ball of fire in search of blood to consume. If one came across the temporarily vacated skin, rubbing it with pepper or salt would prevent her reentry and ensure her demise. *Hags,* however, are believed to be an extinct species today, the last one having been exterminated some 70 years ago. The most famous example of possession by spirits is that of Conrad, a nasty and irritable ghost who squatted in a woman's belly. Nasty buggers who kill children—offering their hearts to the devil for sacrifice or using them in brewing magic potions—*heartmen* appear to come and go with the sugarcane season. A small man who inhabits bottles and better known elsewhere in the West Indies, the *baccoo* has a range of characteristics as wide as those of humanity. The *ballahoo* is a cow-sized spectral dog whose appearance is accompanied by the clinking of chains. Other African beliefs continue to exercise influence. A form of magic, *obeah* (from the Akan word *abayi* meaning "sorceror") still enjoys an underground prestige. Today, as in the past, the practice of *obeah* relies both upon superstition and the effective use of herbs or "bush medicine." There are potions for success, for controlling one's rivals, for sexual attraction, and for leashing in an errant husband. Traditionally, these are served in *coucou* or *coco* tea. While many of the potions may have a purely fanciful effect, there is no doubt that some of these herbal remedies do have a consequence. In fact, some are thought to act upon the nervous system to produce a psychotic state. The power of others—such as the dreaded *duppy dust* (pulverized bones or grave dirt)—works through inducing fear. A matchbox containing a small dead lizard has been known to throw the receiver into a state of shock as will the receipt of a small bottle containing feathers or a vile-appearing liquid. It is widely believed that *obeah* men have the ability to "read up the dead," inducing them to enter the living. Practitioners have traditionally carried a bag of charms containing such "tools" as bits of broken glass, pieces of clay, feathers, and rusty nails. In theoretically Anglicized and Christianized Barbados, *obeah* is even recognized in the law courts. A statute giving the practice of *obeah* felony status is still on the books, and in the early 1960s a man charged with the murder of his wife's lover had the charge reduced to manslaughter after claiming his actions were due to temporary insanity under *obeah*.

religion today: Although Barbados is frequently portrayed as a religiously fervent society, women make up the greater part of the believers. Over half the male population has no links with organized religion, and the overall attendence rate is 60 percent. These days, men increasingly appear to prefer the camaraderie of the rum shops to preaching in the pews. The type of bible-thumping fundamentalism taught on the island—full of restrictions and not geared to deal with life in modern day secular society—holds little appeal for today's young men.

Religious Sects

Despite the domination of the island's religious life by the Church of England since the inception of colonization, the number of religions have proliferated. Altogether, there are more than 140 religious denominations including such ideologically diverse groups as Jews, Hindus, Muslims, Mormons, Bahais, and Catholics. Other churches include the Canadian Pentecostal, Seventh Day Adventist, Jehovah's Witnesses, the Church of the Nazarene, the New Testament Church of God, the African Methodist Episcopal Church (A.M.E.C.), and the Christian Scientists. Evidence of the strength of religious belief abounds. The island's villages all feature "storefront" revivalist churches; the Sunday afternoon CBC TV program, "Time to Sing," showcases a different choral group each week; and the weekly newspaper column "Gospel Bag" serves as a religious calendar which also publicizes new record releases by local gospel groups. Today, outside the 50 percent of the population who are Anglican, the Methodists, Moravians, and the Roman Catholics command the greatest support. The most prominent African-related sects are the Jamaican-rooted Rastafarians and the more traditionally Christian indigenous Tieheads. A survey of the historical influence and significance of each of these groups follows.

Anglicans: The Church of England (the Anglican Church), established for centuries as the official religion, has always enjoyed the widest following. Until its dis-establishment in 1969, it was *the* established religion. As far as former British colonies go, Barbados is one of the few in which the Church of England has remained so powerful. And, aside from Roman

Catholic Malta, it was (until 1969) the only one where clergy were paid by the state. The first Anglican church was housed in a small, primitive structure in Bridgetown. It was replaced with the Church of St. Michael which was consecrated in 1665. Destroyed in 1780, it was replaced by the present structure nine years later which then became St. Michael's Cathedral in 1824. The parish churches were central to rural life in the past. Today, with the advent of TV and other entertainments, this is less true.

Catholicism: Formal practice was suppressed before the 1800s. Any priests landing on the island were promptly put on the next boat out, and a 1650 statute prohibited any form of worship save that established in England. When Cromwell sent off Irish Catholic dissidents to work as "white servants" (read "slaves") for seven years, the priests sent off with them were singled out for especially harsh treatment. In 1839, the first Vicarate Apostate was established in the West Indies, and a bishop was appointed and headquartered in Port of Spain, Trinidad. Construction was begun on the island's first church in 1840, but owing to the poverty of the island's few Catholics, it was not completed until 1848. Fire then destroyed it in 1897, but another was consecrated in 1899. Since then the Catholics have remained a small minority.

Methodism: The first missionaries arrived in December 1788. Finding a few of their faith among the immigrants, it was nevertheless a tough struggle to establish the faith in the face of repression. They encountered so much virulent hostility that they had to stick around Bridgetown and were given no opportunity to reach the slaves. In 1823, their recently built church was pulled down, its furniture destroyed, and proclamations posted about town stating that Methodism was to be exterminated. Led by Ann Gill, the believers resisted. Persecution had died down by the time of Emancipation, and the faith attracted many believers among the former slaves. Today, they have over 20 churches scattered across the island.

Moravians: The first missionary arrived in 1765 and so began the sect's conversion efforts. They set up their first mission at Sharon in the Parish of St. Thomas. The Moravian's strong support for the slaves secured them safety during the 1816 slave uprising. Today, the congregations of the Church of the United Brethren are predominantly black.

Rastafarians

The most prolific of all the Caribbean's religious sects, Rastafarianism is also the most horrendously misunderstood. One reason for this is that its hip and cool posture—commercialized internationally through the commercial exploitation of reggae music—fosters imposters galore. In fact, there are so many of these "wolves in sheep's clothing" that it is getting more and more difficult to find the genuine article. But dreadlocks alone do not a Rastafarian make. Although their appearance may be forbidding, true Rastafarians are gentle, spiritual people who really do believe in "peace and love." The name itself stems from Ras, the title given to Amharic royalty, combined with Tafari, the family name of the late Ethiopian Emperor Haile Selassie; the term Rastafarian thus denotes a follower of Ras Tafari or Haile Selassie. The great black nationalist leader Marcus Garvey set the stage for Rastafarianism when—speaking in a Kingston church in 1927—he prophesied that a black king would be crowned in Africa. In 1930 Ras Tafari, the great grandson of King Saheka Selassie, was crowned Emperor of Ethiopia. Taking the name Haile Selassie ("Might of Trinity"), he further embellished his title with epithets like King of Kings, Lord of Lords, His Imperial Majesty the Conquering Lion of the Tribe of Judah, and the Elect of God. The Ethiopian Christian Church, of which he was a devout member, considered their kings to be directly descended from King Solomon. In the midst of a severe economic depression, Jamaica in 1930 was ready for a new religion. Promoted by early leaders such as Leonard Howell, Rastafarianism soon gained currency among the island's rural and urban poor. Publicized worldwide by the media during the early 70s through the 80s, it gained recognition and followers worldwide.

cosmology: Comparatively speaking, Rastafarianism may best be likened to a black version of messianic Judaism or fanatical Christian sects still found in the US today. The parallels are striking. Haile Selassie is the Black Messiah, and Ethiopia is the Promised Land. God is black, and Rastas are one of the lost tribes of Israel. They have been delivered into exile through the hands of the whites and are lost wandering in Babylon, this "hopeless hell," known to the world as Jamaica or Barbados or wherever the believer resides. The ultimate goal is repatriation to Ethiopia where they will live forever in heaven on Earth. Neither Selassie's reputation as a despot, his death in 1975, nor his lack of support for Rastafarianism during his lifetime have fazed Rastas in their beliefs. Selassie is now customarily referred to with reverence as a living god who has simply moved on to another plane of existance. This follows a pattern typical of messianic cults throughout the world in which the leader lives on in the spirit after his death. Rastas generally regard Christianity with suspicion. Although some Rastas (notably the late Bob Marley among them) have become members of the Ethiopian Orthodox Church, the white Christian God is generally regarded as a dangerous deceiver because his religion denies blacks their rightful destiny (to rule the earth) and expects them to be humble while awaiting death and the passage to an imaginary heaven. For the Rasta, heaven is attainable in the here and now.

rituals, taboos, and symbolism: Rastas are basically vegetarians. Vegetables, fruit and juices are dietary staples. Fish less than a foot long may be consumed but shellfish, fish without scales, and snails are prohibited. Rastas prefer to eat *I-tal* (natural) foods, and they avoid cooking with salt and oil. They strongly object to cutting hair or shaving. Although Rastas are nonsmokers and teatotallers, their consumption of ganja (marijuana) is legendary. Its many names ("wisdom weed," "wisdom food," "the healing of the nations") reflects the Rasta reverence for the plant. The very act of smoking is considered to be a religious ritual. Like the Catholic communion cup, the pipe Rastas use to smoke ganja is known as a chalice. Rastas usually pray to Jah Rastafari or recite variations on verses taken from Psalms 19 and 121 before smoking "the herb." They also cite other biblical passages which they believe sanction and santify the smoking of ganja. (Not all Rastas smoke ganja however, nor is it necessary to smoke ganja in order to be a Rasta). Rastas claim they suffer no ill effects even after decades of continued daily usage. Indeed, they maintain that they are healthy *because* they use ganja. Although not all Rastas sport locks nor are all wearers Rastas, dreadlocks are seen as connecting the Rasta with the Ethiopian lion; Rastas cite biblical passages (Leviticus 19, v. 27; Leviticus 21) to support this practice. The lion is a symbol of Rastafarianism, and as a representation of Haile Selassie, the Conquering Lion of Judah, it may be seen everywhere. Rastas represent the spirit of the lion in the way they carry themselves, in their locks, and in their challenging attitudes towards contemporary social values. Their colors—red, black, and green—are the colors of the Garvey movement; red represents the blood of Jamaican martyrs, black is the color of African skin, and green represents Caribbean vegetation as well as the hope of achieving victory over the forces of oppression.

Rastafarianism in Barbados: Introduced in 1975, Rastafarianism began to spread through the island like wildfire. However the activities of deceitful dreadlocks and the presence of borderline psychotics in their ranks draped the Rastas with a rapscallion image. As fashion faded so did the appeal of the dreadlocked facade. Today, many Rastas are sincere. Many of the island's sportsmen and artists are Rastas. Some of these include journalist and calypsonian Adonijah, poet and actor Winston Farrell, and calypsonian Ras Iley.

The Tie Head Movement (Apostolic Spiritual Baptists)

The most colorful and flamboyant Christian sect is also the only one indigenous to Barbados. Founder Granville Williams spent a 16-year sojourn in Trinidad. There he met up with the Spiritual Baptists—revivalists with African roots. Returning in 1957, Adams spread the word that God had come to him in a vision and personally authorized him to preach the gospel, and he began his Barbados career preaching outside at Oistins.

Meeting a tremendously tumultuous response, he established the Jerusalem Apostolic Spiritual Baptist Church at Ealing Grove and then the Zion Sister at Richmond Gap. The sect's most distinctive feature is its dress. Both men and women sport wrapped cloth turbans. Their colorful gowns are each symbolic of particular qualities. Red stands for strength and the blood of Christ; gold is for royalty; blue stands for holiness; silver-grey symbolizes overcoming; brown represents happiness; white stands for purity; green means strength; and cream symbolizes spirituality.

services and rituals: As with other revivalist sects, the Tie Heads incorporate Christianized but African-like religious styles. Foot stomping, hand clapping, and dancing frequently accompany religious rituals. Even such stiff and sultry Anglican hymns as "Abide With Me" can be made danceable. Acceptance means that you must be baptized again. After a dipping in "living water," the novice adherents are schooled in doctrine. Devotees are then isolated in "The Mourning Ground," a section of the church devoted to prayer and meditation. After a week to ten days, the new member emerges spiritually cleansed and revitalized.

membership: With about 7,000 adherents, the Spiritual Baptists are an up-and-coming sect. Their membership is also 40 percent male—a remarkable achievement on an island where men appear to do their worshipping at the rum shop on Sunday mornings while the women predominate in the pews.

MUSIC

While Bajan music has roots sunk as deep as on any island in the Caribbean, in light of its smaller size and anglophilic nature, Barbados has developed less of a body of music than its larger cousins to the N and S, Jamaica and Trinidad. Still, music is so much in the Bajan's blood that it's said a child can dance before he or she can walk. Along with indigenous musical brews, Barbados has some very fine calypsonians and a small posse of reggae musicians as well. While very much a

Introduction 65

domestic scene, the island's concert venues are occasionally enlivened by performers from abroad—brought in by individual promoters like the Barbados-Cuban Friendship Association, or during the Barbados/Caribbean Jazz Festival held annually in May.

roots: The old Bajan work songs as well as the island's calypsos have deep African roots tempered by Caribbean colonialism. The ethos of musical expression in Barbados—indeed, in Black music in the Americas as a whole—stems from the struggle of a people wrenched out of their own cultural milieu and thrown into unfamiliar circumstances as well as with strangers of diverse cultural backgrounds. The only possession the Africans could bring with them was the space inside their heads; slave owners had no control over cultural memories. But even these memories, already dulled by the cruel voyage overseas and the horrors of slavery, were further confused by the mingling of members from various tribes. As is so often the case in the Caribbean, a cultural synthesis emerged which forged the old into the new. What the slaves could remember, they practiced—often in the face of prohibition (playing drums, for example). What could not be remembered—or only half remembered—they improvised and expanded, often merging African and European elements. While in Jamaica to the N indigenous forms like mento, ska, rock steady, and reggae emerged, Barbados developed tuk music and calypso. Today, these share the island's music scene with imports like rock, reggae, soul, steel band music, and disco.

reggae: Originally emanating from the steamy slums of Jamaica, reggae has swept the world and gone international. No one is quite sure exactly from where it came, but it appears inseparably linked to the maturation of the Rastafarian movement. Reggae may be defined as the synthesis of electrified African music with the influences of ska, rock steady, and American rhythm and blues. Some give the Wailers credit for transforming reggae into its present format. No sooner had the band gained international fame in the early 70s than its members went their own separate ways, with the band's major singer-songwriter Bob Marley changing the name to Bob Marley and the Wailers. By the time of his death from brain cancer at the age of 36 in 1981, Robert Nesta Marley had become an international superstar. His influence remains strong to this day, and no one has yet quite succeeded in filling his shoes. Although reggae is not strongly developed on Barbados, there are a few bands and the music permeates the island.

steel band music: Of Trinidadian origin, this unique orchestral sound has spread all over the Caribbean. Despite its low life beginnings—when it was a scorned child of the lower classes—it is now the darling of every tourist board. From its humble origins, the orchestras have grown as large as 200 members. Although it is often maintained that the instruments are the progeny of African drums, they have much more rhythmically in common with African marimbas. However, in truth, they are far removed from either. The *pan*—as the individual drums are known—is made from a large oil drum. First, the head—along with six to 12 inches of the side—is severed. Then, the top is heated and hammered until a series of large indented bumps emerge. Each of these produces a musical note. Each *pan* is custom designed. While some produce many notes to carry the melody, the bass *pans* have only three or four notes. Bands are now divided into three major sections. The "ping pong" (or soprano *pans*) provide the melody using 26-32 notes; the larger pans ("guitar," "cello," and "bass") supply the harmony; and the cymbals, scratchers, and drums supply the groundbeat. A contemporary steel drum orchestra in Trinidad generally contains 20 or more *pans*; those found on Barbados commonly have considerably fewer.

tuk bands: From the start, slaves on Barbados suffered from musical repression. In 1675, the code against the beating of drums was enforced after an uprising and, as of 1688, drums or any other loud musical instrument would be burned if discovered. But the impulse to drum still survived and resulted in the onomatopoetically named tuk band—named after the "tuk tuk" sound of its large log drum. For the past 125 years or so, the tuk band has provided the rhythmic foundation for every major celebration. While reminiscent of British military bands, its base is African. A pennywhistle player sets the tune and tempo; the kettle drummer changes the movements and style; and the bass drummer throbs along in time. When a

Tuk band performance

band appears, villagers may dress as bears or donkeys—swaying lasciviously in time with the music. Men sometimes don dresses, stuffing them with rags in imitation of pregnancy. These characters have been given colorful names such as Donkey Man, Stilt Man, and Mother Sally.

Calypso

Perhaps no music is so difficult to pinpoint, and none is quite so undefinable as calypso. Next to reggae, it is the best known music to come out of the English speaking Caribbean. Its rhythm is Afro-Spanish. Sometimes the Spanish elements dominate, sometimes the African. Call-and-response is employed frequently. It *is* strikingly African in the nature and function of its lyrics. While the tunes don't vary a whole lot—there are some 50 or so—the lyrics *must* be new! And, without exception, they must also pack social bite. Like reggae, calypso is a political music—one which more frequently than not attacks the status quo, lays bare the foibles of corrupt politicians, and exposes empty programs. The songs often function as musical newspapers providing great insight into society. And, as even the briefest listening will reveal, calypso is also a very sexual music. One of the most frequent themes is the wrath of a scorned woman focused on an unfaithful male.

origins: No one can say precisely where or when calypso began. Each island claims it for its own, and certainly all of the islands had music similar in style to calypso. In fact, some of them were also called calypso. However, these styles were all influenced by Trinidadian calypso. Partially because of the popularity of Trinidad's calypso and also partially because the same businessman who had the island's calypsonians under contract owned a group of record stores on the other islands, calypso on the smaller islands came to resemble the Trinidadian style. The true origins of calypso remain shrouded in mist. The famous Trinidadian calypsonian Atilla the Hun (Raymond Quevedo) maintained that the calypso was "undoubtedly African." According to Quevedo, the first calypsos were sung in the fields by the *gayap*—a group of organized communal workers which has equivalents in West Africa. These work songs—which can be found in every African community in the Americas—still exist. And, their more ribald counterparts, which served to spread gossip concerning plantation folk, paralleled modern day calypso. However, it is more likely that they were merely an influence. Certainly, there are many African elements present in the music including the use of dynamic repetition, call-and-response patterns, and the rebuking of socially reprehensible behavior—a frequent theme in African traditional songs. Whatever its roots, calypso seems to have reached its stylistic maturity in the 1870s. It was originally accompanied by rattles, a scraper called a *vira*, drums, and a bottle and spoon used like a West African gong. During the 40s and 50s, calypsonians first began twisting words—executing swift ingenuity—to contrive rhymes that also produced a wide range of rhythmic effects in the vocal line. Lines which vary in length as well as short phrases or cries, juxtapositioned between the lines of verses, also serve to enliven and add gaiety to the music's spirit. Calypso music has incorporated elements of jazz, salsa, Venezuelan, East Indian, and R&B music. But—like all great classic musical forms—it has been strengthened rather than inundated by their influence.

the calypsonians: As with any other form of contemporary popular music, the singer is at the focus of the music. Like the American and British rock stars, the calypso kings are sexual objects. One qualification is to be unemployed—the image of the witty indigent—bordering, but not entering, criminality. Another is to be very dashingly and wickedly attractive to swooning women. Like the *griot* musicians of West Africa, the calypso singer lives through donations. And flamboyant titles—whether it be the Mighty Sparrow or Atilla the Hun— serve to reinforce the high-and-mighty image. Crowned King in a tent as a feature of Caribbean carnivals, he becomes the symbol of masculine prowess incarnate.

early Bajan calypso: Although the influence of Trinidadian calypso began spreading in Barbados during the early years of this century, it was decades before calypso attained any degree of popularity on the island. To those preoccupied with trying to be as properly British as they could an indigenous musical form like calypso appeared to lack class and culture. The average calypsonian wandered around from bar to bar strumming a guitar. During the 30s, the best known calypsonians included Frank Taylor, Da Costa Allamby, and Mighty Charmer. Only the latter made much of a splash. He had a hit in 1947 with "My Dear Mammy." However, the local stuff seemed to lack appeal compared to the Trinidadian variety. So Mighty Charmer made the pilgrimage to Trinidad and hit it big there with his tune "Flying Saucer." Influenced by the Mighty Sparrow (Francisco Slinger), his lyrics grew more and more satirical. Charmer was succeeded in the tradition by the Merrymen—the Barbadian Beatles. Developing a trademark beat called the "Caribeat," the Merrymen, led by Emile Straker, began by recycling old calypsos like "Sly Mongoose," "Millie Gone to Brazil," and "Brudda Neddy".

contemporary Bajan calypso: Finally calypso began to catch on in the early 60s. With the advent of radio and a larger number of performers arriving from Trinidad for performances, calypso's popularity mushroomed. By the mid-60s, the pool of talented performers had grown to include the Mighty Gabby, Mighty Viper, Lord Deighton, Mighty Dragon, and Lord Summers. The years 1968 and 1969 saw major competitions. In the early 70s, however, calypso was eclipsed and sent into retreat by a new music called spouge. Introduced by its inventor Jackie Opel, a former calypsonian who had developed the style while in Jamaica, this reggae-calypso hybrid dominated the music scene from 1969 to 1974. Although Opel died in an auto accident in late 1970, groups such as the Blue Rhythms Combo, the Draytons Two, Sandpebbles, and the Outfit continued the short-lived tradition. After the 1974 revival of the Crop Over Festival, calypso began to grow in acceptance once again. Today more than half of the songs deal with political issues. Bajan calypso has truly matured.

the Mighty Gabby: Foremost practitioner of Bajan calypso, Gabby holds out in his tent, Battleground, where he expounds on favorite topics including the foibles of island politicians. He

The Mighty Gabby

has won the Crop Over Festival competition successively in 1968, 1969, 1976, and in 1985. His real name is Tony Carter, and he has been singing since age 6, competed in a calypso contest as a teenager, and spent time in New York from 1971–76. Some of his more famous songs include "Jack," which deals with the controversial concept of limiting beach use, "Miss Barbados," which concerns the Canadian selected to represent Barbados in an international beauty pageant, and 1985's "Culture" which deals with the threat posed by the imported "trash" coming over the airwaves. One of his most recent tunes, "Chicken and Ram" deals with the infamous Mrs. Ram who allegedly sold diseased chickens to restaurants. Infuriated by the tune, Mrs. Ram sued and lost. In concert, Gabby dances and sways expressively—swinging his mike like a bat on "Hit it" and folding his arms and jumping like a chicken during "Chicken and Ram." Also a protest folksinger of note, he was voted Folksinger of the Year in 1977, 1978, and 1979. Gabby has two albums out, *One In The Eye* and *Across the Board,* on Ice.

the current crop: Today, Gabby has his rivals, and tops among them is Red Plastic Bag. Among his claims to fame is the song "Mr. Harding Can't Burn," which won him his first calypso crown. Another song, "Holes," pontificates lamentingly over the miserable condition of the island's roads. Other prominent performers include Romeo, Bumba, Viper, and Grynner (pronounced "Grinder"). The latter often tours with Gabby. His album on Ice, *King of the Road March,* is a greatest-hits compilation. It includes his most famous composition "Leggo I Hand," the story of a band of Rastafarian musicians accosted by the police.

THE ARTS

Theater

dinner theater: Entirely formulated and produced for the tourist trade, supper shows provide the visitor with sheer entertainment rather than a feel for the island and its history. "1627 and All That Sort of Thing" is presented on Sun. and Thurs. evenings under the stars at the Barbados Museum. During the show, a dance troupe dramatizes the lifestyle of a Bajan village. Held Tues. night at Balls, an old sugar estate, "Barbados, Barbados," a musical comedy, is based on the life of the semi-mythologized whorehouse manager Rachel Pringle. "Plantation Tropical Spectacular II," held in the garden of the Plantation Restaurant, presents an evening of song and dance.

other drama: Catch a performance by the Green Room Players or Stage One Theatre Productions. Watch for shows at Queen's Park Theatre, the Steel Shed, Combermere School Hall, and The Auditorium (on George St.). There are two major opportunities to catch theater on Barbados. During Feb. and March during the Esso Arts Festival performances of the island's three best current plays are staged. And during Crop Over the Farley Hill Concert, held in the park atop Farley Hill, and Cohobblopot, held at the National Stadium, both feature dramatic performances as part of their entertainment.

dance companies: Ebullient yet disciplined, dance on the island combines African zeal and exuberance with European conservatism. All types of dance troupes—from ballet to avant garde—flourish on the island. The foremost ballet schools are the Penny Ramsey and Sheila Hatch schools. Mary Stevens singlehandedly introduced modern dance to the island when she founded the Barbados Dance Theater Company in 1968. It has drawn on African roots—introducing a new version of West African spider-hero *Anansi* and the *hag*, a mythical woman who sheds her skin nightly—transforming herself into a ball of fire in search of blood to consume. Generating from the 1975 merger of the Rontana Dance Company with the Awade Drummers, the Rontana Dance Movement presents percussion-attuned choreography. A semi-professional company which formed out of the revolutionary late 60s theater group the Yoruba Yard, the Yoruba Dancers give occasional performances. Founded in 1981, the Dance Experience—a group of young dancers who incorporate jazz, folk, and modern techniques in their performances—are frequently accompanied by the Wesahh Singers. Founded by Patrick Cobham, Country

Theatre Workshop—who perform regularly at the Plantation Spectacuar—is yet another group. In addition to those performing regularly at hotels, many companies strut their stuff during the Esso Arts Festival held in February and March and at the Farley Hill Concert held during Crop Over.

Art

For such a small island, Barbados certainly is a wellspring of artistic talent. As any visitor to the island's galleries can attest, Barbados has a large number of talented artists who rival those of any other Caribbean island. Because it was created on behalf of the British expatriate plantocracy, most of the island's early art reflected the needs and values of the colonial power structure—and, like the planters themselves, most originated in England. The most famous early sculpture is that of Admiral Nelson which stands in Trafalgar Square, and the island's most famous painting is one by Benjamin West which hangs in the St. George Parish Church. Struggling to survive, the liberated slaves had little time to do artwork at first but, given time, the island's art movement began to grow. Formation of the Barbados National Arts Council in the mid-50s was a milestone in the island's history. Tourism has contributed to the art boom by providing patrons.

murals: As it has all over the Americas—from San Francisco to Santo Domingo—mural art has flourished on the island. On Barbados, mural painting originated with the paintings done on the exterior of shops on Bridgetown's Baxter's Road and Nelson St. which were colorful advertising billboards. Similarly, vendor's carts still display cute, often cartoonish ads. When in 1981 it became Barbados's turn to host the Caribbean Festival of Creative Arts (CARIFESTA), mural painting began in earnest. During the festival, the murals that festoon the Barbados Community College, the Springer Memorial School, and the Eagle Hall Post Office were created.

painters: Many painters seek to record fast disappearing aspects of Bajan life such as windmills, great houses, donkey carts, and chattel houses. One of the finest painters of the latter is Fielding Babb. Other painters of traditional Barbados include Oscar Walkes, Briggs Clarke, twin brothers Omowale and Sundiata Stewart, Kathleen Hawkins, twin sisters Winifred and Harriet Cumberbatch, and Adrain Compton. Artist Ena Power specializes in painting flowers. David and Indira Gall use local images to project symbolic messages.

museums: The Art Collection Foundation (ACF) has recently launched the National Art Collection. View the Collection at Barbados National Bank on Broad Street. Older treasures including prints may be viewed at the Barbados Museum.

art galleries: Foremost among these are the Barbados Arts Council Gallery at Pelican Village, tel. 426-4385, and the monthly rotating exhibits at the National Cultural Foundation's Queen's Park Gallery, tel. 427-2345. Coffee and Cream Gallery—located in Paradise Village, St. Lawrence, Christ Church—represents about 40 island artists. Also displaying jewelry, it doubles as a coffeeshop and bar. It's open from 11-5:30 Tues. to Saturday. Set in the ruins of an old mill at the home of Barbados Art Council founder and painter/papermaker Norma Talma in the south coast village of Enterprise, Talma Mill Gallery is open by appointment only, tel. 428-9383. Fine Art Framing (tel. 426-5325) and The Studio Art Gallery (tel. 427-5463) in Bridgetown also hold exhibits occasionally. Maryam's (tel. 436-4703), located in a downtown Bridgetown restaurant, holds frequent exhibitions. Set in the Bridgetown waterfront, Origins (tel. 426-8522) contains both paintings and "wearable" art. Located inside the Sandy Lane Hotel in Sandy Lane, The Barbados exhibits arts and crafts such as jewelry, hand painted silk, batik, ceramics, and paintings. Set in a garden in Christ Church's Marine Garden, Bertalan Gallery (tel. 427-0414) showcases William Bertalan's metal sculptures. Painter and ceramicist Golde Spieler operates out of her workshop at Shop Hill in St. Thomas. Painter Jill Walker sells her work at her chain of Walker's World shops found islandwide. Outdoor arts and crafts displays are found at the annual Crop Over and Holetown festivals.

Literature

Rooted in oral tradition, the island's literary culture began with the legends and folklore that grew up with the combination of transplanted European and slave cultures. Most of the works originally published concerning the island were written by outsiders. The first of these, Richard Ligon's *A True and Exact History of the Island of Barbadoes,* was published in 1657. Just as it took generations to gain the right of recognition as humans for Barbadians, so did it take hundreds of years for the local literature to evolve and gain acceptance. The first publicity indigenous literature received was on the 1940s and 1950s BBC program called "Caribbean Voices" and through the literary magazine called *Bim*, edited by the late Frank Collymore, which began publication in 1942. Much of Bajan literature deals with the questions of cultural identity, synthesis, and racial strife. Some of the most famous Bajan writers include Oliver Jackman, Geoffrey Drayton, Austin Clarke, and John Wickham. One of the most important writers—not only in Barbados but in the entire Caribbean—is George Lamming, who rebelled against the traditional novel, refusing to give heed to normal conventions of plot and characterization. His novel *In the Castle of My Skin* is a masterful account of Bajan village life, one which should be required reading for any visitor. Another well known poet is H. A. Vaughn. Edward Braithwaithe is an internationally known poet.

FESTIVALS AND EVENTS

Holidays

1 January	New Year's Day
1 May	May Day
30 November	Independence Day
25 December	Christmas Day
26 December	Boxing Day

Christian holidays observed are Good Friday, Easter Monday, and Whit Monday. Other holidays are Caricom Day in early July and United Nations Day in early October. There are four major festivals on the island:

The Holetown Festival: Celebrating the arrival of the first settlers and held since 1977, this February festival commences with a week-long celebration. Although the date commemorated (17 February 1627) may possibly be incorrect, this festival really swings irregardless. You may hear medieval hymns sung in the churches and experience the sights and sounds of and smells of the carnival held at the fairgrounds. The St. James Parish Church is filled with exotic blooms along with a display of its antique silver. Evening activities include a performance by the Royal Barbados Police Force band and the Mounted Troop—with torches blazing on their lances. Other features are food stalls and folksinging and dancing.

Oistins Fish Festival: This two-day festival in April celebrates the island's fishing industry. Contests are held in fish-

Crop Over costume

ing, boat racing, fish "boning," and crab racing—all to the clamor of steel bands. There are food stalls galore and arts and crafts booths. The Coast Guard even puts on an exhibit.

Crop Over Festival: The summer's highlight, this all-island festive explosion happens from mid-July through early August. It's a recently revived version of the festival from the island's early days which celebrated the sugar cane harvest—a Caribbean version of Thanksgiving. Calypso music rings out from the performers' tents and the sweet smell of Bajan cooking permeates the festival grounds. Features include the "Bridgetown Market," a delight for epicures; the "Cohobblopot," a pastiche of dance and drama which frames the crowning of the King and Queen of costume bands; and the "Pic-O-de-Crop Show," when the year's King of Calypso is revealed. The climax comes with "Kadooment Day" when a flurry of costumed performers and bands take to the streets during the day followed by the explosive gyrative bursts of fireworks illuminating the nighttime sky.

The National Independence Festival of the Creative Arts: Each November contests are held in the fields of music, singing, acting, dancing, and writing. Their denouement is marked by the announcements of winners on 30 November, Independence Day.

FOOD AND DRINK

A limited variety of available produce combined with a skimpy household budget means that Bajans have always had to be both cautious and resourceful when cooking—a set of conditions which has produced innovative culinary delights. Bajan cooking has incorporated a number of influences from different cuisines including West African, English, French, Spanish, Amerindian, Indian, Chinese, as well as recipes from other Caribbean islands. Although many Bajans raise their own pigs and chickens, meat is a luxury item, and the staple food is rice supplemented by sweet potatoes, yams, and beans. Bajans who can afford them have traditionally relied for protein on dairy products, imported salt beef, codfish, and pork, local pork and mutton, and imported frozen beef. The Hotel Association sponsors the "Bajan Table," an annual culinary exhibition. Taking place in early October, hotels, restaurants, and individuals are awarded prizes for dishes in different categories. A celebration of indigenous culinary skills, the National Independence Festival of Creative Arts (NIFCA) awards highly prized bronze, silver, and gold medals on Independence Day (November 30). American fast food has also made its indelible mark on the Barbadian culinary psyche. But it has yet to take the place of indigenous cuisine in the hearts and minds of locals.

snacks: Street vendors sell a wide variety of tasty, deep-fried snacks. Likened to "slabs of wood," dried and salted codfish had traditionally been imported from North America to feed slaves. Once viewed with disdain for this reason, it has lost its stigma and codfish balls and cakes are now considered to be culinary delights. Made from boiled and finely minced salted dried cod which has had boiled pumpkin and grated raw yam added, they are mixed up well—with beaten eggs, milk, butter, salt and pepper—and fried in boiling lard. They are often sold one or two in a bun in rum shops. A *cutter* is a French roll with a slice of meat, ham, a fried egg, or cheese inserted. Roasted corn is a roadside treat. Deriving from an African dish called *kanki* or *kenke, conkies* consist of corn meal, coconut, pumpkin, sweet potatoes, raisins, and spices mixed and steamed inside a banana leaf. Traditionally for some unknown reason, housewives prepare *conkies* on Guy Fawkes Day. *Travellers* are syrup-covered snowballs sold by pushcart vendors. Sweets or sweeties include guava cheese, coconut sugar cakes, tamarind balls, sugar cocks, nut cakes, glass cakes (peanut brittle), ginger-flavored sweetie boots, and shaddock rind.

local specialties: One of the dietary mainstays is peas and rice. One or several different types of peas (such as blackeye, pidgeon, green, cow peas or lentils) are combined with cooked rice which has been flavored with salted pig tails or salted meat. In local restaurants macaroni pie (i.e. macaroni and cheese) and sweet potato pie are similar accompanying side dishes. Directly related to African culinary staples such as *foo foo* or *kush kush*, *cou cou* (or *coo coo*) is a cornmeal and okra pudding which is customarily served with gravy and salt fish. It is sometimes jestingly referred to as "organ dust," because its grainy texture resembles the debris left by the wood ant. *Jug* or *jug-jug* is a mixture of guinea corn and green peas cooked with salt pork and beef. Its name is a corruption of the Scottish dish *haggis*. When Scots were exiled in Barbados after the 1685 Monmouth Rebellion, they brought with them their favorite dish—a mixture of oatmeal, well seasoned and steamed like a pudding, with minced liver and suet mixed in. Bajans substitute whole grain millet for oatmeal; salted or fresh meat, peas, fat, and herbs are minced and blended with the grain. It is a traditional Christmas dish. *Cohobblopot* or *pepperpot* is a very spicy stew made using different meats and casareep. Another island dish with African origins, *calalu* is crab and okra stew made with dasheen leaves, pork fat, and grated coconut. Originally from the Indian subcontinent, *roti* (meaning "bread") consists of a *chapati* (a stovetop-baked, circular-shaped unleavened bread) wrapped around curried meat. Vegetarian versions are also available. Many dishes are supplemented with the ubiquitous hot sauce, a mixture of peppers, vinegar, and mustard with onions, tumeric, and other spices added.

flying fish: One of the island's staples, flying fish are fried, steamed, or baked. These seven- to nine-inch flying fellows travel in schools as small as 50 and as large as 1000 members. Harvested offshore between December and June, they are frozen or dried for use during the rest of the year. They may be served steamed, fried, or baked. A special seasoning used in their preparation incorporates onion, garlic, black pepper, red pepper, parsley, thyme, paprika, lime juice, salt, and any other spices available. One prime local delicacy is flying fish melts—a word derived from the now obsolete term milts, referring to the roe or spawn of fish. In addition to flying fish, Bajans also consume tuna, dolphin (not the mammal), kingfish, red snapper, bonito, chub, and smaller fish such as jacks, sprats, and fray.

sea urchins: Known locally as *sea eggs*, white sea urchins are gathered at the beach. The roe of several urchins are combined into one emptied shell and, topped with a sea grape, they are ready for market. Traditionally, they are either steamed or fried with chopped onions and sweet pepper until golden brown. Bajans believe them to be an aphrodisiac.

pudding and souse: This is one of the island's oldest and most legendary dishes. Its preparation is almost an art form. First, white *pudding* is prepared using grated sweet potatoes, thyme-seasoned pumpkin, sweet marjoram, and shallots. To create black *pudding*, pig's blood is then mixed in. The resultant *pudding* is salted and stuffed into pig intestines which have been rinsed with lime juice. Tied at both ends with strings and suspended in pots of boiling water, the puddings are rotated continually until they are cooked. *Souse* is made by placing the chopped and boiled head and feet of a young pig into a bowl of brine containing hot red peppers and lime juice. It is customarily served with chopped onions, cucumber slices,

Holetown vegetable market

and cut peppers. A traditional Saturday night meal, it may be fried up as breakfast on Sunday mornings.

other pork dishes: Resourceful to a fault, it is said that the only part of a pig that the Bajans cannot turn into a dish is the hair. Devised to cover the mid-week days when funds and fresh food might be short, *stew food* combines ground provisions (i.e. roots such as yams and breadfruit plus greens) with finely chopped pig heads, trotters, snouts, and tails. For another dish, several pounds of pig is "corned" (pickled) in a stone urn along with saltpeter, sea salt, spices, and water. Removed after several weeks, it is desalted through soaking and then combined in a stew with onions, butter, gravy, tomatoes, white beans, parsley, thyme, and pepper.

vegetables: A surprisingly large variety is available. These include roots such as yams, cassava, sweet potatoes, and white eddoes (taro). Others include cabbage, okra, spinach, cristophenes (a type of gourd), onions, and tomatoes. Originally introduced from Tahiti by a British sea captain in 1792, breadfruit has become an island staple. Covered with a bright green skin, it has a white starchy pulp which may be boiled, fried, or pickled.

fruit: Since Barbados can't grow enough of its own owing to land and climatic limitations, much must be imported from other islands. Fruits found include the mango, mammee apple, pomegranate, genip, avocado, grapefruit, shaddock, Chinese orange, tangerine, guava, lime, sapodilla, golden apple, dunk, sugar apple, soursop, custard apple, and Barbados Cherry. The latter has the highest vitamin C content of any fruit in the world: just one contains the full daily requirement! Containing the digestive enzyme papain which is used as a meat tenderizer, the melon-like paw paw (papaya) is one of the world's most delicious tropical fruits. The sour pulp of the Indian tamarind tree, extracted by sucking, is a delicious treat. Pleasant smelling but slightly sour tasting, the hogplum has often been used to fatten up hogs and cattle.

fruit drinks: Served by Rastas on streetcorners, coconut water is a popular drink. Lemonade is made using fresh limes. A variety of punches are made with mangoes, guavas, papayas, passion fruit, tamarind pods, cherries, soursops, golden apples, and gooseberries.

also widely available. Dark and Stormy is a 30 proof canned mixture of rum, ginger, and quilaia bark extract.

Rum

The name of this, the premier Barbados beverage, probably comes from the archaic term "trumbullion"—a drunken tumult resulting from drinking—or from *saccharum,* the Latin word for sugar. Producing the first and finest rum in the world, Barbados had, by the mid-18th C., developed a thriving rum trade—selling to other West Indian islands, to North America, to England, and to Ireland. Rum was even brought to West Africa where it became a very popular barter item for slaves. For hundreds of years the British Navy dispensed a daily rum ration, a blend including Barbados rums; this practice ended in 1970. Barbados became one of the exporters of the new light-bodied rum at the end of the 19th C.

manufacture: There would be no rum without molasses. Molasses is what remains after most of the sugar has been extracted from sugarcane juice. Molasses is distilled in American white oak wooden pot stills to form dark rum. As the wood adds color and flavor, the longer it is aged the better. A small amount of caramel (burnt sugar) is also added. Light rum is aged for a shorter time in modern metal stills.

marketing: Because of the sugar glut, most Caribbean islands strive to prop up their fragile, import-dependent economies with rum exports. Unlike the US-controlled Commonwealth of Puerto Rico (whose brand Ron Rico is nearly simultaneous with the word "rum" itself), Barbados has no special access to the US market. But the island's major exporter, Mount Gay, strives to make up for this deficiency with its elite appeal. It pushes hard to have its Eclipse brand be the choice of the American sailing set. And—quite amazingly, considering the wealth of varieties available to the imbiber—it has succeeded.

Recently, it has been joined in competition by Hanschell Inniss, Ltd. with its Cockspur brand. Although both brands taste nearly identical, Mount Gay has the clear advantage because

other beverages: Once dispensed by the formerly ubiquitous but now extinct mauby lady, mauby is a drink made using a bitter tree bark which—after boiling with spices—is strained and sweetened. It may also be brewed to make a nonalcoholic beer. Ginger beer is a similarly prepared beverage. Prepared from the fresh or dried red sepals of this colorful plant, sorrel is a Christmas drink which is also packaged commercially. It is often mixed with rum. Soft drinks include the non-alcoholic Giant Malt and Ginseng Up from St. Kitts, Coca Cola, Joe's beverage (carbonated concoctions), Plus Action Drink, alcohol-free Tiger Malt, and Barbados Bottled Water. Locally brewed Banks beer and Jubilee Ale is available in every bar. Imports—including brews from Trinidad and Jamaica—are of its distinctive packaging which incorporates a map of Barbados on the label. Interestingly enough, the vagaries of historical circumstance have set distillers competing with each other in unusual ways. Panicking in the face of overwhelming competition by the island's two major distillers (Mount Gay and West India Rum Refinery), the local taverns impelled the legislature to pass the Rum Duty Act of 1906 which forbade the two refineries from selling rum in anything smaller than 10 gallon containers. Accordingly, both refineries have built up separate companies for bottling. Thus, local brands may be aged by Mount Gay but bottled by West India!

rum on Barbados: Possibly no fluid has such a socially solidifying effect anywhere in the world as on Barbados. Not only do the island's inhabitants consume an ungodly 250,000 cases per year, they also do so in an enviable atmosphere of conviviality. For the female Bajan, church is equivalent to social life; men invest their Sunday morning spiritual endeavor imbibing spirits—in that second pillar of the community, the rum shop. Rum is "fired" on social occasions and at all rites of passage: births, christenings, marriages, funerals, and the like. It is drunk either straight from the bottle, using a small "snap" glass, on the rocks, mixed with water, or with a chaser. A small bottle is called a "midi," and a larger one a "flask."

Politicians are notorious for trading rum for votes, the traditional practice being to supply a repast of rum and corn beef to voters both before and after elections.

mixed drinks: A rum punch is made with four parts water, three parts rum, two parts of falernum or other syrup, and one part lime juice—otherwise known as "one of sour, two of sweet, three of strong, four of weak." This is supplemented with a dash of Angostura bitters, a few grains of nutmeg, and a sprig of mint. A planter's punch has the identical ingredients; the difference lies in the glass and decoration. Poured in a long glass, the latter is adorned with chunks of mango, papaya, or other seasonal fruit. An orange slice and a toothpick-stabbed cherry are added for decorative effect. The name "punch" was taken from the large puncheons or casks used to hold up 120 gallons of liquid. *Corn and oil* is a mixture of rum and falernum. Falernum was originally a discovery of Bajan Henry Parkinson who combined ground almonds, brown sugar, clove powder, ginger root, with crushed limes. Parkinson's descendant Arthur Stansfield registered it in 1934. A famous local concoction is *sangaree,* a longtime favorite of the upper classes. To make it a wine glass of sherry, madeira, or port is added to a half-pint tumbler with cracked ice along with a half-teaspoon of port, and a half-teaspoon of Curacao or Dom. Soda water is added along with a slice of lime and with a topping sprinkle of grated nutmeg. The Barbados bombshell is a cocktail made from rum, Pernod, freshly pressed lime juice, and grenadine syrup. Drinks such as pina coladas and banana daiquiris were developed especially for the tourist trade. Pina coladas are made by combining cream of coconut with pineapple juice, rum, and crushed ice. New liquors on the market produced by Butler Bell, the late Prime Minister Tom Adams' butler, include hibiscus-flavored Amoroum and Cane.

PRACTICALITIES

TRANSPORT

by air: The best way to get a deal on airfares here is by shopping around. A good travel agent should call around for you to find the lowest fare; if he or she doesn't, find another agent, or try doing it yourself. If there are no representative offices in your area, check the phone book—most airlines have toll-free numbers. In these days of airline deregulation, fares change quicker than you can say "Bim," so it's best to check the prices well before departure—and then again before you go to buy the ticket. The more flexible you can be about when you wish to depart and return, the easier it will be to find a bargain. Whether dealing with a travel agent or with the airlines themselves, make sure that you let them know clearly what it is you want. Don't assume that because you live in Los Angeles, for example, it's cheapest to fly from there. It may be better to find an ultrasaver flight to gateway cities like New York or Miami and then change planes. Fares tend to be cheaper on weekdays and during low season (mid-April to mid-December). The most prominent carrier serving the Caribbean from the US is now American Airlines. And, with two flights per day (to Miami via San Juan) arriving and departing, it is one of the most convenient airlines to take. From either its Miami or San Juan hubs convenient connecting flights are available to and from virtually every major city. If you need to change your reservation while in Barbados, a reservation counter is located inside the Cave Shepherd Department Store on Broad St. right in the heart of downtown Bridgetown. Pan American flies nonstop from Miami and New York. Battered and beleaguered

Eastern Airlines is trying to reestablish itself in the market also. Service to Barbados commenced in Dec. 1989; they now fly nonstop from Miami. BWIA flies direct to Baltimore, Miami, New York, and Toronto and to Frankfurt, London, and Stockholm on its European routes. Air Canada and Wardair fly nonstop from Toronto. British Airways flies nonstop from London. It takes approximately the following times to reach Barbados from these gateway cities: New York, 4 hrs, 20 min; Miami, 3 hrs, 40 min; Toronto and Montreal, 5 hrs; San Juan, 1 hr 30 min; Caracas, 2 hrs and 30 min; Rio de Janerio, 8 hrs; London, Frankfurt, and Brussels, 9 hrs. Barbados may also be reached by air from everywhere in the Caribbean.

by sea: Sadly, there's no regular passenger service between Barbados and other major Caribbean islands, and none at all from North America. So, unless you are willing to take a cruise ship—which, in addition to costing more than flying, allows only a very limited stay, and often isolates you from locals—there is no regularly scheduled alternative. Cruise ships serving Barbados include P and O lines from Southampton; Hapag and Lloyd from Bremen; Royal Cruise and Royal Viking from San Francisco; Sitmar Cruises from Fort Lauderdale; Royal Caribbean Cruise Lines and Cunard Line from Miami; and a host of others departing out of San Juan, Puerto Rico. These only stop at the island for a day or two with the exception of the Cunard's "Sail n'Stay" package which combines a week's cruise with a week's accommodation at their Cunard Paradise Beach Hotel. One potentially rewarding opportunity if you can afford it is to sail your own yacht to Caribbean waters and travel about on your own. It's possible to crew on a boat coming over from Europe; most boats head for the southern Caribbean.

exploring by ship: A cargo and passenger ship sails from Bridgetown for other islands twice a month. Contact Eric Hassell & Son, Ltd. (tel. 426–5068) for departure dates and times. Caribbean Safari Tours and Tropic Air (tel. 428–8062) offer flights to nearby Union Island and travel from there via a C.S.Y. (Caribbean Sailing Yacht) charter. Another alternative is to fly to St. Vincent and hop a passenger ferry through the Grenadines.

package tours: As they say, all that glitters is not gold. And this cliche may be old but certainly remains pertinent when it comes to package tours! If you want to have everything taken care of, then package tours are the way to go. However, they do have at least two distinct disadvantages: Everything (or most things) have already been decided for you, which takes much of the thrill out of traveling; and you are more likely to be put up in a large characterless hotel (where the tour operators can get quantity discounts), rather than in a small inn (where you can get quality treatment). So think twice before you sign up. Also, if you should want to sign up, read the fine print and see what's *really* included and what's not! Don't be taken in by useless freebies that gloss over the lack of paid meals, and other basic amenities.

hitchhiking by yacht: Hitchhiking by boat through the Caribbean can be easy if you have the time and money to wait for a ride and are at the right place in the right season. Best time to head there is about mid-Oct., just before the boat shows and the preparation for the charter season. Along with those at English Harbor on Antigua, the marinas on St. Thomas (at Red Hook and at Charlotte Amalie) have the greatest concentration of boats and the most competition for work of any island in the Caribbean. Many times it's easy to get a ride from one island to another. Just hang around the docks or pubs and ask! As far as working on yachts goes, it's hard work, low wages, and long hours, and you must have a real love for sailing and the sea. Depending upon whether you are working on salary or for piece work, the salary may or may not depend on how many hours are actually involved. Usually you are constantly doing something from early morning until late at night. Some boats may be more lax than others, but it generally involves pretty continuous work. Check out *Sail* magazine or *Yachting* for the addresses of charter companies. But it's really unnecessary to write: most people are employed on the spot.

arriving by air: Immigration cards are dispensed on the plane and stamped upon arrival. Be sure to retain yours and have B$20 for the departure tax. (Cruise ship passengers are exempt). Be certain to request more time than you think you'll need. If you later decide to stay longer than 28 days, you will have to extend your visa, a time consuming process which requires money and photos. If you have nothing to declare, you will be speeded through customs. Among the forbidden goods are meat and frozen foods, flowers, plants, fruits, guns, and any household pets.

getting around: Blue-with-yellow-stripe Transport Board buses and yellow private minibuses cover all of the paved roads, but you'll need to have patience. Despite the small area involved, always allow plenty of time to get to any island destination. Bus service is inexpensive but painfully inefficient and slow: an example of government bureaucracy at its worst. As Bajans put it, "we complain, complain, complain, until we are blue in the face, but things don't improve." Buses are packed during peak hours (7–10 AM, 4–7 PM), when traffic is near gridlock in and around Bridgetown anyway, so avoid riding at these times. Under normal circumstances, it takes about an hour from Bridgetown to Bathsheba and about half that from Bridgetown to Speightstown. Fares are $1 (exact change) regardless of distance. Tokens are also available in the bus terminal at the information windows. **routing:** The major routes are as follows. No. 1 travels along the West Coast from Bridgetown to Speightstown and on. No. 2 runs to Rock Dundo. No. 3 runs to Turner's Hall via St. Andrew's Church and Hillaby. No. 4 runs to Shorey Village via Welchman Hall Gully, Harrison's Cave, and Flower Forest. No. 6 runs between Bridgetown and Bathsheba. No. 7 runs to Bowmanston via Gun Hill. No. 7A runs to Sergeant Street (village) via Gun Hill station, Bridgetown, and Codrington College. No. 12 runs to Sam Lord's Castle and the Crane Beach Hotel. No. 13A runs to Silver Sands via the S coast. All of the buses lead to or from Bridgetown except those on the Speightstown to Bathsheba (once every two hours) and the Speightstown to Oistins (hourly) routes. The latter is one of the most notoriously unreliable of all the buses; avoid it during rush hour. Bridgetown has three terminals—the largest is on Fairchild St. The other

Minibus, Bridgetown

major terminal is at Speightstown. Otherwise, buses stop at round signs marked "TO TOWN" or "OUT OF TOWN" depending on direction. Yellow private minibuses, which sound from the outside like purring mechanical cockroaches owing to the reggae music flooding their interiors, ply the nation's roadways. Just like the houses, they are named, and they have unique slogans and paintings on their rear ends. Generally, they run over the most heavily populated (and therefore profitable) routes; destinations are marked on a board in the window. Shared taxi vans (also B$1) now cover some routes (such as Bridgetown to Christchurch). Their destination isn't marked so you'll need to ask. Jitney buses, owned and operated by some hotels, shuttle tourists to and fro for free or for a small charge. Identified by the letter "Z" on their license plates, local taxis are expensive. Be sure to agree on the price *before* entering. Knowing the fare will prevent your being deceitfully done in.

Taxi Fares

Between Grantley Adams Airport and

Atlantic Shores	B$16
Bathsheba, Cattlewash	B$36
Belleplaine	B$42
Bridgetown Harbour	B$26
Callenders	B$12
Crane Beach	B$18
East Point	B$25
Gibbes	B$33
Heywoods	B$42
Holetown, Porters	B$30
Long Beach/Silver Sands	B$12
Oistins	B$13
Prospect, St. James	B$27
Rendezvous	B$18
Sam Lord's Castle/Pollards	B$20
Speightstown	B$42
St. Lucy's Parish Church	B$45
Any point N of St. Lucy's Parish Church	B$50

Between Bridgetown/Bridgetown Harbour and

Airport	B$26
Bathsheba, Cattlewash	B$36
Callenders	B$20
Crane Beach	B$30
East Point	B$38
Gibbes, St. Peter	B$25
Harrison's Cave	B$24
Heywoods	B$27
Hilton, Grand Barbados Resort Garrison	B$7

Holders, Paynes Bay	B$16
Holetown, Porters	B$20
Long Beach/Silver Sands	B$26
Oistins	B$17
Rendezvous	B$16
Sam Lord's Castle	B$33
Speightstown	B$27
St. George's Church	B$12
St. John's Church	B$30
St. Lawrence, Dover	B$13
St. Lucy's Parish Church	B$30
Any point N of St. Lucy's Church	B$35
Welchman Hall Gully	B$23

renting a car: Renting a car may be an option you'll want to consider. Cars may be rented at the airport from Avis and Hertz. If you show a valid US or International driver's license, a temporary license will be issued for B$10. This is available from Hastings, Worthing, and Holetown Police Stations and at the Licensing Authority whose offices are at Oistins, Christ Church; the Pine, St. Michael; and Folkestone, St. James. The best alternative, however, is to get the license when you arrive at the airport where there is a police window. Car rental companies can also make arrangements. A permit is also required for motorbikes (70–90 cc maximum available) or mopeds; helmets are required by law. Expect to pay from B$300 per week for a four-passenger "mini-moke" (a hybrid between an Austin Mini and a jeep) to B$600 for a six-passenger automatic saloon. Most companies require a rental of three days or longer. Produce a credit card or face paying a substantial deposit. Smaller companies frequently offer better deals. An important consideration is insurance. If you are not covered, you must pay the first B$600 in damages if you have an accident. Even if it's only a scratch, it could easily amount to this much after repairs. It costs about B$10 per day extra for insurance; keep in mind that this only covers the insuree(s) who is (are) renting the vehicle. If you loan out your rental vehicle, not only will it not be covered but this practice is illegal. Likewise, if you rent from a private party you may save but you'll receive no insurance coverage. Gasoline—an astronomical B$1.10 per litre (for premium)—is extra. As you should do everywhere, read the contract thoroughly—especially the fine print. Ask about unlimited mileage, free gas, late return penalties, and drop-off fees.

rental agencies: For a full list of the 36 car rental companies, check the yellow pages. Some of the more prominent are detailed here. In St. Michael's: Hill's Garage (tel. 426-5280) which offers free pickup and delivery to and from the airport; Barbados Rent-A-Car (tel. 425-1388, 428-0960/3737), P & S Car Rentals (tel. 424-2050/2907); Courtesy (tel. 426-5871/5219); Auto Rentals Limited (tel. 428-9085); National (tel. 426-0603); Johnson's (tel. 65168); with locations in Hastings and in Bridgetown, Dear's (tel. 429-9277, 427-7853); and Sunny Isle (tel. 435-7979). Sunset Crest Rent-A-Car (432-1482) rents mini mokes as well as 4-door automatics. For scooters and motorbikes try Lynn's Rentals (tel. 435-8585). Finally, don't forget the alternative of renting a bicycle, one of the most economical and ecological ways to get around. Outlets include M. A. Williams (tel. 427-1043/3955) in Hastings and Fun Seekers Inc. (tel. 435-8206) in Rockley.

driving in Barbados: Don't forget that you drive on the *left* hand side of the road. On an island this small, it's difficult to get lost. All too often, the island's 830 miles (1280 km) of public roads are poorly marked so getting anywhere can be an adventure in itself! The greater part of the road system was laid out with 17th C. donkey carts in mind, so there are a number of blind corners. Potholes reflect poor maintenance. While Barbados may have one of the most extensive road networks of any island its size, it also may possess the largest quantity of poorly paved surfaces. Drivers frequently disobey the speed limits so exercise caution. Limits are usually 35 kph (21 mph) in town and 60 kph (37 mph) in the countryside. A notable exception to this is on the Spring Garden Highway connecting Bridgetown with St. James which is 80 kph. Two proposed highways will link Fontabelle with Black Rock and Wildey with St. James, and others are also planned. However, when you envision the word "highway," keep in mind that you are talking about the equivalent of what would be an ordinary country road stateside. When rounding a roundabout, remember to give way to traffic from the R and, when that side is clear, you may go. Keep going R until you see the road you want—then take it. Be aware of special island vocabulary when taking directions. "Gap," for example, may signify entrance to a road, a driveway, or a short road. Just as in England all roads lead to London, Barbados's numbered routes all lead to or from Bridgetown. Parking in Bridgetown is denoted by blue "P" signs. Upon parking, entrepreneurs are likely to approach you offering to either wash your car, "mind" your car, or both. Since street parking is scarce, be aware that there are several parking lots. However, owing to the congestion and the confusing one way streets, it's preferable to avoid the town entirely with your car and just take the bus in.

TOURS

One option for visitors with not a great deal of time or with a yen to savor a few different experiences is to take a tour or excursion. Many of these include hotel pickup and dropoff in their pricing. In addition to those listed, large resorts like Sam Lord's Castle offer their own tours for guests.

internal air tours: While there's no internal flight system, one can tour Barbados via a number of small airlines. One is Acro Services (428–8628/9) located at the airport. Skytours offers an air tour (tel. 428–5010/7101) which also includes a buffet, rum punch party, and transport to and from your hotel.

by submarine: Perhaps the most unusual activity available on the island is an underwater voyage on the Atlantis Submarine. Brainchild of Canadian Dennis Hurd, this US$3 million recreational sub is one of a small fleet deployed at tourist concentrations throughout the world; the others are at Kona and Honolulu (Hawaii), Catalina Island (near Los Angeles), St. Thomas, Grand Cayman, and at Guam. After you arrive for

Atlantis Submarine

check in, you can munch on an ice cream from a vendor or there's a Pepsi machine; if you want a drink, there's a nearby a/c bar located off of Hincks St. inside a noisy video parlor. Before you depart, a videotape supplies orientation. Then, a launch takes you out to the 28-passenger sub. After the previous passengers disembark, you board. As you're only going down 150 ft (50 m) for 45 min, there's no need to worry about mishap. Besides, the 49-ton vessel holds food sufficient for three days. The Atlantis II cruises over the artificially sunk wreck of the Lord Willoughby. A running commentary provides information on all of the corals, sponges, and fish that you pass. Fish finder and coral finder charts are conveniently located. Although dives run from day until night, fish fans can see them best early in the morning and from 3-4 PM. After your voyage, you return to the center where a dive certificate is awarded. To book call 436-8929/8932 or 1-800-535-6564 (Caribbean Appetizers) stateside.

greathouse tours: During the winter season, tours are conducted of a selected greathouse every Wednesday by the National Trust (tel. 426-2421, 436-9033).

group tours: Sightseeing taxi tours are available; a six- to seven-hour tour costs around B$150 for a group of one to four people. The most established sightseeing bus tour operator is L. E. Williams (tel. 427–1043/6006/6007/2257) who, on their "80 mile tour," offers free drinks along with lunch at the Atlantis Hotel. Some of the more notable sights they take you to include Animal Flower Cave, Cherry Tree Hill, and St. John's Church. A more personal and unusual tour is offered by John B. Austin (tel. 435–8542, 428–2474) who operates the Tropical Traveler, a tour which takes you in a small van to some of the lesser known island locations. You will visit Gun Hill, the Potteries on Chalky Mount, Hacketon's Cliff, Codrington College, along with other sights. Free drinks and a lively, informative discourse by John, a highly knowledgeable native Barbadian, are included in the price. Remac (tel. 422–0546) offers three types of tours. Another alternative, run by Sally Shearn, is VIP Limo Services (tel. 429–4617), an eight-hour limo tour custom designed according to your specifications.

rum tour: One of the more unusual tours is "Where the rum comes from" (tel. 435–6900) which combines a chance to tour the Spring Garden Highway Mt. Gay rum plant with a buffet lunch. As a warmup, drinks are dispensed gratis as a four-man steel band plays under the shelter of a green and white canopied tent. Lunch—set out on tables under a green corrugated zinc-roofed pavilion—consists of a choice of chicken, stew, macaroni pie, rice, salad, plus coffee and dessert. The short but informative tour illustrates the distilling process.

air excursions: One- or two-day air excursions to neighboring islands (such as St. Vincent, Dominica, Martinique, St. Lucia, Grenada, the Grenadines, and Tobago) are offered by Caribbean Safari Tours Ltd. (tel. 427–5100).

ACCOMMODATIONS

The major industry is tourism, and Barbados is *not* for low budget travelers. The cost of lodging is high—from US$35 d to $400 or more per night. And the 5 percent room tax along with a frequently applied 10 percent service charge makes this island even more expensive! It's cheapest to visit this island off season (mid-April through mid-December), and the major resorts have three or four sets of rates: winter, summer, shoulder, and (sometimes) Christmas. There are no campsites, and camping is forbidden. Accommodations here range in size from beefy 300-room hotels to small guesthouses. In addition to luxury resorts, there are self-catering apartments and furnished villas and cottages. The majority of the structures are designed to blend in harmoniously with the landscape. Hotels, guesthouses, condos, etc. are listed in the back of the book. It's a good idea to get the current rates from the tourist board. If they don't list the rates, it's just that they haven't supplied them to the board, so use the address or phone number listed in the chart to contact them. There are also rental agents on the island. If you arrive without reservations, the Board of Tourism has offices to help you in both the airport and the harbor. Finally, while reservations may not be necessary for the large hotels except during the season, it would be prudent to reserve and send a deposit to the smaller establishments so you can be certain of your booking. Otherwise, your vacation might end up costing you substantially more than you had counted on.

apartment and condominium rentals: Located at Derricks on the St. James coast, Alleyne, Aguilar, and Altman (tel. 432–0840) have a large list of villa rentals. Abroad, you may try Caribbean Home Rentals, Box 710, Palm Beach, FL, tel. (305) 833–4454; Villas and Apartments Abroad, 19 East 49th St., NY, NY 10017, tel. (212) 759–1025; and Travel Resources, Box 1043, Coconut Grove, FL, tel. (305) 444–8583.

NIGHTLIFE AND ENTERTAINMENT

Few locations for their size can rival Barbados's breadth and scope of nightlife. While the island has the usual plethora of Caribbean pseudo-cultural events comprising limbo dancing, belly dancing, fire eating demonstrations and dancing on broken bottles barefooted, it also features high quality theater performances. Also available are discos, English-style pubs, rum shops, and local dances featuring sound systems.

dinner entertainment: Marriott's Sam Lord's Castle offers a special eight-course dinner in its antique dining room. Served on the Queen's china complemented with Waterford crystal, the meal commemorates the banquet served to Queen Elizabeth II during her visit. The Shipwreck Party features an outdoor buffet (flying fish, steak, chicken, salad, baked potatoes), a steel band, Egbert the fire eater, a flaming limbo duo, and Roslyn "the Golden Girl" calypso dancer. Yet another Sam Lord production is "Bajan Fiesta Night": A "village" is created in the pool area with each hut offering a different specialty; a floor show follows. A "Night of the Buccaneers" takes place on Thursday evenings at the Barbados Hilton; it showcases a performance by the Country Theater Workshop. On Mon. and Thurs. nights, the Apple Experience in Hastings presents "Bajan Night" featuring music, limbo and belly dancing, and fire eating. The Ocean View also offers the seasonal "Xanadu Follies." For other dinner and entertainment features see the dinner theater listing under the "Theater" section.

English-style pubs: There are a number of these including the Mill Pub and Restaurant, The Windsor Arms, and the Cricketeers at Coconut Creek Hotel on the W coast. The Coach House in Paynes Bay, St. James features live bands most nights as does The Ship Inn in St. Lawrence Gap. The Sir Francis Drake is right across the street.

clubs: Two a/c equipped intimate clubs downtown, September's, on Bay St. and Higher Level, are active on Fri. and Sat. nights. Featuring an open air terrace with the lights of Bridgetown gleaming off in the background, the Warehouse, newly rebuilt after a devastating 1989 blaze, has live bands on its bandstand below. Set right on the water's edge at the Careenage, Waterfront Cafe, also similarly devastated and rebuilt, features nearly nightly entertainment focusing on jazz and folk. On the other side of the Careenage, the Station Break and the Shoreliner present a "floating nightclub" every Fri. night from 9–? The special feature of Harbour Lights (open 9:30–4:30)—set right on the beach overlooking Carlisle Bay—is dancing to live bands under the stars. Live bands are on five nights per week; unlimited drinks (B$15 cover) are dispensed on Wed. There's a mostly youthful crowd here, and a selective door keeps out hustlers. Located on the beach at Hastings, Sandy Bank provides bands and caters to a youthful crowd. A barrel of rum punch is dispensed *gratis* every Mon. from 6 PM until the cask bottoms out. Also located in Hastings, Apple Experience features live entertainment on Mon., Thurs., and Sat. The liveliest area on the island for nightlife is undoubtedly in St. Lawrence Gap. And After Dark is unquestionably the island's classiest as well as its most iconoclastic club. Originally only a jazz bar, it is now divided into two distinct sections: a disco and a jazz room. The twin bars feature rows of hanging sparkling crystalware, with fine mahogany and pine walls and counters. There are also beautiful chandeliers and plenty of mirrors. A passageway leads to the jazz bar which has comfortable stuffed armchairs and a wide screen TV which plays jazz videotapes when the band breaks. Open 5 PM–5:30 AM, After Dark caters to an older crowd, and, unlike other clubs, it has a large local clientele. To one side of After Dark is The Backyard which is also a really nice outdoor bamboo-style disco—catering largely to beach boys and their clientele. This is a great place for socio-anthropological observation. On the other side, the Ship's Inn features bands nightly. Unfortunately, the band plays inside, and the only dancing area is the narrow path right in front of them. Although it's another big beach boy hangout—lotsa cool young dudes done up in dreads and gold chains—you might see any type of tourist inside. The restaurant/bar area features a unique, nautical-style atmosphere with eclectic displays of sea-oriented paraphernalia. As with the Backyard, the cover is redeemable in drinks, and some 4–500 people circulate here on Fri. and Sat. nights. A British-style pub, the Duke of Edinburgh is across the street. Out on the main road and farther down the stretch near Divi's, check out the Pepperpot Entertainment Centre. In St. Thomas, the Bagatelle Great House's restaurant converts into a sophisticated nightclub after hours.

Practicalities 99

The liveliest clubs in Holetown are The Beach Club, which features a different band nightly, and The Hippo at Barbados Beach Club down the road towards Bridgetown, whose specialty is male and female dancers. Piano bars include the Music Man Inn and Rockley.

local dances: These gatherings are one of the best ways to enjoy yourself you can find. And they're found easily—through posters and in the newspapers. Generally, they occupy small rectangles spread over a full page in the *Weekend Nation*. Each notice has the picture(s) of the sponsor(s) along with their name(s), occupation(s), and when and where the dance will take place. The sponsors rent the place for the night, jack up the drink prices slightly to make money, and charge B$3–5 admission. Attendance is the key to profit, and, while a dance may lose money, it can also make up to $600 or so. The dances are divided into certain categories. A "dance" usually plays reggae, oldies, spouge, and calypso. A "grand dance" simply has a more impressive title. A "splash down" is frequently a

Dance posters, St. Michael

Ice cone cart at cinema, Bridgetown

more informal event, and a "supa fete" caters to a younger crowd and includes more dub music.

movies: Kung fu, sex, and violence. These thematic threesomes dominate the fare at the island's cinemas. Award-winning films arrive on occasion, but *only* on occasion.

others: Known as "the street that never sleeps," Baxter's Road is always fun. It may be difficult *not* to hang out in local bars for there are an estimated 1,000 or more rum shops on the island. Located in Clapham, Henry Bailey Observatory opens its doors to stargazers every Friday night. Church socials, listed in the paper, are a good way to meet locals.

concerts: There are a number of venues. In Queen's Park, the major hall is the Steel Shed. Inside, smoothly swirling ceiling fans hang from the rounded corrugated iron roof. The comfortable green upholstered chairs can be moved across the red painted concrete floor. The Queen's Park Theatre, in Queen's Park House just a bit farther on, shows plays on occasion. The Frank Collymore Hall, named after the eminent writer and linguist, is inside the Central Bank Building.

SPORTS AND RECREATION

beaches and swimming: There're over 70 square miles of beaches in colors ranging from virgin white to coral pink. The seas are rougher along the Atlantic on the N and E coasts; on the "lee" side, the W and S coasts are generally calm. Along the E coast exercise caution while swimming. Don't swim after eating or allow your kids to swim unsupervised. Legally, all the island's beaches must provide unrestricted access. However, you can expect to pay for the use of beach chairs.

scuba and snorkeling: Barbados is an exceptionally fine place to do either. A large number of companies offer instruction/rentals with PADI and/or NAUI certified teachers. If you're inexperienced in diving, expect to train for a few days in a swimming pool first. Plan to spend about B$30 for lessons and about B$60–70 per one tank dive including boat fee. Although gear is loaned out free of charge on board excursion cruises, snorkelers would do well to bring their own equipment because otherwise gear rents for B$8–10 per hour. (One place that snorkeling gear is provided *gratis* is on daytime boat excursions). Locations for renting snorkeling and scuba equipment include Dive Boat Safari (tel. 426-0200, ex. 395), the Dive Shop (tel. 426-9947), and Willie's Water Sports (425-1060)—all in St. Michael; Exploresub Barbados (tel. 435-6542,

428-7181, ex. 349), Underwater Barbados (tel. 428-9739), and Best Western Sandy Beach Hotel—all in Christ Church; and Jolly Roger Water Sports (tel. 422-2335, ex. 116, 432-7090), Coral Reef Club (tel. 422-3215, 432-2068), the Divi Hotel, Blue Reef Watersports (tel. 422-3133), and Sandy Lane Hotel (tel. 432-1311)—all in St. James. The ruins of the deliberately sunken freighter *Stavronikita* lie at the Folkestone National Marine Reserve here. For information on scuba diving, call Brian Stanley at the Barbados Subaqua Club, tel. 427-5190.

surfing: The E coast is famous for its waves. Surfing spots include Bathsheba, just inland from Bow Bells reef off South Point, at Gravesend near the Hilton, Rockley Beach (on the SW coast between Worthing and St. Lawrence), and at Enterprise Beach near Oistins.

wind surfing: Conditions for wind surfing are said to be among the best in the world. Try Windsurfing Barbados (tel. 429-8216) at the Hilton, Club Mistral (tel. 428-9095) at Christ Church, and Jolly Roger Water Sports (432-1311) in St. James. Steady breezes at Maxwell, Silver Sands, and Round Rock make for great windsurfing.

angling: Some of the best fishing is to be had off of the northern and southern coasts. The prize catch is a blue marlin. Offshore anglers can expect to reel in yellowtail, snapper, mackerel, jacks, small barracuda, snook, and tarpon.

deep-sea fishing: You can expect yellowfin tuna, dolphin (dorado), mackerel, bonefish, sailfish, barracuda, yellowfish, blue marlin, and wahoo. Charters (available for half or full day) include Blue Jay Charters (tel. 422-2098), Dive Shop Ltd. (tel. 426-9947), Jolly Roger (tel. 432-7090, 422-2335, ext. 116), Loisan II (tel. 427-5485), Sandy Lane (tel. 432-1311), Cap'n Jack (tel. 427-5800-02/428-2793), Southern Palms (426-7171), La Paloma (tel. 427-5588/429-5643), Challenge (tel. 436-5725), or the Barracuda (tel. 426-7252/7898). Also try Pakis Water Sports in St. Michael. Expect to pay in the range of B$300-450 per half day.

sea excursions: Many boat trips are available. Most include lunch and or cocktails and transportation to and from your hotel. *The Bajan Queen* (tel. 436-2149/2150) offers water cruises as does *The Jolly Roger* (tel. 436–6424). Both offer party atmosphere, a buffet meal, a live band, and free use of snorkeling gear. *The Bajan Queen* also has a rope by which you can drop right into the water. Sailboats and yachts (see below) also offer more intimate excursions.

night cruises: These are usually party, party, and more party. With unlimited free booze and a live band, a good time is had by all. *The Bajan Queen* (tel. 436-2149/2150) caters to a mixed crowd while *The Jolly Roger* (tel. 436-6424) appeals to the college set. Painted a sleek red and white, *The Bajan Queen* has live reggae band and a buffet dinner with Bajan cuisine. Departures are at 6 PM, and transport is provided to and from your hotel. On Thurs. night *The Jolly Roger* features the renowned local group The Merrymen.

glass bottom boats: Best on the west coast owing to the calm sea; there are a number of private firms on the beach offering trips. Also try Blue Reef Watersports (tel. 422-3133), Dive Shop, Ltd. (tel. 426-9947), Jolly Roger Watersports (tel. 432-7090), and Sandy Lane (tel. 432-1311).

The Bajan Queen, *Bridgetown Harbour*

regattas: Several yacht races are held every year. The season's highlight is the Atlantic Rally for Cruisers (ARC) when over 200 yachts arrive from Gran Canaria for the race's dramatic climax. Many of these stay put for the Mount Gay Regatta which is held around Christmas time.

tennis: An abundance of courts are found on the island. A parish-by-parish list follows: Paragon Tennis Club (on Brittons Hill) and Cunard Paradise Beach, both in St. Michael; Casuarina Beach Club, Rockley Resort Hotel, and Southwinds Hotel and Beach Club in Christ Church; Crane Beach Hotel and Ginger Bay Hotel and Beach Club in St. Philip; Sandy Lane Hotel and Sunset Crest Club in St. James; and Cobblers Cove and Heywoods in St. Peter. Typical charges are B$4-12 per hr. In addition to those found at hotels, public hard and grass courts are maintained at Folkestone Park in Holetown and at the Garrison (B$2 ph charge).

golf: Originally opened as a nine-hole course in 1946, the Rockley Resort Hotel's greens were opened in redesigned form as an 18-hole course in 1946. Just outside Bridgetown, the most popular course, the Sandy Lane Golf Club, has an 18-hole layout. The three-day Sandy Lane Open, the Barbados Golf Association's main annual event, is played here in November. Another course is at Heywoods Resort Hotel, St. Peter.

squash: Courts include the Barbados Squash Club, Rockley Resort Hotel, and Casuarina Beach Club in Christ Church; Heywoods in St. Peter; and a number of other courts.

horseback riding: English-style riding along scenic trails. Contact Brighton Riding Stable (tel. 425-9381), Caribbean International Riding Stables (tel. 423-1086), Wilcox Riding Stable (tel. 428-7809/8388) and Ye Old Congo Road Stables (tel. 423-8293/6180), Country Corral Riding Stables (tel. 422-2401), and Valley Hill Stables (tel. 423-0033). Expect to pay around B$40-50 ph.

polo: Venues are the Barbados Polo Club in St. James and Brighton Stables in St. Michael.

running: The Run Barbados International Road Race Series is held the first week in December. There are two courses: one following a 26-mile and 385-yard (42,195 meter) marathon along paved roads and by the sea and a 10-kilometer run in and around Bridgetown. Attracting competitors worldwide, its top prizes include air fare and hotel accommodation so that competitors may return to enter the next year's race.

aerobics and Nautilus: For those who are worried about missing their workout while on vacation, there's no reason to fret. A number of facilities offer classes. Contact Family Fitness Centre (tel. 429-9287), Dancersise Fitness Centre (tel. 427-8564), Body Electric Exercise Studio (tel. 428-1890), Profile Health and Beauty Club (tel. 432-1393), Executive Health Club (tel. 427-2564), Radiant Health Club (tel. 436-1024), National Fitness Centre (tel. 429-7600), Speightstown Mall's Paramount (tel. 422-5965), and the Universal Health Club (tel. 429-8273).

bridge: Located in Belleville, the Barbados Bridge League welcomes visitors to its games of duplicate bridge held from Mon. to Thurs. and on Sat., tel. 427-4839.

hiking: Although not a hiker's paradise, the island has a number of paths; many of them run along the gorgeous Atlantic coast. Bring a good pair of shoes because the crusty coral coast can be sharp. And bring a small water bottle because, when out on the coast, there are no facilities without traipsing inland. One of the great conveniences for the walker or hiker is the now-antiquated standpipe. Here, you can get a refreshing blast of clear, clean coral-filtered water. From Jan. through March the Barbados National Trust (tel. 426-2421) and the Duke of Edinburgh Award Scheme host early Sunday morning (6 AM) rural five-mile walks. Usually, you assemble in front of an old sugar plantation. With around 300 participating, it's an excellent way to meet Bajans. Walkers are divided into three groups: fast, medium, and slow. The Outdoor Club of Barbados (tel. 436-5328) offers excursions three times per week. Food and transport are included.

Cricket

If one passion can be ascribed to Bajans, it must be love for this, the national sport. It's never hard to catch a match. If it's not going on along some back road or lot, then you'll find it at an elite International Test Match, usually played between January and April or at a club match in the first division competition (May to mid-December). Internationally famous for its almost religious reverence for the sport, Barbados has given the world the three "Ws"—Frank Worrell, Everton Weekes, and Clyde Walcott. Considered by some to be the island's national religion, cricket is tightly interwoven with the island's moral fabric. The expression "it's not cricket" stands as a byword for what is not upright moral conduct. Cricket, more than any other activity or attribute, has gained Barbados international recognition. A source of national pride, it is one of society's unifying bonds. It has been partially responsible for taking the island's stratified and isolated classes and bringing them together—a process which was a necessary precursor to independence.

history: Originally the exclusive cultural property of the upper classes, cricket reflected society's tiered apartheid-like structure. Wanderers, formed in 1877, along with its successor, Pickwick, were both white as a ghost in composition. But, while Wanderers catered to the merchants, Pickwick drew its membership from the plantocracy. Drawing from the growing pool of black and mulatto professionals, Spartan maintained the standards for its "class." Its blackballing of black public health inspector Herman Griffith—because he was felt to fall below their social station—led dissidents to found the Empire Club. One of the game's classic players, Griffith became the first black ever to captain a Bajan team. This upper class Bridgetown-centered sport soon spread island-wide. Workers, farmers, and carpenters took up the sport and founded their own leagues; plantation overseers encouraged their workers to play—often providing a field and second hand equipment—because they took notice of its importance as a form of social bonding. Of course the *pukka* Barbados Cricket Association turned up its nose at these lower class leagues. But the spir-

Cricket

ited rivalry between plantations gave birth to the Barbados Cricket League—a revolutionary event which initialized the process of breaking down class and racial barriers. However, the true lower class was still excluded from participation.

cricket heroes and mascots: Over the years cricket has thrived to the point that Barbados's greatest heroes are now cricketeers. One of the three "Ws," Frank Worley, was knighted by Queen Elizabeth in 1964, and he peers from the face of the B$5 bill. Lethally lithe left hander Garfield Sobers—whom no less a personage than the Mighty Sparrow, the greatest living calypsonian, has dubbed "the greatest cricketer on earth or on Mars"—was knighted by the Almighty Queen on the Garrison Savannah, where some of the earliest recorded matches took place. Today, a cricket hero garners moola as well as hoopla: a top star may receive B$50,000 per year, a fortune in Barbadian economic terms. And top players, even those of lesser standing, can find jobs teaching and coaching abroad with relative ease. Flannagan, a traveling mascot, entertained followers by attacking Barbados's opponents during the 30s and 40s. Today, King Dyal—unfailingly dressed in a flashily colored three-piece suit—regularly appears, as he has for nearly three decades, to root for the opposition!

cricket today: Despite the slight slip in performance, the sport's popularity remains high if not fanatical. You'll see Bajan youth practicing everywhere, using anything that remotely resembles equipment to sharpen their skills—for cricket remains one of the few outlets for social mobility available to them. Taken together, the Association and the League, the two main cricket clubs, host 100 matches on Saturday afternoons between early June and mid-September. International matches are major events running for five days from 10:30 AM to 5:30 PM daily for five consecutive days. Barbadians picnic on the grounds, munching on local cuisine and shipping it down with hits of rum. You can count on Kensington Oval, the largest ground, being crammed to its 15,000 capacity on Test Match days when the local team faces off against Australia or England. Local club matches may pack in crowds as large as 4,000 to the smaller grounds. For current information on matches, call the Barbados Cricket Association, tel. 436-1397.

other spectator-only sports: In addition to cricket, Bajans are afficianados of other spectator sports. The more than 100 softball leagues—which play a modified version of the game using tennis balls and mahogany bats—hold contests on Sun. mornings. Affiliated with the Twickenham Rugby Union, the Barbados Rugby Club competes regularly against visiting teams and naval ships. For more information, contact Victor Roach, tel. 436-6883. Both men and women play hockey, and an international festival is held annually in August. Coordinator is Mike Owen, tel. 436-3911. The center of horseracing for over eight decades, Garrison Savannah plays host to the Barbados Turf Club's two annual seasons: from Jan. to May and from Aug. to Nov. on alternate Saturdays. Entrance to the grandstand is B$10. Including competition from Trinidad, Martinique, and Jamaica, the Cockspur Gold Cup Race usually takes place in early March. For information call 426-3980. Holding forth at its grounds at Holders, St. James, the

Barbados Polo Club (tel. 432-1802) plays on Sat., Sun. and Wed. during the August-to-April season.

OTHER PRACTICALITIES

money and measurements: Monetary unit is the Barbados dollar, which is divided into 100 cents. Notes are issued in denominations of 1, 5, 10, 20, and 100, and coins are minted in amounts of 1, 5, 10, and 15 cents, and $1. Current exchange rate is US$1 = B$1.98. There is no black market. Most banks impose a service charge of B$1-2 plus stamp duty of 10 cents per check cashed. You may evade the service charge by changing a larger amount of money. Cash brings slightly less than traveler's checks, and there is no service charge. You must produce an air ticket and identification to change your money back to foreign currency, and you lose around 2-3 percent; you can do so at the airport, but the bank opens at 8 AM so if you have an early morning flight be sure to do it the evening before. Major credit cards are accepted by banks, shops, and restaurants. The metric system is used, and gasoline and milk are both sold by the liter. While road distances are given in kilometers, road speed signs and car speedometers use miles per hour. Land elevations are expressed in meters. The island operates on Atlantic Standard Time which matches Eastern Daylight Time during the summer.

banking hours: Banks are open 9-3, Mon. through Thurs., and Fri., 9-1. Barclays is open Mon to Thurs., 8-3, Fri., 8-1 and 3-5. At the airport, Barbados National Bank is open 8-midnight daily. Money can also be changed at your hotel but at a slightly lower rate.

visas: Citizens of the British Commonwealth and the following nations do not require visas for stays of up to three months: Austria, Belgium, Columbia, Denmark, Finland, West Germany, Greece, Iceland, Republic of Ireland, Israel, Liechtenstein, Luxembourg, Netherlands, Norway, Peru, San Marino, Spain, Surinam, Sweden, Switzerland, Tunisia, Turkey, USA, and Venezuela. (American citizens may enter with a passport, driver's license, or voter's registration card). Citizens of most other countries (except Communist ones) may stay without visas for 21 days providing they have onward tickets. All others must have visas; applications should be accompanied by two photos and a letter from a travel agent on letterhead certifying booking. Business travelers should have a letter from their company giving details of their business and confirming financial support for the applicant. If you are arriving from South America, you may be asked to produce a yellow fever vaccination certificate. In order to extend your stay, you must apply at Customs House at The Wharf in Bridgetown, tel. 426-9912.

broadcasting and media: The two major dailies are the *Advocate* and the *Nation*. The *Advocate's* motto—spread across a narrow scroll folded into divisions—lies right under its blue banner. "For the cause that lacks assistance/against the wrongs that need resistance/for the future in the distance/and the good that I can do." Regrettably, it's all downhill after the motto. The paper relies heavily on sensationalistic banner headlines with minimal coverage of the world outside Barbados. One suspects that they must be big Nancy Reagan fans because "Just Say No To Drugs" is frequently interspersed throughout the pages. With a pink on yellow masthead and a ubiquitous "dainty, vivacious, and sexy" cover girl, the always hilarious *Weekend Investigator* is also a product of the *Advocate's* newsroom. Considered outrageous by the island's prim and proper, it resembles an American soft core porn mag of the 1950s. The letters column will have you rolling on the floor in stitches. Its photographers also exploit young women (domestic and foreign) by shooting them on the beaches and in the discos. Its saving grace is the wonderful column written by calypsonian The Mighty Gabby. *The Nation* is slightly better than the *Advocate*, but *only* slightly. Its weekend edition features the right wing rantings of columnist Gladstone Holder, a Lyndon La Rouche defender. Its most controversial and outspoken columnist is Jeanette-Layne Clark. More independent and radical than the daily newspapers, the excellent monthly *Caribbean Contact* is an ecumenical newspaper which supplies news and views from around the Caribbean. The *New Bajan* is the island's news magazine, and *Bim*, published twice a year, is the Caribbean's leading literary journal. The *West Indies Chronicle*, published by the West India Committee in London, and *British Trade Topics*, published by the British High Commission in Port of Spain, are also available. Tourist literature of value includes the annuals *Time Out in Barbados Magazine*, *The Ins and Outs of Barbados*, and the biweeklies *The Sun Seeker* and *The Visitor*—as well as the monthly calendar-format tabloid *What's On*. Imported newspapers and magazines are unconscionably expensive. Two rags with surprisingly high circulation given their dear price are *The National Enquirer* and the always hilarious *Weekly World News*. Imported from Trinidad are two papers—the *Sunday Punch* ("The Love Paper") and *The Bomb*—which make the local press seem intellectual! The state-owned Caribbean Broadcasting Corporation (CBC) has two AM stations (CBC, 900 AM; VOB, 790 AM) and one FM (Liberty, 98.1). The Barbados Broadcasting Service operates BBS, 90.7 FM. The newest FM station is Yess Ten Four at 104.1 FM. Barbados Redifusion Service operates a wired service featuring the "Voice of Barbados" program (790 AM). CBC introduced TV service (Channel 3) in 1964, and there are roughly 200 TVs for every 1,000 Bajans. It shows CNN from 6–10 AM, Mon. to Fri. and Sat. and Sun. from 9–1. Broadcasting hours are 5 p.m. to 11:45 PM Mon. to Fri. and 1 PM to 12:30 AM on Sat. and Sun.

health: World-renowned for its purity, water is safe to drink everywhere. Medical care is usually on a first-come, first-served basis. Bridgetown's 600-bed Queen Elizabeth Hospital (tel. 436-6450) is the main hospital; eight health centers and 10 other health clinics are scattered across the island. Although the quality of medical and dental services is among the highest in the Caribbean, it's not quite up to US standards.

conduct: Men and women alike tend to dress conservatively. If you want to be accepted and respected, dress respectably. Bathing attire is unsuitable on main streets as is revealing female attire. Going shirtless or wearing too short shorts is also *verboten* on streets. While there are a few louts about, Bajans are among the most polite, gracious, and hospitable

Suggested dress code

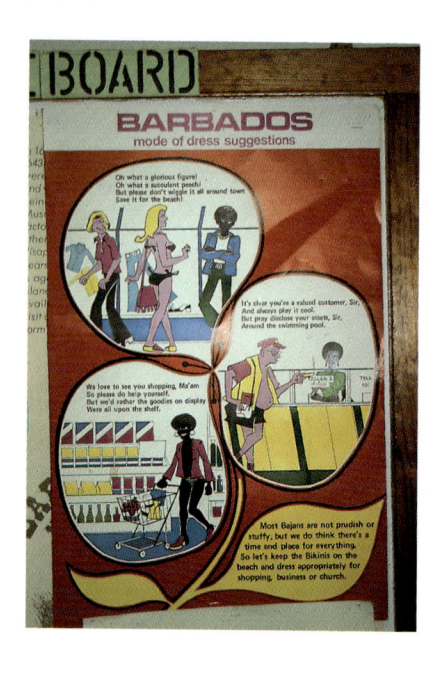

people in the entire Caribbean, if not the world. While the contact with outside has brought some of the bustle along with a considerable amount of its hustle, the island still has the feel of a large village. Be sure to ask people's permission before you take their picture. Generally, adults are reluctant to have their picture taken. Some feel that you are going to make fun of them; others that you are somehow financially benefiting from their picture. Children are willing subjects. Traditional Barbadian culture focuses on politeness. Inquiries are usually prefaced by a "Good Morning", "Good Afternoon," or "Good Evening." These simple courtesies go a long way. Remember to respect private property while visiting ruins: Be sure to ask permission first. All beaches on Barbados are public by law from the vegetation line down to the water. Certain hotels have attempted to restrict usage by charging visitors an entrance fee; however, you can just circumvent paying by entering the beach area to the side. Expect to be charged, however, if you use private facilities like lounge chairs or changing rooms. And, remember that you are sharing the beach: Don't litter or make excessive noise. Expect to find hustlers hassling you on the beach. The most effective treatment is to firmly say "no thank you" from the start, or it will be impossible to get rid of them. Viewing the merchandise will only draw the interchange out, and you may end up purchasing something just to make them go away!

women traveling alone: A large number of women come to Barbados alone or in groups, and the attitudes of some of them have led local males to assume that they are part of your adventure in paradise. You should have no problems with men if you simply say "thanks but no thanks" when you are offered the priceless chance by men to spend the night with their "big bamboo." Expect to be confronted and challenged aggressively by males even if you are with a guy. Part of the reason for the male chauvinist attitudes prevalent here is the state of male-female relations on the island. Another is the influence of Western movies and television programs. Traveling will be a relatively hassle-free experience as long as you exude a certain amount of confidence.

environmental conduct: Respect the reefs. Take nothing and remember that corals are easily broken. Exercise caution while snorkeling, scuba diving, or anchoring a boat. Dispose of plastics properly. Remember that six-pack rings, plastic bags, and fishing lines can cause injury or prove fatal to sea turtles, fish, and birds. Turtles may mistake plastic bags for jellyfish or choke on fishing lines. Birds may starve to death after becoming entangled in lines, nets, and plastic rings. In order to protect your own hide, never go snorkeling without tying a float (such as a bright beach ball or a white plastic gallon container) to your wrist or ankle to serve as a warning to speedboat or jetski drivers. Correspondingly, jetski afficionadoes should keep a keen eye out for snorkelers and bear in mind that most people come to the beach to *escape* hustle and bustle. Those interested in preserving the environment or in gaining a further appreciation would do well to contact the Barbados Environmental Association, Box 132, Bridgetown. They have occasional lectures at the Barbados Museum as well as nature walks.

photography: Film isn't particularly cheap here so you might want to bring your own. Kodachrome KR 36, ASA 64, is the best all-around slide film. For prints 100 or 200 ASA is preferred, while 1000 ASA is just the thing underwater. For underwater shots use a polarizing filter to cut down on glare; a flash should be used in deep water. Avoid photographs between 10 and 2 when there are harsh shadows. Photograph landscapes while keeping the sun to your rear. Set your camera a stop or a stop and a half down when photographing beaches in order to prevent overexposure from glare. A sunshade is a useful addition. Keep your camera and film out of the heat. Replace your batteries before a trip or bring a spare set. Finally, remember not to subject your exposed film to the X-ray machines at the airport: hand-carry them through.

film developing: Sun Colour limited has one-hour photo developing and printing available at their Cave Shepherd (Broad St.) and their Sunset Mall (St. James) stores. Their Windsor store in Hastings is open 24 hours.

what to take: Bring as little as possible, i.e. bring what you need. It's easy just to wash clothes in the sink and thus save lugging around a week's laundry. Laundromats, in the form of "laundermats," are available at selected locations; a wash is around B$3.50. Remember, simple is best. Set your priorities according to your needs. With a light pack or bag, you can breeze through from one town to another easily. Confining yourself to carry-on luggage also saves waiting at the airport. See the chart for suggestions and eliminate unnecessary items.

What to Take

CLOTHING
socks and shoes
underwear
sandals or thongs
T-shirts, shirts (or blouses)
shirts/pants, shorts
swimsuit

hat
light jacket/sweater

TOILETRIES
soap
shampoo
towel, washcloth
toothpaste/toothbrush
comb/brush
prescription medicines
chapstick/other essential toiletries
insect repellent
suntan lotion/sunscreen
shaving kit
toilet paper
nail clippers
hand lotion
small mirror

OTHER ITEMS
passport/identification
driver's license
travelers checks
moneybelt
address book
notebook
pens/pencils
books, maps
watch
camera/film
flashlight/batteries
snorkeling equipment
extra glasses
umbrella/poncho
laundry bag
laundry soap/detergent
matches/lighter
frisbee/sports equipment
cooking supplies (for apartment hotel living)

theft: There should not be a problem if you're reasonably cautious. By all means don't flash money or possessions around and, in general, keep a low profile. Don't leave anything unattended on the beach, and keep off the deserted beaches at night. Never, never leave anything in an unoccupied vehicle. Bajans are forbidden to use credit cards, and there isn't much of a market for hot cameras, so cash is the aim of thieves. Remember that locals who form sexual liaisons with foreigners often do so with pecuniary gain in mind. And, if you give one of them access to your hotel room, it's a bit sticky to then go to the police and make a charge.

services and information: Unlike some other islands, Barbados has a fairly reliable phone system, including a good supply of pay phones. To use a pay phone, wait for a dial tone *before* inserting your 25 cents; calls are limited to five minutes, after which you'll need another coin. Unlimited free local calls are included in the basic service so local calls made from your hotel room are free of charge. Available at limited locations—including the airport, Carlisle Bay Centre, and at the harbor—card phones use a pre-paid phone card which makes them ideal for overseas calls. The number for local information is 119. The island's area code is 809. Tourist information centers are at the airport. The best available map is the $1/50,000$ scale government Ordnance Survey map with an index prepared by the National Trust, but the regular old giveaway map should be sufficient for ordinary use. In addition to one-hour and same-day laundry services, a number of self-service laundromats (termed "laundermats") are located in the major towns and resort areas. Sun Colour Ltd—which has shops at Cave Shepherd, Broad St. and with branches in Hastings and Sunset Mall—offers one-hour film developing. In operation Mon. to Thurs., 6–9 PM, and Fri. to Sun., 6 PM–6 AM, the Rape and Crisis Center provides confidential counseling and referrals.

postal service: District Post Offices stand in every parish. Put outgoing mail in red pillar postal boxes. Letter rates are 25 cents local, 50 cents within the West Indies, 65 cents to North America, and 75 cents to Europe. Parcel post packages may be mailed from the General Post Office headquarters in Cheapside, Bridgetown. An express delivery service guarantees delivery within 48 hours. Collectors will want to visit the Philatelic Bureau. With a deposit account, first day covers will be mailed to your address.

libraries: The Central Public Library stands next to the Law Courts on Coleridge St., Bridgetown, tel. 426-1744. Open Mon. to Sat., 9-5. Among its collections' treasures are old books and newspapers about Barbados which may be examined. Branches are located in Christ Church, St. George, St. James, St. Peter, St. Philip, and St. Thomas parishes. Books may be borrowed for a B$20 refundable deposit.

nuptials: Getting married is a big industry on the island. And there are a number of places to do it—from aboard a yacht to the chapel of your choice. There is a six-day residency requirement along with a B$100 charge for a marriage license which must be accompanied by a B$13 revenue stamp obtainable from any post office. Three days are required to process the application.

hair stylists: Primadonna (tel. 435-7303) offers "hair designs," manicure, and pedicure. The Hair Club Beauty Salon (tel. 427-9655, 436-2165) specializes in special services for "women of colour." Many others can be found by consulting the Yellow Pages.

embassies: The US consular section is on the first floor of Trident House in Bridgetown, tel. 426-3574. The Canadian High Commission stands at Bishops Court Hill, St. Michael, tel. 429-3550. The UK's address is Lower Collymore Rock, St. Michael, tel. 426-3525. The Federal Republic of Germany is at Banyan Court, Bay St., St. Michael, tel. 427-1876.

dining out: Many tourist restaurants are in the B$60-70 range. If you have a prepaid package at a luxury resort such as the Coral Reef Club, you may be able to take advantage of "exchange dining" which will allow you to dine at, for example, Cobbler's Cove. Most dinner shows and buffets have an all-you-can-eat policy, but you are limited to "firsts" on the meat, fish, or chicken. Generally, a 5 percent tax and 10 percent service charge are added on top of the base price except in the case of fixed price buffets. If in doubt, ask. While a large number of restaurants are mentioned in the text, it is beyond the scope of this book to evaluate them in detail. Consult the current issues of *Dine Barbados* or *The Ins and Outs of Barbados.*

budget dining: There are a small number of local restaurants in Bridgetown with some food (but mostly light snacks) for sale in rumshops islandwide. Restaurants offering counter service are generally less expensive. Snackettes have the most reasonable food, and some of the minimarts serve takeaway items. All prepared food in Barbados is supposed to have a 5 percent tax added, even if it's a takeaway item, but the local restaurants generally include this in the price. A variety of food and related items are sold on the street. One of the most popular items is drinking coconuts. These are young coconuts which the vendor opens with a machete. He hacks off a piece from the edge which, after you're finished eating, serves to scoop out the soft white jelly inside. If you want more water than jelly or lots of jelly, just tell the vendor, and he'll hand pick for you. Since much of the island's food is imported, supermarket prices are guaranteed to shock.

rum shops: Since most Bajans eat at home, they usually only snack around. And a major place for both snacking and socializing is the rum shop. Often doubling as a general store, the shop customarily displays buns, pastries, and other goods inside glass cabinet(s) on the counter. Food is generally consumed inside. Men usually buy a "mini" or a "flask" of rum, ask for some cold water to dilute it, and swallow it right down. If you need music to help your digestion, you won't go wanting in the rum shop. Jukeboxes sport an incredibly variegated mix of music including R&B, Prince, calypso (Gabby, Grynner, Red Plastic Bag), C & W, etc.

tips for vegetarians: This is definitely a carnivorous society so the more you compromise your principles, the easier time you'll have. For example, in many cases, rice and peas are flavored with pork, and there is no plain rice available. If you're a vegan (non dairy product user), unless you're cooking all of your own food, you're in trouble! Outside of the tourist restaurants and the Chevette chain of fast foods, vegetables in general, and salads in particular, are near to nonexistent. Since the bulk of the vegetables go to feed hungry tourists and a larger number are also imported, prices tend to be very high. Locally grown fruits, such as papaya, when purchased from hucksters, tend to be much more reasonable. If you do eat fish, you should be aware that locals eat it fried and that it may have been fried in lard or in the same oil as chicken or pork. Cheese cutters (sandwiches) will serve you well in a pinch as will saltfish cakes on a bun. Macaroni pie (macaroni and cheese) is commonly available and may serve as a main course. If you eat a lot of nuts, plan on bringing your own because those available locally are expensive. The same goes for dried fruits such as raisins. Finally, bear in mind that—outside of tourist restaurants—fish may be in short supply at times. Note: Places serving vegetarian food are frequently listed in the text.

Shopping

Opening hours vary but stores are generally open from Mon. through Sat. with some stores closing for an hour in the afternoon. Things are pretty much dead on Sunday, a day when it may be difficult to find even a food market open. Other than local handicrafts, there isn't much to buy that can't be found cheaper (or at nearly the same price) somewhere else. Unmistakably Bajan souvenirs include rum and falernum. One of the nicer things to carry back with you is some "dark crystal" sugar. While the "brown sugar" sold in the US is actually bleached sugar darkened with molasses, this is the genuine article. Dorly manufactures rum in bottles shaped like Barbados Harbour policemen for those who want an unusual souvenir. And, for unique souvenirs or for a chance to please that stamp collecting relative, don't forget to visit the philatelic bureau inside the General Post Office at Cheapside, Bridgetown. Finally, a less conventional (and quite educational) alternative is to visit one of the many auctions; these are published in the classified section of the Sunday newspaper.

crafts: These are found in Pelican Village on the Princess Anne Highway near Bridgetown as well as in many of the island's shops. Handicrafts include pottery, woven baskets, rugs, mats, coconut shell accessories, straw and *khus-khus* fans, bottle baskets, mahogany-fashioned wooden crafts, and shell and coral jewelry. The best place to buy crafts and souvenirs is at the Self Help Cooperative, located on Broad St. near the Careenage. Founded in 1907 by Lady Gilbert Carter, cooperative members sell a wide variety of goods including local pottery, crochet work, loupha-fashioned dolls, and home-produced peanut butter, stewed guava, guava jelly, gooseberry syrup, local cherry wine, and other delights. Open Mon. to Fri., 8–4, and Sat., 8–12. Run by the Industrial Development Corp., Pride Craft has a wide variety of goods at a large number of shops. Another major location is Temple Yard in Bridgetown where the Rastas present their arts and crafts. Chalky Mount in St. Andrew produces traditional pottery. Another location is Earthworks Potteries where ceramicist Goldie Spieler holds forth heartily handbuilding heaps of clay into everything from chattel houses to microwave—safe modern pieces. Bridgetown's Articrafts, inside Norman Centre on Broad St., features the work of artist, designer, and handweaver Roslyn Watson who is noted for her tapestries and basketry. Guardhouse Gallery is in Grand Barbados Resort. A chain of shops islandwide, Best of Barbados showcases the varied work of Jill Walker.

department stores and malls: Including a number of individual franchises, Da Costas on Broad St. sells everything from duty free goods to fabrics to sewing machines. Cave Shepherd, also on Broad St., is the island's largest department store. Another air conditioned mall on Broad St., Norman Centre features The Book Shop, a record store, Mother Care, and T-shirt and jewelry shops galore. Located at Bridgetown Harbour and on Broad St., Harrison's offers a cornucopia of duty free goods. Also on Broad St., Mall 34 has 24 shops carrying everything from greeting cards to fashionable clothes. Small but diverse, Med-X Mall, also on Broad St., has a health food store and restaurant, an ice cream parlor, dry cleaning, a stamp counter, and a pharmacy. Located at Rockley and Hastings respectively in Christchurch, Quayside Centre has a number of shops and restaurants, and Hastings Mall has 32 shops. Chattel House Village, opened in 1989 at St. Lawrence Gap, consists of a group of newly constructed chattel-style houses which sell local crafts and clothing including beachwear.

antiques: While prices have risen and the best goods are siphoned off abroad, many great antiques are retained on the premises of the island's greathouses. Buyers will do well to check the Sunday papers for auction sales listings. Spread out in the interior of a greathouse at Greenwich, St. James, Greenwich House Antiques has the widest selection in the Caribbean. Aficionados can literally spend hours browsing through it! Another alternative is Antiquaria which displays its wares on three floors of an old townhouse on St. Michael's Row, opposite the cathedral, in Bridgetown. La Galeria Antique is at Paynes Bay in St. James.

markets: Always a source of entertainment and of unique souvenirs, the local markets are a great place to strike up an acquaintance as well as stock up on produce. Try the Cheapside market in Bridgetown as well as the Oistins fish market.

books: Like all imports, these are very expensive here. Although the largest bookstores are in Bridgetown, The Cloister has branches around the island. A secondhand bookshop is on Bay St. The most memorable books to buy here are the publications of the National Cultural Foundation (particularly anything scribed by G. Addington Forde) and the National Trust. You might also wish to check out books by local authors; a good collection is in Robert's Stationary in High St.

imported goods: These luxury items include a variety of clothing—such as cashmere sweaters, French hand-beaded and Italian handbags, and shoes; crystal ware from France, Ireland, England, and Sweden; bone china items from England, France, and Denmark; an international assortment of gold and silver jewelry; the highest quality Swiss and Japanese timepieces; leading brands of perfume; and a variety of Japanese cameras and other famous Japanese goods.

duty free shopping: In order to purchase these at duty free prices you must produce your travel documents. Some goods (spirits, tobacco, electronic and camera equipment) must be delivered for pickup at the airport or harbor before departure. Or you can just buy it there directly before departure. Be sure you know your prices; just because an item is marked "duty free" doesn't mean that it is.

American customs: Returning American citizens, under existing customs regulations, can lug back up to US$400 worth of duty free goods provided the stay abroad exceeds 48 hours and that no part of the allowance has been used during the past 30 days. Items sent by post may be included in this tally, thus allowing shoppers to ship or have shipped goods like glass and china. Over that amount, purchases are dutied at a flat 10 percent on the next $1,000. Above $1,400, duty applied will vary. Joint declarations are permissible for members of a family traveling together. Thus, a couple traveling with two children will be allowed up to $3,200 in duty free goods. Undeclared gifts (one per day of up to $50 in value) may be sent to as many friends and relatives as you like. One fifth of liquor may be brought back as well as one carton of cigarettes. Plants in soil may not be brought to the US.

Canadian customs: Canadian citizens may make an oral declaration four times per year to claim C$100 worth of exemptions which may include 200 cigarettes, 50 cigars, two pounds of tobacco, 40 fl. oz. of alcohol, and 24 12-oz. cans/bottles of beer. In order to claim this exemption, Canadians must have been out of the country for at least 48 hours. A Canadian who's been away for at least seven days may make a written declaration once a year and claim C$300 worth of exemptions. After a trip of 48 hours or longer, Canadians receive a special duty rate of 20 percent on the value of goods up to C$300 in excess of the C$100 or C$300 exemption they claim. This excess cannot be applied to liquor or cigarettes. Goods claimed under the C$300 exemption may follow, but merchandise claimed under all other exemptions must be accompanied.

British customs: Each person over the age of 17 may bring in one liter of alcohol or two of champagne, port, sherry or vermouth plus two liters of table wine; 200 cigarettes or 50 cigars or 250 grams of tobacco; 250 cc of toilet water; 50 gms (two fluid ounces) of perfume; and up to £28 of other goods.

German customs: Residents may bring back 200 cigarettes, 50 cigars, 100 cigarillos, or 250 grams of tobacco; two liters of alcoholic beverages not exceeding 44 proof or one liter of 44 proof plus alcohol; and two liters of wine; and up to DM300 of other items.

BARBADOS BOARD OF TOURISM OFFICES

BRIDGETOWN
Harbour Road (P.O. Box 242)
Bridgetown, Barbados
(809) 427-2623

GRANTLEY ADAMS AIRPORT
Christ Church, Barbados
(809) 428-0937/5570

BRIDGETOWN HARBOUR
Bridgetown, Barbados
(809) 426-1718

NEW YORK CITY
800 Second Ave.
NY, NY 10017
(212) 986-6516
(800) 221-9831

LOS ANGELES
3440 Wiltshire Bvd.
Suite 1215
LA, CA 90010
(213) 380-2198
(800) 221-9831

TORONTO
Suite 1508, Box 11
20 Queen St. West
Toronto, Ontario M5H 3R3
Canada
(416) 979-2472/2137
(800) 268-9122

MONTREAL
615 Dorchester West Blvd.
Suite 960
Montreal, Quebec H3B 1P5
Canada

GREAT BRITAIN
263 Tottenham Court Rd.
London W1P 9AA
(011) 441-636-9448

WEST GERMANY
Rathenau Platz 1A
6000 Frankfurt 1
West Germany
069-280982

FRANCE
Barbados Board of Tourism
c/o Caribes 102
102 Ave. des Champs-Elysees
75008 Paris, France
42 62 62 62
42 25 62 62

SWEDEN
Barbados Board of Tourism
c/o Hotel Investors (Sweden) Ltd.
Tuhus 2, Skeppsbron
S111-30 Stockholm
Sweden
(08) 24 06 07

BRIDGETOWN AND ST. MICHAEL'S PARISH

BRIDGETOWN

Despite its small size, Bridgetown possesses a vibrancy which cities many times as large might envy. Its clamor and bustle reflect the industry and energy of the island's people. Here, you'll find historical buildings intermingled with modern offices, dreadlock-sprouting coconut vendors slashing open coconuts with machetes for waiting businessmen clad in suits and ties; and hucksters hurrying to market, produce riding smartly atop their heads.

history: Bridgetown was founded on 5 July 1628 when the soon-to-be governor Charles Wolverstone arrived along with 63 other settlers. The site was selected for its harbor and definitely *not* for its proximity to a large swamp which made it an unhealthy place to live during its early years of development. The present name has evolved from its early appelation "The

Indian Bridge Towne"—which referred to the bridge left by the Caribs. Through the years it has been known as "The Bridge," "The Bridge Town," and "St. Michael's Town." Its fine harbors at Careenage and Carlisle Bay gave it predominance over Holetown which was settled a year earlier. Street names downtown also date back to the city's founding—in honor of such prominent early settlers as High, Tudor, James, and Swan. The last was a surveyor who laid out the town and thus had the secondary business street named after him. Hurricanes and fire, however, have done in the earliest buildings. Originally a fine town of broad streets and attractive stone storehouses, Bridgetown was reduced to a mass of rubble by the 1780 hurricane. Only 30 houses were left standing, and 3,000 died. Bridgetown never recovered from this, the most devastating single catastrophe in the island's history. Over the years, the town has played host to such luminaries as Winston Churchill, Aldous Huxley, Paul MacCartney, Queen Elizabeth II, Mick Jagger, George Washington, Sting, and Henry Morgan.

arriving by air: Grantley Adams International Airport is located in the southeasternmost portion of Christ Church Parish. After disembarking, you can expect long lines at Immigration. There are also only two teller windows open at the bank; the Tourist Information may be able to change a small amount if you have cash. Curiously, if you want to use the restrooms, the two pay phones encased in pillars, or the free lines to selected hotels, you must backtrack through Immigration! Once you've finished your business inside, you can expect to breeze through customs. Plenty of taxis are available but, if you don't have a lot of luggage, you can take one of the infrequent 12A buses out on the main road towards Bridgetown. If you wish to go towards Crane Beach or Sam Lord's Castle, you must cross the road and wait on the other side. In any case, have your B$1 exact change ready.

getting around: The main bus terminal stands next to the Charles Duncan O'Neal Bridge on Fairchild St. From here buses leave for Bathsheba, Sam Lord's Castle, and other locations to the S and E. Ask at the information counter for the bus gate and probable time of departure. Although this is a new terminal, the bus system hasn't improved. Expect phenomenally long lines during rush hour. There are two other bus terminals in town. One is the Jubilee (or Lower Green St.) bus terminal at the end of Broad St. which has buses mainly to Holetown, Speightstown, and other points N. Another and much smaller is the Pelican terminal located off of Princess Anne Highway after Temple Yard and the G.P.O. but before Pelican Village. From here No. 1-D goes to District D (Dunscombe) in St. Thomas. No. 2 goes to Rock Dundo via Rock Hall. No. 3 goes to Turner's Hall via Hillaby and St. Andrew's Church. No. 4 goes to Rock Hall via Holetown.

CENTRAL BRIDGETOWN SIGHTS

Trafalgar Square: The city's heart—alive and pulsating, the square features vendors wending their way to market, policemen directing traffic, and kids cajoling each other as they pass on their way to school. Lord Nelson has gazed over the hustle

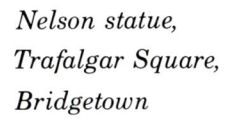

Nelson statue,
Trafalgar Square,
Bridgetown

CENTRAL BRIDGETOWN

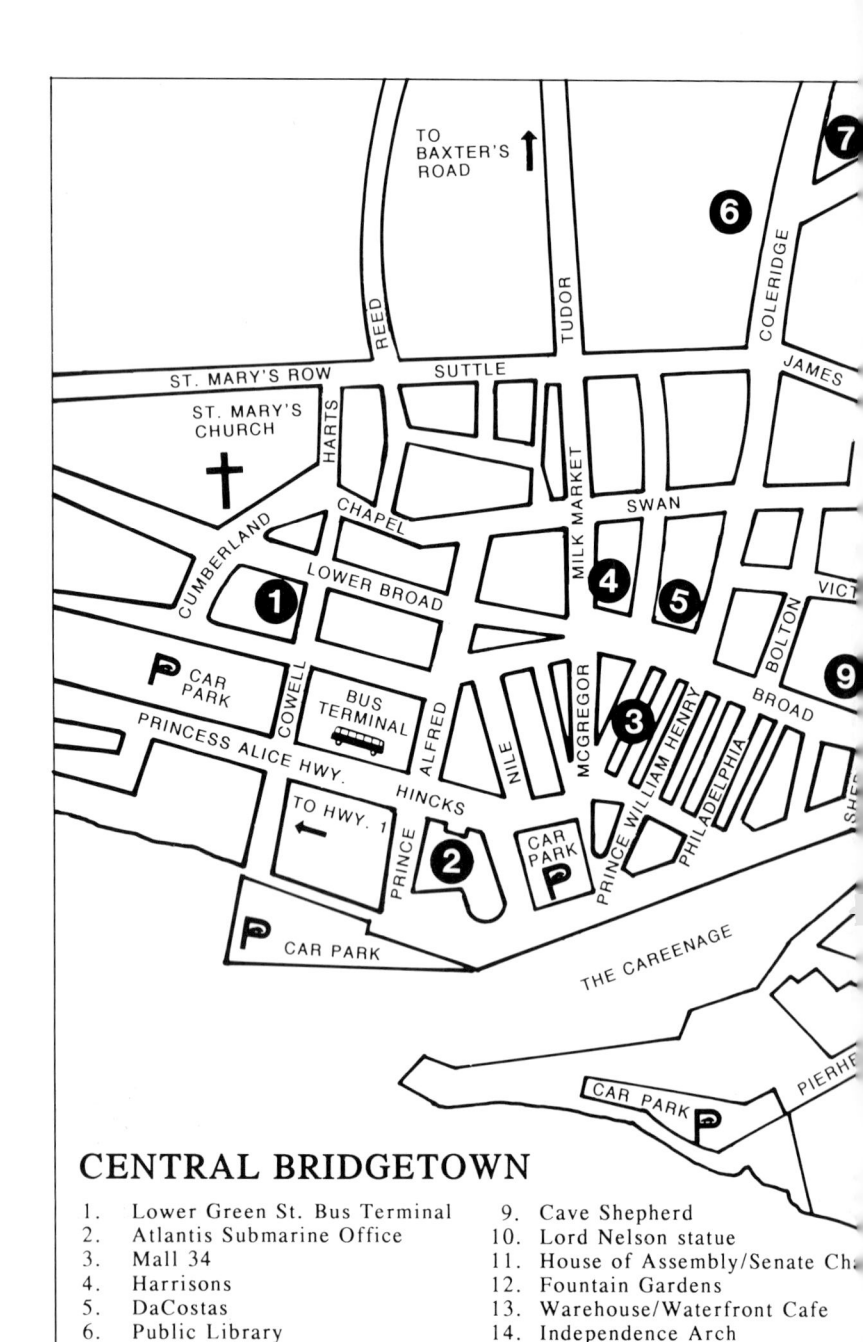

1. Lower Green St. Bus Terminal
2. Atlantis Submarine Office
3. Mall 34
4. Harrisons
5. DaCostas
6. Public Library
7. Montifiore Fountain
8. Synagogue
9. Cave Shepherd
10. Lord Nelson statue
11. House of Assembly/Senate Cha
12. Fountain Gardens
13. Warehouse/Waterfront Cafe
14. Independence Arch
15. Central Bank Building

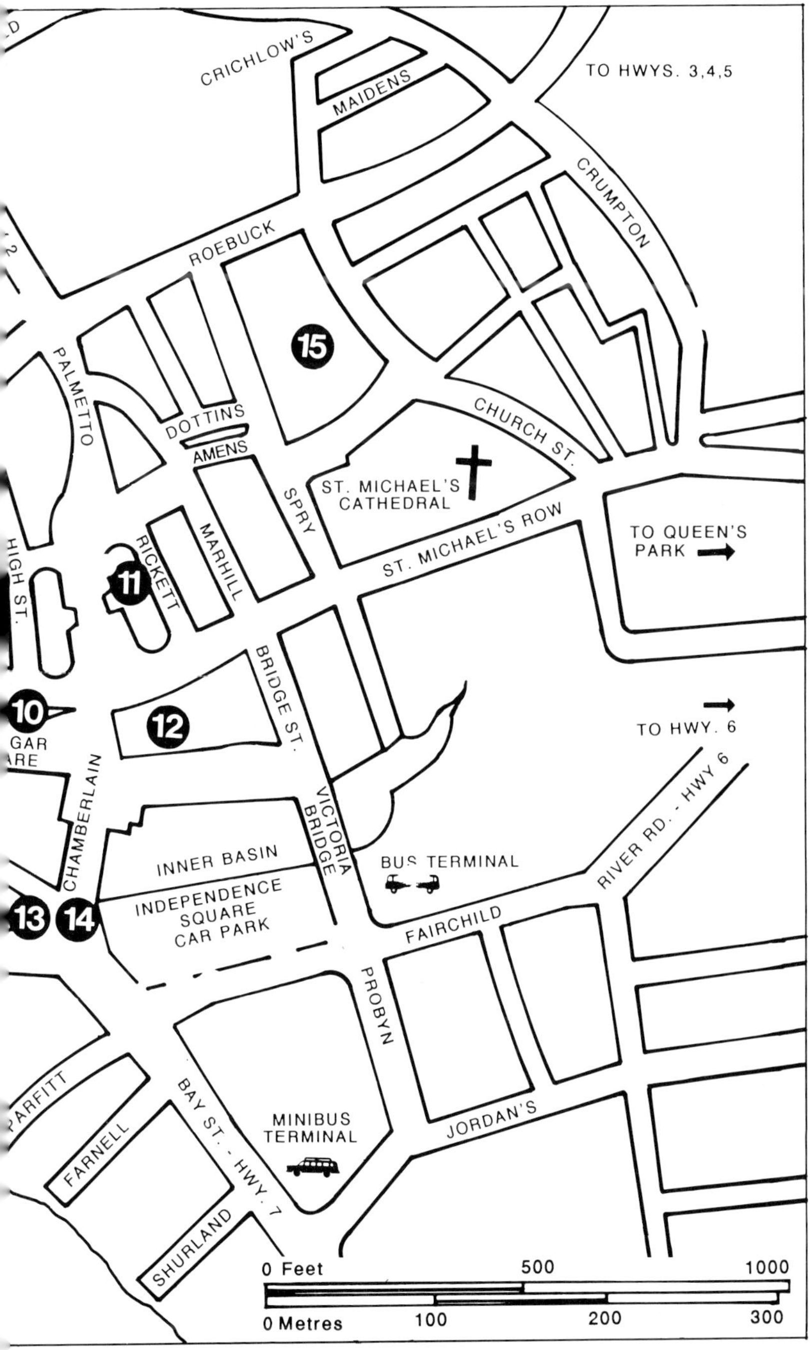

CRICHLOW'S
MAIDENS
TO HWYS. 3,4,5
CRUMPTON
ROEBUCK
PALMETTO
15
CHURCH ST.
DOTTINS
AMENS
SPRY
ST. MICHAEL'S CATHEDRAL
ST. MICHAEL'S ROW
TO QUEEN'S PARK
HIGH ST.
RICKETT
MARHILL
11
BRIDGE ST.
10
12
TO HWY. 6
GAR
ARE
CHAMBERLAIN
VICTORIA BRIDGE
RIVER RD. - HWY 6
INNER BASIN
BUS TERMINAL
13
14
INDEPENDENCE SQUARE CAR PARK
FAIRCHILD
PROBYN
PARFITT
BAY ST. - HWY. 7
MINIBUS TERMINAL
JORDAN'S
FARNELL
SHURLAND
0 Feet
500
1000
0 Metres
100
200
300

and bustle—silently reliving his victory at Cape Trafalgar—since just before dawn on 22 March 1813. In the midst of his search for France's Admiral Villaneuve, he steamed into Carlisle Bay, thus making a great impression on the Bajans. In their grief at his death, they managed to raise £2,300 for the statue in only a few weeks. Purchasing Eggington's Green, they renamed it Trafalgar Square and installed the statue as its *piece de resistance*. Sculpted by Sir William Westmacott, it is 17 year older than its London cousin. Traditionally, visiting schoolchildren have been instructed to salute it. It has also been a center of controversy. Cries for its removal have been voiced periodically since 1833, one of the most notable being calypsonian the Mighty Gabby's call to "take down Nelson and put up a Bajan man." Although garbage has been dumped at his feet and protesters have used him as a backdrop, Lord Nelson has stood imperturbably through it all, maintaining a stiff upper lip and portraying an expression of forbearance. The only change in the statue's lifestyle over the decades has been the end of the tradition of wreath-laying on the Trafalgar anniversary, a practice halted in 1962. These days, taxi drivers waiting for customers hang out at his heels. Be sure to read the fantastically verbose inscription on the pedestal. An ironical footnote to bear in mind with reference to all of the above is that, writing home, Nelson had described Barbados as being both "barbarous" and "detestable." Before passing on, be sure to swing your binoculars upward to focus on the young Lord's finely crafted head.

Fountain Gardens: Situated to the SE of the Public Buildings in Trafalgar Square and incorporating the Mediterranean Dolphin Fountain and the War Memorial, this area functions as a watering hole—one of the town's best spots for *limin'*. Inaugurated in 1865 in commemoration of the introduction of piped water into the city in 1861, the fountain has recently been restored to its former magnificence. Originally constructed in 1925 to commemorate those who died during WWI, the obelisk-shaped grey granite War Memorial is adorned with bronze panels featuring the island's coat of arms and the names of those Bajans who died during the two great wars. Its coral stone basin is of local design.

Fountain Gardens, Bridgetown

The Public Buildings: The Houses of Parliament across the road, where the House of Assembly and the Senate convene once a week, date from 1872. The Senate and House meet in the East Wing. The Assembly's stained glass windows include personable portraits of all the Kings and Queens of England including one who ruled without benefit of royal blood—the Great Protector Oliver Cromwell. He is placed in the rearmost window by the visitor's gallery, as if to signal his outsider status. The ornately carved Speaker's Chair was an Independence Day gift from India. The much smaller Senate chamber features enormous framed photos of Queen Elizabeth and Prince Philip; the coats of arms on the wall are those of the once all-powerful plantocracy. The extra seats in the chamber are reserved for the Governor General and the Queen. At the building's entrance stands the statue of Sir William Conrad Reeves who served as Chief Justice from 1886–1902. Reeves, considered by the average black Bajan of the time to be an "Uncle Tom," became the first Chief Justice with African blood in the British Empire. Staunchly supported by the island's elite, Reeves placated the Colonial Office through compromises. His moderate proposals—such as increased educational opportunities and lowering of the voting age— saved the island from falling into the grip of the Crown Colony system and, consequently, he was accorded knighthood and the position of Chief Justice. **visiting the House:** Seeing the House or Senate in session is an experience no visitor should miss if the opportunity avails itself. The visitor's gallery in the house overlooks the chamber below. At the beginning of a session, the enormous brass scepter, which resembles a refined, ornate version of a club, is carried in and placed in a receptacle to the front. The bewigged Speaker then enters and takes a seat in the ornate chair. The Chairman of Committees sits to his R. To find out when the next, unfortunately all-too-rare session is, call 426–5331/3717/3712.

The Careenage and beyond: On the other side of Trafalgar Square in the eastern portion of Carlisle Bay, this marina is so named because wooden hulled sailing vessels were careened (turned on their sides) for repair here. Although the larger ships berth at the Deep Water Harbour to the W of town, smaller boats, including the city's fishing fleet, still patronize the Careenage. This marina occupies the outer reaches of what was once the Constitution River, which was actually not a river at all but the arm of a bay. Today, its inner stretch has been covered with landfill. Warehouses on either side are preserved by owners DaCosta & M. N. Musson. For 300 years the Careenage reigned supreme—acting as the center of communications and mercantile activity for the island, but it has been eclipsed by the modern Bridgetown Harbour. Nowadays, it is more of note as a spiffy berth for sleek yachts, and it supports a beehive of nightspots. Two bridges span its length and separate its outer and inner basin: the Charles Duncan O'Neal Bridge, named after the founder of the Democratic League and

Independence Square and the Careenage, Bridgetown

the Workingman's Association (see "History") and the Joseph Chamberlain Bridge (1872), named after the Colonial Secretary who helped Barbados out with financial aid after the 1898 hurricane. This latter bridge once swung up and down, splitting into two halves to admit ships, but mechanical problems have rendered it stationary. At the W end of the Careenage stand the Pierhead and Willoughby's Fort. Now occupied by the Coast Guard, the latter was constructed on what was then Little Island in 1656. Once located across from the island and now lying adjacent to it, the Pierhead was pastureland before it held warehouses. Waterfront Cafe, a tourist watering hole with a spectacular view, was once one of these warehouses. Heading E from the Pierhead, Independence Square, near the main bus terminal, is a popular center for political rallies during election times. The Independence Arch commemorates a memorable event in Barbadian history. Consecrated on 1 Jan. 1858 by American Reverend Joseph S. Meyers, St. Ambrose Church lies in the district's heart, a deliberate move on the part of the Right Reverend who was disgusted by the filth and vice he found present there.

Barbados Mutual Life Assurance Building

Broad Street: A major center of activity, crowded Broad Street should perhaps be renamed "Bustle Street." A shopping area since the 17th C., Broad Street was originally known as Cheapside, a name which still is applied to the end where the General Post Office and the farmer's market are located. It was also known as Exchange Street or The Exchange, owing to the presence of the Merchant's Exchange. Today, as the main shopping street in town, it is worth a stroll for its atmosphere. Its classic architectural landmark is the Barbados Mutual Life Assurance Building (1895). At night, it becomes a special place for promenading—with popcorn and peanut vendors galore.

St. Michael's Cathedral: Honoring the archangel, the present day edifice stands on the site of the original small, primitive structure. It was replaced with the Church of St. Michael which was consecrated in 1665. This was destroyed in 1780 and replaced by the present structure in 1789 which, in turn, was extensively renovated and changed after it was damaged by the 1831 hurricane. It became St. Michael's Cathedral in 1824. Although it remains essentially Georgian in appearance, it also incorporates Gothic Revival-style additions including pointed arches in the round-topped windows and trefoil clerestory windows. Its sadly neglected military cemetery is filled with the tombs of dignitaries and soldiers—many of them in their teens and early twenties—who fell victim to plague and yellow fever. Be sure to note the inscription commemorating Robert Hooper and the painted memorial to Thomas Duke, Treasurer in 1750. Note the Braithwaite memorial, the Francis Bovell memorial, and the monument recording the tragic death of Mrs. Letitia Austin. Sir Grantley Adams, the island's first premier, also lies interred here. Also note the barely legible tablets set into the floor, which date from the 17th C. A good time to visit is on a Sunday afternoon when Sunday School is in session. The nation's barristers, clad in wigs and gowns, assemble here for the annual Assizes Service. Note the processional cross. At Sunday morning services, the angelic voices of the choirboys—clad in high ruffed surplices and red gowns—ring out clear and true. They sang at Westminster Abbey during the summer of 1971.

vicinity of St. Michael: Behind the Cathedral on the other side of St. Michael's Row stands Cathedral Square and the Masonic Temple. The latter once housed Harrison College, originally founded as Harrison's Free School by Thomas Harrison in 1733 in order to provide free education for indigent boys. Towering above both is the 11-story Central Bank Building, the highest structure on the island. It contains a small theater and art gallery. The building is flanked on its N side by the huckster mecca of Roebuck Street. The monument and plaque out in front of the building was erected in 1989 in order to commemorate the meeting place of the first Parliament 300 years before. James Street, nearby, was once the property of the Quakers until they were swindled out of it.

Queen's Park House: This former military home currently houses Queen's Park Theatre. Constructed in 1786, it replaced the original structure which was destroyed in the hurricane of 1780. The commanding general of the British West Indies lived here until 1906. It is surrounded by Queen's Park which was first opened to the public in 1909. Nearly totally derelict in appearance—rather like an abandoned grandmother clad in rags and decaying—the Park was given lots of TLC by the Parks and Beaches Commission in 1970. The playground to the R of the theater/gallery borders an enormous thousand-year-old African baobab tree which, as the island's largest, measures 61.5 ft. (18.5 m.) in girth. At night the park appears to acquire its own characteristic ambience, becoming a quieter

Baobab tree, Queen's Park

and more mysterious place. The monkeys and birds sleep in their cages, dark shadows behind the grills. You might see a gospel group rehearsing in the pavilion, using a Casio synthesizer for accompaniment.

in and around Queen's Park: Nearby, note the facade on the adjacent Ministry of Agriculture. To the N is "The Square" of Harrison College which was founded in 1733 as Harrison's Free School—the nation's oldest and most prestigious secondary school. Another historic building, which once housed Queen's College, is on Constitution Rd.

synagogue: On a side street extending from James St. to Magazine Lane stands a building which once contained the Jewish synagogue, a successor to the original which was totally destroyed by the 1831 hurricane. The island's Jewish community consisted of Sephardic Jews who probably emigrated from Brazil in the 1650s. Isolated and ostracized, they were listed separately on the census and heavily taxed. By the 1850s, most of the community had migrated and only 71 remained, half of that number nonpracticing. By 1926, there was only one, and the synagogue was dismantled. While some of its treasures may be seen in the Barbados Museum, two of its five cemetaries have disappeared, and its four chandeliers were sold to an American. The building—under restoration by the current Jews—now retains only its cemetary to serve as a reminder of an era past.

Prince William Henry Street: Commanding the frigate *Pegasus,* Prince William Henry (later to become King William IV) arrived in 1786. He and his entourage laid waste to the town's principal brothel belonging to a Ms. Rachel Pringle Polgreen on Bay St. The street was named to commemorate his visit. Both sides of Hincks St. near to its base—from the car park to W. S. Munroe—are filled with Bajan color and character.

public library: The historic public library stands on Coleridge St. It was a gift of Andrew Carnegie and was opened in 1906. Easy to pass by, the diminutive and nonfunctioning Montifiore Fountain, the centerpoint of the triangle facing the Public Library was a gift of John Montifiore way back in 1864; it was relocated here from Beckwith Place in 1940. Each of its four marble statues represents a different human ideal: Justice, Fortitude, Temperance, and Prudence. A complex on this street includes the Police Station, Law Courts, and the Magistrates' Courts.

Tudor Street and environs: Parallel to Coleridge St. is Tudor Street where the Quaker meeting house once stood. While one end of this street leads into Broad Street, the other end terminates in Baxter Road: "The Street That Never Sleeps." From dusk to dawn, evening after evening, Bajans party hard—up and down, in and out of the street's numerous rum shops and restaurants. The odors of frying fish and chicken permeate the air, and jukeboxes blare almost to dawn. Renowned for its atmosphere, Suttle Street, a respectable neighborhood now transformed into a trader's mecca, runs into St. Mary's Row, the street's extension. Completed in 1827, St. Mary's Church was built to accommodate the overflow from St. Michael's. Lower Green Station, another bus terminal, stands across the street here.

Temple Yard: As is reflected elsewhere in its culture, Barbados represents a synthesis between Africa and Britain. In the case of Temple Yard, the African elements predominate, merging art and craft in a colorful melange of shape and form. Here, in a series of conjoined rudimentary wooden stalls, the island's top Rasta artists show their stuff. Ceramicist Ayem, a graduate of the Jamaica School of Art, produces sculptures, reliefs, hangings, plaques and paintings. Sculptor Ras Congo has his own small house here. Innumerable crafts—wrought from bamboo, leather, coconut, seashells and other materials—are represented. Rasta culture is everywhere in evidence: from representations of lions to the red, green, and gold maps of Africa, to the images of Marcus Garvey and Bob Marley. Music blasts from small restaurants selling *I-tal* (vegetarian) and Bajan dishes (like rice and stew). Also present is open use of marijuana and a hard sell atmosphere. This location came into being after the government moved them off of the various sidewalks where their parked stalls were causing congestion. A minibus terminal is here, and Cheapside market stands a bit farther on as does the new General Post Office, a kissing cousin in design of the Central Bank Building. Along Princess

Alice Highway, which parallels the coast, lies Trevor Way, named after a young man who was killed nearby. Beautified by the Rotary Club and maintained by the National Conservation Commission, this small but flourishing park offers a stand of cabbage palm and mahoe as well as a great view of Carlisle Bay.

Pelican Village: Located across from Pelican Bay and near temple yard, this complex—built on land reclaimed from the sea—contains cheap handicrafts as well as serious art. The Barbados National Council has its art gallery here. A craftsman who began his career as a tailor, Karl Broodhagen has his sculpture gallery here. He's well known for his cast bronze heads including the one of Sir Grantley Adams which stands on a pedestal at the Government Headquarters on Bay St. "The Freed Slave," his most famous sculpture, stands at the center of St. Barnabas Roundabout at the border between St. Michael and St. George parishes. Courtney Devonish, a scion of island pottery village Chalky Mount, operates out of a work-

Statue of "The Freed Slave"

shop here as well. While he has work representative of traditional pottery, some of his other pieces reflect his Italian training. Pelican Restaurant is the place to stop to collect some energy before exploring farther. The Industrial Development Corporation operates a sales shop nearby.

mosque: Although you won't find it in any tourist brochure, this amazing anachronism is sandwiched between two chattel houses on New Kensington Rd. off of Fontabelle opposite a house labeled "Bombay Villa." This large two-story mosque has green tinted windows and is constructed of green and white painted concrete.

Medford's Mahogany Craft Village: Near Baxter's Road, this woodcarving center is run by self-taught artist Reggie Medford who builds a wide variety of pieces from massive mahogany roots. Open Mon.-Fri., 9–5, Sat. 8:30–12:30.

Bridgetown harbour: Inaugurated in 1961, construction was begun in 1957. More than 90 acres of land were added by filling in the sea with more than 730,000 cubic yards of quarried gravel, thus eliminating Pelican Island which lay 1800 feet (600 meters) away. On this former "dependency" now stands the offices of the Port Manager and Harbour Master. The huge sugar warehouse, which can hold up to 80,000 tons (half of the annual crop), was built at the same time. The port can clear up to 2,000 tons of cargo per day. There's also a 50-acre duty free Industrial Park. Kensington Oval, nearby, features wildly-competitive cricket matches.

UWI Cave Hill Campus: Located N of town off of Highway 1, the nation's only university has some handsome architecture. Check out the view from the library's window. The grave of Sir Frank Worrell, the legendary West Indian cricketeer, lies within the complex. Heading N from Cave Hill, near Batt's Rock, a high-walled house was once a "lazaretto" or home for lepers. It was subsequently converted to house the island's first radio station whose antenna still dominates the landscape to its rear.

Belleville District: Dating from 1882, this earliest of suburban developments—many of whose homes have been restored—is home to Erdiston, the Teachers' Training College. At 10th Avenue in Belleville, Roland Tree House, the Barbados National Trust's headquarters (tel. 426-2421/9033), is not a house built in a tree but rather one named after a man named Tree—the Trust's founder. Constructed in 1893, this classic Victorian is furnished with period furniture and a fine exhibit of old photos of local architecture. Every Thurs. ladies clad in Victorian garb show visitors around.

along Highway 4: Crowning a hill overlooking Belleville, Government House, official residence of the Governor General, was constructed in 1736. It was originally called Pilgrim House, after its owner Quaker John Pilgrim, and has suffered major damage during hurricanes. The home and its gardens may be viewed on special open days. The upper-class residential area of Pine Gardens is in the vicinity. Bishop's Court Hill, at its end along Highway 4, is named after the home of the island's Anglican Bishop. Farther on, past Collymore Rock, a commercial district contains Bank's Breweries with Wildey Industrial Park to its rear. Farther along the highway is the Barbados Institute of Management and Production.

along St. Barnabas Highway: This highway, lined with modern technological facilities, connects Grantley Adams International Airport with Speightstown. It flanks such ultramodern edifices as the Caribbean Development Bank and the Caribbean Broadcasting Corporation. It also runs past Pinelands, an ugly housing development that dates from the 1960s. Karl Broodhagen's sculpture "The Freed Slave," his most famous work, stands at the St. Barnabas Roundabout in St. Michael. This massive statue—erected in 1986—depicts Bussa, the leader of the 1816 slave revolt—standing in a defiant posture, his hands still wearing broken chains. Turning to the W, the Two Mile Hill road leads to Ilaro Court.

Ilaro Court: Less than two miles from Bridgetown, this greathouse is a must for visitors. Framed by trees on a bluff, its stark white walls surround doors and windows incorporating various architectural techniques. Vivid green hoods frame the decorative wrought ironwork of its windows. Designed and planned by American Lady Gilbert-Carter whose husband served as Governor from 1904–11, its interior features paintings, a grand piano, and East Asian tables. Inside the lounge, the walls are adorned with beautiful tapestries and prints of old sailing merchant vessels. The covered arcade overlooks the rolling countryside. Adjoining the lounge, the upholstered green and white chintz furniture gleams in contrast to the pale brown glow of the pine floor and the subdued pale grey walls. The house surrounds a rectangular courtyard which overlooks a swimming pool and flowering plant garden. Long polished doors in the dining room lead out to the open verandah. Two glass chandeliers reflect light playing on the chippendale chairs, two circular dark mahogany tables, and a collection of old china. The five bedrooms are adorned with Regency dressing tables and slender four poster beds; lily ponds and fountains embellish the grounds.

HEADING TOWARDS CHRISTCHURCH'S GOLD COAST

Although the best sites are out and around the island, many locations of historic interest surround the city. In addition to the ones mentioned so far, others are enroute to Christchurch's tourist strip.

Carlisle Bay Centre: Cruise ship passengers purchase a package ticket to this "day on the beach" resort. It features a restaurant (with daily lunchtime specials), shops, water sports facilities, and tuk band and steel band performances. Facilities are also available for use by outsiders, tel. 427–4735/6.

Esplanade: Located on Bay St., this area provides a great view of Bridgetown harbour complete with romantic red sails in the sunset before dusk. Before its purchase by the government at the end of the 19th C., the now-demolished house which once stood here dealt in smuggled goods. A bust of Sir Grantley Adams stands in the gardens.

ST. MICHAEL

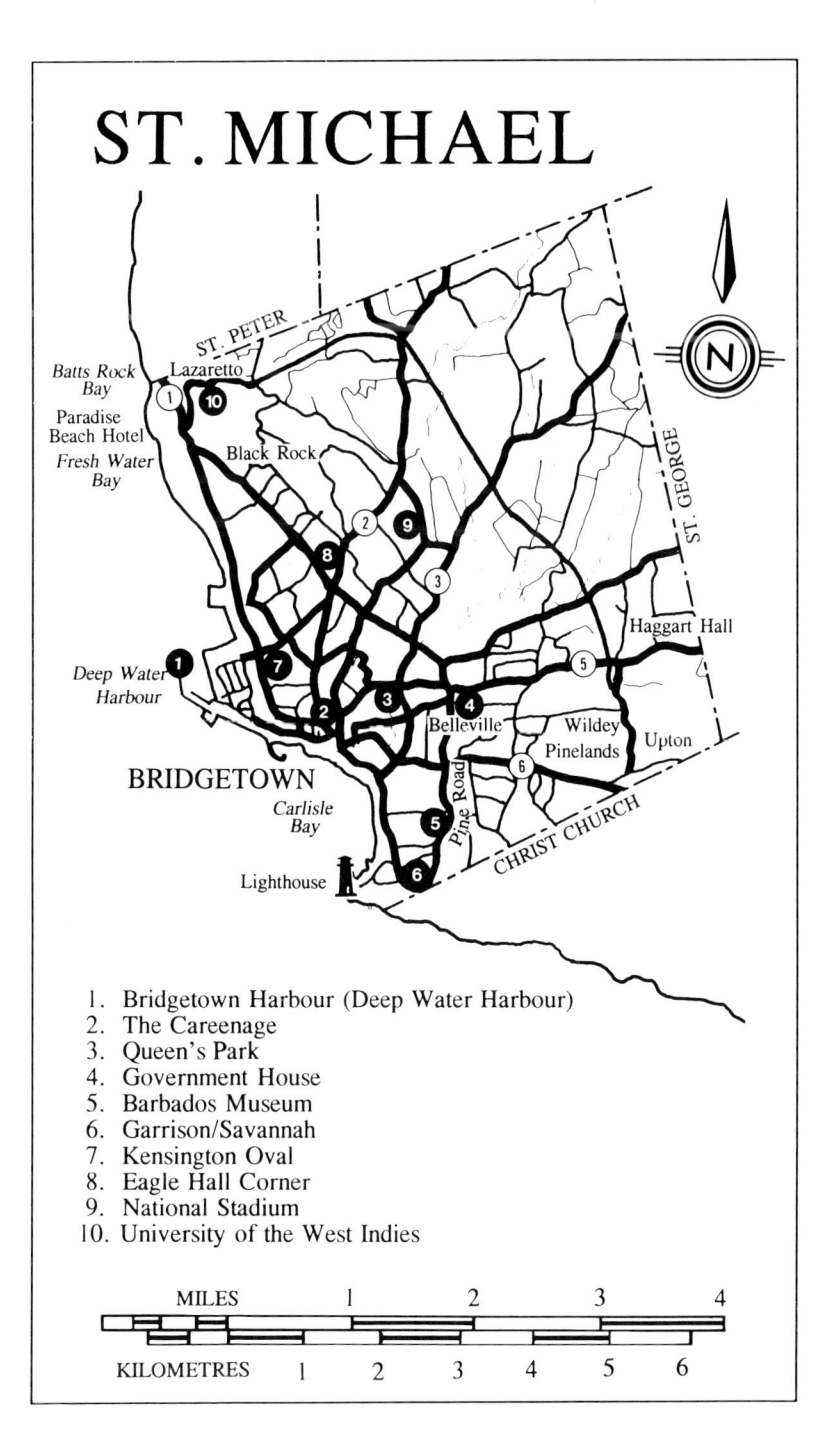

1. Bridgetown Harbour (Deep Water Harbour)
2. The Careenage
3. Queen's Park
4. Government House
5. Barbados Museum
6. Garrison/Savannah
7. Kensington Oval
8. Eagle Hall Corner
9. National Stadium
10. University of the West Indies

Government Headquarters: Surrounded by begonias, poinsettias, and hibiscus, modern Government Headquarters with its semi-circular driveway stands on Beckles Road. The bronze bust in front of the flower-bordered circular driveway leading to the headquarters commemorates Sir Grantley Adams, the "father" of modern Barbados.

St. Paul's Church: Rebuilt in 1831, St. Paul's Church was once used as a garrison church. The names of many British soldiers are inscribed in stone between the aisles. The regimental crests, plaques, and flags on the wall are those left by members of the Irish regiment the Connaught Rangers whose religious needs spurred construction of the original structure.

Crofton's House: At the corner of Bay Street and Chelsea Road, this is one of those major "sights" in the Caribbean—like Alexander Hamilton's house in Christiansted on St. Croix—that have no basis in fact. In his first and only visit abroad, Washington arrived in Barbados on 3 November 1751. He stayed here with his half-brother Lawrence in the hope that the climate would cure Lawrence's illness. Any of the houses in the area might very well have been *the* house, but since it's fun to look at old houses anyway, you might as well have a look! Standing directly opposite is the privately-run Yacht Club which is housed in a former military building. Farther down the road, right behind the Seaview Hotel, is a gem of a natural tract featuring palm trees, casuarinas, hummingbirds—all bordering the beach. Standing at Needham's Point, Charles Fort—the largest of those constructed along the S and W coasts during the 17th and 18th C.—is named after King Charles II of England, the "Merry Monarch" who reigned from 1660-1685. A number of cannon are here.

The Garrison: The collective name for St. Ann's Fort and the Savannah, its parade ground. A British garrison was permanently assigned here from 1694-1906, after which it was replaced by a volunteer force. Use your imagination to visualize batteries of troops—garbed in red and white starched uniforms—drilling in formation here. The Savannah contains a playing field (used for soccer and rugby) and a racetrack. Every Easter Monday a kite flying festival is held here. The arms on the cupola tower of the former British Regiment guard house, now transformed into the Savannah Club, belong to William IV. The fort, located behind an obscuring ugly Victorian structure, dates from 1702; its signal tower was constructed around 1819 as part of the increased security in reaction to the 1816 slave rebellion. In addition to its defensive functions, the fort also served to relay messages to other parts of the island. Signal stations in other districts could hear about a slave uprising, the arrival of a ship, an impending attack, or an upcoming Council meeting. Today, it is manned by the Barbados Defence Force. Inside, one can still see the thick walls enclosing the store room, the armory, and the powder magazines. Situated behind the fort overlooking the sea, lies a cemetery chock full of the bones of old soldiers. In the area nearby known as Needham Point, just before the Garrison, are the Hilton Hotel and a Mobil Oil Refinery. There's also a fine beach here; the recently restored military cemetery stands to the Hilton's E. The former abodes of colonial era government officials stand around the Savannah; blocks of handsome arcaded red-painted brick buildings follow. Dating

Barbados Museum, St. Michael

from the post-1831 hurricane era, they were originally used to house troops. Formerly the hospital for St. Anne's Fort, the red brick structure to the S of the Savannah along Highway 7 has now been subdivided into flats. Nearby, St. Mathias Gap leads from the highway to St. Mathias Church. Consecrated in 1850, this church superceded St. Paul's as the Garrison Chapel.

Barbados Museum: This lovingly conceived and executed complex serves as a superb introduction to Barbados—one that no visitor should miss! Housed in the old military detention barracks (constructed between 1817 and 1853), most of the galleries here were once cells that held prisoners. As you tour the structure, visualize them lying about rotting in rags. Built with rusticated limestone and yellow brick, it has an arched carriageway running through the entrance; the marble fountain here was once at the local synagogue's entrance for Jews to wash their hands before attending a service. The clock, menorah, and one of the benches also come from here. You enter at the shop where, among other things, there are wonderful antique postcards for sale. The first dioramas in the Harewood Gallery are of flora and fauna and can help you appreciate what you see—both above and below water. One diorama illustrates the life of the island's coral reefs. The displays continue as you round the corner into the Jubilee Gallery which illustrates the nation's history, largely through Amerindian and colonial artifacts. Among the highlights are a cowrie shell inscribed with the Lord's Prayer, antique medical equipment, old guidebooks and other memorabilia relating to the early tourism industry, and a July 22, 1789 copy of the *Barbados Mercury*. Also be sure to take note of Stewart Howard's caricature of the German officers a century ago. The final gallery of the wing contains a map collection. Outside and to the L, the Warmington Gallery displays mock-ups of a typical bedroom and living rooms such as might be found in the home of a 19th C. planter. If you're hungry or thirsty, the cafe next door has menus uniquely executed on paper bags! The Challenor Gallery displays military memorabilia. Next door, switch on the lights and enter the Cunard Gallery which contains a fine collection of antique prints and paintings, the best of which are Will Holland's hilarious sendups of the West Indian plantocracy's lifestyle. The final two galleries are exceedingly diverse. One displays a very fine collection of African musical instruments, sculpture, ceramics, and woodcarving. The gallery to the rear displays hundreds of pieces of late 18th C. china, glass, snuff boxes, rare furniture, and silver. One of the more interesting displays is a case featuring British ceramics which stylistically imitate Ming Dynasty pottery. The room's finest piece, however, is the Scotch snuff mull made from a ram's horn which includes implements and a moustache comb. Also note the carved ivory diptych and the Staffordshire ceramic figures. The newly refurbished children's galleries bring history alive with historical dioramas and doll houses. Open Mon. to Sat. 9–6. Also be sure to note that the museum's courtyard serves as the location for the performance of "1627 and all that," and the museum may be toured during the evening if you attend.

PARISH PRACTICALITIES

accommodations: Cunard Paradise and Grand Barbados to the N of Bridgetown along the coast, and Hilton International at Needham's Point, are the major hotels.

budget accommodations: The outlying suburb of Belleville is a center for reasonably priced accommodations. The Crystal Crest (tel. 436-6129), Pine Road, has rooms for US$22 including breakfast and dinner. Others, ranging around US$20 pn EP, include The Great Escape (tel. 436-3554), 1st Ave, and Broome's Vacation Home (tel. 426-4955/2937, 429-3937/4192) in Pine Gardens. Fortitude (tel. 426-4210) is on lower Wellington St. Stox Inn (tel. 427-4370), at Industry Hall on Bay St. just minutes on foot from downtown, is one of the lowest priced guesthouses on the island, but it's also extremely spartan. You also might try De Splash Inn Guest House, Passage Rd., (tel. 427-8287), and Superville Guest House (tel. 427-5668), 3rd Ave. in Pickwick Gap on Wilbury Rd.

dining out: On Pinfold St. near the Jewish Synagogue, The Recess, set inside Alexander House, has a menu which features burgers, subs, and potato dishes. Just off Broad St. at the corner of Tudor and Milkmarket, Cat's is popular with both locals and visitors. Geared towards the nautical crowd, the Boatyard is set on Bay St. at the edge of Bridgetown. The Waterfront Cafe and Fisherman's Wharf, both overlooking the Careenage, are perhaps the best known seafood restaurants. Somewhat less expensive and open at times (such as Sun. evenings) when others may be closed, the Look Out Bar and Restaurant, Prince Henry St., features local dishes. Offering a choice of dining either under a hanging fern filled pavilion or out on a garden terrace, the Brown Sugar is in Aquatic Gap. The Schooner and Golden Shell restaurants are in the Grand Barbados Hotel in Carlisle Bay. Set in a former rum store dating from 1803, the Barracks, at the Island Inn in Aquatic Gap, emphasizes local food. The Hilton and The Pebble, the latter of which also caters to vegetarians, are at Needhams Point. One of the more reasonable but yet comfortable places to eat lunch is at the Barbados Museum's restaurant.

budget dining: One of the friendliest and most reasonably priced places to eat lunch (around B$8) is Norma's on Spry St. You might find members of the House of Assembly eating here after their Tuesday afternoon sessions. Every Fri. Queen's Park Restaurant serves a buffet lunch for B$15; meals average B$9 on other days. One of the more moderate and better places is the cafeteria inside Cave Shepherd near the American Airlines kiosk on the third floor. They offer local cuisine like fried flying fish, cakes, coffee, etc.; there's also a bar and takeaway counter. Also try the new hanging restaurant overlooking the street. Da Costa's has the Munch Wagon and Ho Kwong (buffet Chinese). On Marhill St. near Trafalgar Square, Encore features a variety of reasonably priced food; items include sweet potato pie, macaroni pie, and salads. Chefette, across on Broad St., serves fast food pizza, chicken, *roti*, burgers, salads, and ice cream. On Palmetto St. nearby, Capricorn has similar prices. The City Centre Bar, across the street, offers counter service. On Chapel St., Bucaneer Barrel, offers local fast food, and Colonel Sanders has the same stuff as stateside. Not real nifty on aesthetics—your food is served on styrofoam—but offering reasonable food with good size portions, E.O.B.'s Cafeteria is adjacent to the Fairchild St. bus terminal and shares its canned music. A sample special is steakfish, salad, rice, macaroni pie, and a small cup of iced mauby for B$10.95; it's also one of the few budget eating spots in town open on Sun. For snacking in the area, vendors are out the door to the L and around the corner. Out on Spring Garden Highway across from the Mt. Gay Rum Plant is the Bajan Food Tent which is open 24 hours a day. It serves delights like flying fish sandwiches (B$3.25) and rice and peas with steakfish (B$15). On Baxters Road ladies tending coalpots sell fried fish for B$8 per large piece; some of the more famous restaurants are Johno's, Enid's, and Collins Bar and Restaurant. Other places to eat are on the way to Christ Church. September's, Lower Bay St., offers a weekday (11–3) lunchtime special featuring a B$12 set plate and a B$20 buffet. Also inexpensive, Friday's Restaurant is nearby. Other local restaurants in the area include The Boatyard—pool table-equipped and having the feel of being on a ship. Mainly for tourists and overlooking the water, it features seafood, a salad bar, and ice cream. Just down the road is the Gasbros Club where you can dine on *pudding and souse* every Friday. If you happen to be out in Belleville, try The Great Escape.

food shopping: One of the main supermarkets, Elmer's, over on Broad St., has a wide range of products. Sample prices: eggs, B$6.26 per dozen including a 50 cents deposit on the box; Windmill Tomato Ketchup (794 g), B$3.70; La Choy Soya Sauce (5 oz.), B$2.50; apples, B$6.72/kg; cucumbers, B$4.31/kg; brown sugar, B$1.75/kg.; Grannie's Choice whole wheat flour, B$3.75/kg; 25 plastic cups, B$4.85; 3 lbs. American parboiled rice, B$3.97. Downtown Supermarket is on lower Broad St. Basix is on Marhill St. Bonnett's is on Suttle St. Budg-Buy Food is on St. Michael's Row. Super Centre Supermarket is on Bridge St. Buy Rite Discount Market has stores on Broad St., Fairchild St., High St., and Swan St. Federal Supermarket is on Nelson St. Rick's Supermarket is on Fairchild St. Goddard's Kensington Supermarket is near the Deep Water Harbour. A mere shadow of former times, Cheapside Market, at the end of Broad St. just before the ultramodern G.P.O., still has hucksters vending their wares. Another outdoor market location is on Swan St. Harry's Vegetable Basket is on Middle St. near Victoria. Chick Growers Ltd, Roebuck St., sells eggs for B$5.88/doz. and chicken for B$2.88/lb. Also on Roebuck is Alleyne Arthur's Discount Store which has some deals. One very fine place to buy food is the Farmer's Discount Center which has a selection of poultry, fruit, and vegetables as well as locally produced molasses and banana essence. On Beckles Rd. off of Bay Rd. near the museum, it's open Mon. to Fri, 8–6; Sat., 8–1. Finally, if you want to economize on your rum, The Grog Shop on High St. features cheap rum straight out of the keg if you bring your own bottle.

bookstores: Cave Shepherd has a very fine bookstore—just take the escalator up. They also sell the Sunday *New York Times* (B$21.60). Robert's Stationary Store, 9 High St., has a fine collection of local books. Airconditioned Bryden's Bookshop, on Victoria St., has an excellent selection. The Book Shop is inside Norman Centre. Days Books is in the Diamond Tower Mall on Marhill St. Island News Stand is on the first floor of De Costa's on Broad St. The Book Place, featuring very reasonable used books and some very eclectic new ones, is on Probyn St. and has another branch on Bay St.

record shops: Records are expensive in Barbados, averaging about B$23 per LP. Cave Shepherd has a small record kiosk. Dance World is on Rickett St. Electronic City is inside Speedbird House on Fairchild St. No. 1 Record Shop is at Independence Square. Manning's is on Broad St.

services: A stamp counter and Mid Town Pharmacy are inside Med-X Mall. The USIS has a small library open 12–3, Tues. to Fri., on Parry St. The local representative for American Express is Barbados International Travel Service (BITS), also on Parry St.

THE NORTHERN PARISHES AND THE SCOTLAND DISTRICT

Containing the entire parish of St. Andrew and comprising portions of St. Peter, St. Joseph, and St. John, the Scotland District was named after its UK lookalike. Take your time while exploring and savour this, the only area to offer much in the way of forest glades, streams, hills, ravines, and gorges. The Scotland District was formed after the sea ate away at the island's coral cap, exposing the soft underbelly of sandstones and clays known locally as Joe's River Mud. During the rainy season, the streams turn into raging torrents carrying along with them everything in their wake. Landslides occur along with the collapse of bridges and losses of patches of vegetation. In 1901 nearly 100 homes and estate buildings were destroyed when 400 acres of land slid downwards toward the sea. Again in 1938, 50 acres of hillside land shifted position, forcing abandonment of 100 houses in Rock Hall Village. The soil's instability can be traced to such activities as overgrazing, cultivation of steep slopes, and deforestation. These problems have a multiplying effect; each serves to intensify the effects of the other. Heavy flooding, in turn, adds to the problem when sand and silt clogs the streams; oil seepages and salt in the land also serve as barriers to cultivation. Aloes and cotton are grown in the district which extends for 22 sq. miles and covers about 1/7th of the island's land area. The other northern parishes included in this section are the three parishes due N of Bridgetown: St. James, St. Peter, and St. Lucy. St. James has the glamorous tourism; St. Peter contains the island's most picturesque town; and St. Lucy, the nation's cap, has some of its most picturesque scenery and most attractive traditional chattel houses.

SAINT JAMES AND THE PLATINUM COAST

Plush and well heeled, the so-called "Platinum Coast," a villa-speckled oasis stretching along the coast of St. James Parish, was once a simple paradise. Gone are the days when schoolboys would bicycle to Freshwater Bay, then, unobserved, strip themselves naked and plunge into the delightful water. Things began changing in the late 20s when Burton Ward, owner of the Walmer Lodge plantation, decided to build a club house at Freshwater Bay. Out of this modest establishment—combining dance floor and rented bungalows—came Paradise Beach, once the West Coast's leading beach resort. Bajans originally shunned the coast because of fear of tidal waves, the lack of the refreshing trade winds that grace the E coast, and the distance from Bridgetown. As any visitor can now see, any time lost in development owing to initial hesitation has been more than adequately made up for! Some of the more outstanding architecture includes two mansions of coral stone: Henrietta, lying to the E of the Sandy Lane Hotel and Ronald Tree's on Heron Beach, completed in 1947. Today one can still wander mile after mile of beach-lined coast, taking in the sights.

Sandy Lane Hotel: During the nearly 30 years of its existence, Sandy Lane has welcomed many of the high-and-mighty. Among those who have sojourned here are Tom Jones, Mick Jagger, Princess Margaret, Jacqueline Kennedy Onassis, Claudette Colbert and David Niven. The hotel was built by the late Ronald Tree who spared no expense in its construction. Portuguese masons worked on the bathrooms and Tree designed much of the furniture himself. Its golf course is the

ST. JAMES

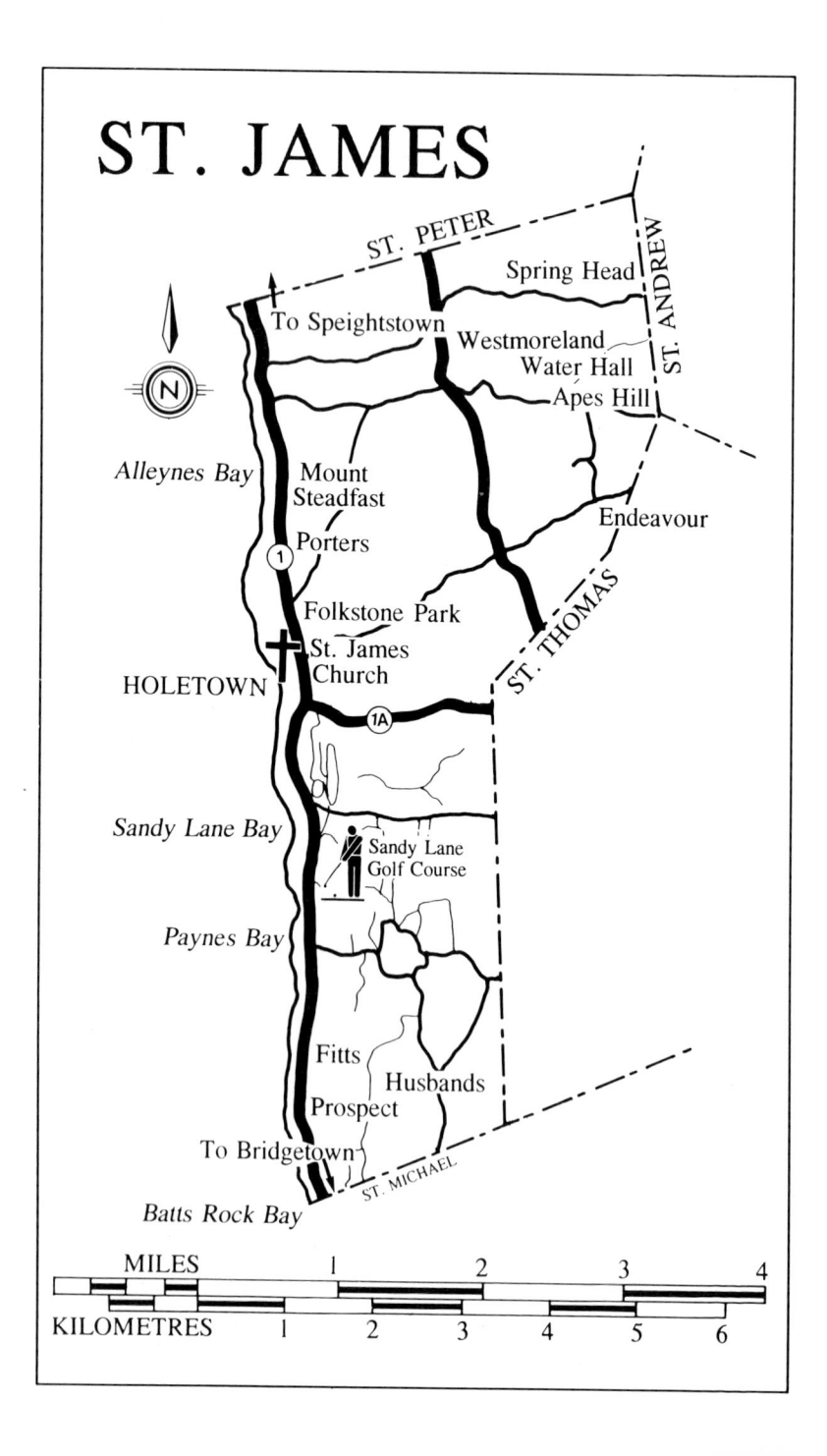

only 18-hole course on the island. Tree brought his wealthy friends with him, and the neighboring 380-acre Sandy Lane Estates contains more than 100 luxurious dwellings valued at between US$350,000 and $3 million each. Nearby Sunset Crest is a French-designed condo complex.

Holder's House: Just S of Sandy Lane in St. James Parish. Constructed some 300 years ago on a ridge, this magnificently restored great house stands at the center of what was once a 500-acre sugar and tobacco plantation. Its two-foot-thick plastered rubble coral stone walls have multiple louvered exterior doors for good air circulation.

HOLETOWN

Hardly a town at all—Sunset Crest Shopping Centre is what saves Holetown from mere village status—it is the parish's hub, off of which all of the resort hotels seem to branch. Despite its development, it still has bits of nature scattered about. Astride a small bridge near the Discovery Bay Hotel, one can observe white egrets arriving to rest in trees at dusk. And the sunsets are still marvelous along the beaches!

history: At one time known as Jamestown in honor of James I, the town is now so named because it offered settlers a "hole" into which they could anchor their ships, and because it also reminded them of the "hole" in the Thames river.

sights: The remains of James Fort lie behind the back of the police station where only two coral stone walls and a cannon remain. The Holetown Police Station was originally part of the gunner's quarters for the fort. The Holetown Monument lies a few yards N of the police station. Constructed of softstone blocks with a wooden cross set on top, it commemorates the 300th anniversary of the landing of the *Olive Blossom* in July 1605—an incorrect date which should actually read "1625" not "1605." On the L side of the road a few hundred yards farther N stands St. James Parish Church. Built in 1785 after its predecessor was razed by the 1780 hurricane, St. James has

St. James Parish Church

one of the few reminders of early church architecture—the porch tower with two crudely carved pillars and a keystone over the door. Fine stone sculptures grace the walls. Among these is one commemorating Sir John Alleyne's two wives and son John; it shows a view of Eton, the famous British public school. The old bell, cast in 1696—prior to the renowned Liberty Bell which was cast in London in 1750—is on display inside the church. The "King William" referred to in the inscription is William III. Check out the 18th C. tombstones and the memorial tablets inside the church, especially the racy one dedicated to Sir John Gay Alleyne's wife which hangs on the side above the steps to the balcony. In part the 1774 plaque reads that she "fweetened the Joys, alleviated the Cares, & enlightened the Pleasures of the nuptial State...."

Folkestone Park: This features tennis courts, a playground, and an artificial reef, formed by sinking the ship *Stavronikita*. A playground and picnicing area for locals, it has shaded benches as well as a small but fairly expensive restaurant. Its small marine museum is open Mon. to Fri., 10–5, Sat., Sun. 10–6; hourly slideshows from 10:30. B$1 admission, 50 cents for children. Note that water sports are prohibited in the areas delineated by buoys. Follow the underwater trail along seven-mile-long Dottin's Reef a mile offshore. Folkestone House nearby is also a former fort.

Bellairs Research Institute: Located next to the Folkestone, scientists here at this division of Canada's McGill University have studied tropical biology relating to sea urchins, flying fish, and plankton; wind and solar power; tropical climatology; sea turtle conservation; and the possibilities involving the use of brackish or purified seawater in agriculture.

Heron Bay: Ronald Tree had this house built in 1947, set amidst 20 acres of verdant splendor. Its grounds include a mullet-stocked pond, a citrus orchard, and a coconut palm grove. Overnight visitors have included the likes of Adlai Stevenson, Winston Churchill, Aristotle Onassis, and the Queen and Prince Phillip. It's right down the road from Colony Club and across from the entrance road to Porters. If you pass it on the beach, follow the beach down to the end and turn R past blooming jasmine and frangipani trees before encountering banyan trees near the main road. An incredible array of striking houses are around this stretch.

Porters House: Near Holetown and opposite Colony Club and Heron Beach stands one of the island's most majestic guesthouses which now serves as a private residence. Although parts of it do date from the 17th C., the greater part of the structure is 18th and 19th C. It is approached by a paved road lined with mahogany trees. To get to the sugar oven next door, retrace your steps, follow the main road and pass by mooing cows to enter the creepy, deteriorating remains.

from Holetown heading N: Along Highway 1, follow the coast through the villages of Mount Steadfast, Weston, and Carlton. Between the highway and the sea at Lower Carlton, St. James stands St. Alban's Church which was once Clarendon Fort; a great view from the seawall.

Vaucluse factory: Off Highway 2A, this sugar cane processing plant is named after a department in southern France's

Porters House, St. James

Rhone valley. Excellent view from Dukes nearby. Jack-in-the-box gully nearby has a variety of trees, but not its namesake.

Portvale Sugar Factory: Located in Blowers in the E part of the parish, this huge collection of sugar manufacturing and harvesting equipment is housed in the Sir Frank Hutson Sugar Machinery Museum which was opened in 1987 when the distinguished engineer was 91.

PARISH PRACTICALITIES

accommodations: One of the foremost resort hotels in the area is the Coral Reef Club. Run by members of the English expatriate O'Hara family, the hotel dates from the early 50s when the tourist industry was just beginning to emerge. Its compact cottage villas, spread out over a large area, are an economic anachronism; today's high land prices would render them unfeasible. The twin themes here are the color white and the flower hibiscus. Everything—from the staff's uniforms to the buildings—is a pristine white. And, although flowers are everywhere—one of the housekeepers is a genius at arrangements—hibiscus is the best represented. The 12-acre grounds, with their labeled trees, form a small botanical garden, and the villas have names like "Coconut"—along with a framed picture and typed description of the tree. Generally speaking the atmosphere here is one of gentle, mellow etiquette: even the birds appear to chirp thoughtfully and politely. Wrought iron work and yellow doors beckon you into the reception and dining area. The Casual Shop, the resort's chief shopping venue, is fortunate to have friendly and vivacious Jennie on its staff. If you reserve a room here, keep in mind that the villas towards the rear have a completely different ambience than those towards the front facing the sea. The latter comprise just 16 out of the 75. The deluxe suites feature a kitchenette, twin-bedded room, private bath, two air conditioners, large living room, and balcony. There's also a pool and two tennis courts on the grounds. For more information and/or res-

Queen's Fort, private home near Coral Reef Club

ervations, call New York, (tel. 800-223-1108) or London (tel. 01-240-2200). Other large resorts in the parish include Buccaneer Bay, Colony Club, Glitter Bay, and Sandy Lane. Hotels include Discovery Bay, the Sandpiper (also managed by the O'Hara family), Barbados Beach Village, and the Royal Pavilion.

dining out: Two of the better known establishments are the Coral Reef Club and Sandpiper Inn. The former features a barbecue with floor show and steelband on Thurs. nights and a buffet on Sun. Another well known restaurant belongs to the Treasure Beach Hotel. Sandy Lane offers a daily afternoon tea, a Sunday traditional lunch, and a Friday evening buffet. You may dine on a pink marble terrace at the Royal Pavilion Hotel's The Palm Terrace. Or you may dine under swaying palms at Piperade at the Glitter Bay Hotel in Porters. Another well known choice is the Colony Club. Other choices in the vicinity include Settler's Beach Hotel. Folkestone Restaurant and Bar, set on the beach in Folkestone Park, offers *cou cou* and flying fish for lunch on Wed. In Holetown, the Balmore House Restaurant is in a colonial-style home. Raffles Restaurant, First St., wins the prize for the most unusual decor. It features zebra-patterned couches, black and spotted painted leopards, and representations of other jungle critters. Informal and moderately priced, Barbados Pizza House offers whole pizzas and slices (B$3.35) as well as fish and chips (B$12.95). Overlooking Palm Beach in Holetown, The St. James Steak House specializes in *guess what*? Set inside Sunset Crest Mall, The Brig is an imitation old English sailing vessel. One of the better known gourmet restaurants is Noelles in Holetown which has two bistros: Le Cafe and The Garden Terrace. Another, in Paynes Bay, is La Cage Aux Folles which features local, Chinese, and international dishes. Also in Paynes Bay, the Bamboo Beach Bar serves a variety of seafood specialities as well as steak and chicken; the Buccaneer Bay Grill specializes in European cuisine. Set beside beach coves at Derricks, the Coconut Creek Club's restaurant serves up a variety of special dishes as does the Carambola and Reid's which are also at Derricks. The Fountain Restaurant is in Barbados Beach Village. Located at Prospect are three restaurants: Rose and Crown (creole fare), Fiesta, and Koko's—a small restaurant perched right on the edge of the sea. Sandy Lane's restaurant is also well known, with a Fri. night International Buffet. At Black Rock, Cunard Paradise Village's restaurant has live music every night. Coach House is an English Pub-style bistro which features a B$20 buffet lunch weekdays with local food.

budget dining: In Holetown, Catamara offers Bajan fare like fried flying fish and peas and rice. The Beach Club features nightly specials. About the only truly budget place to eat in town is the takeaway counter inside the 99 Convenience Store. Holmes Bar, another rum shop in St. James, serves food until the wee hours. Located atop Holder's Hill—off Highway 1, just opposite Tamarind Cove—it has real rural atmosphere, extending right down to the spicy fried chicken.

market food: A cooperative minimart is next to St. James Parish Church. Wick's Discount Wine and Spirits also sells French bread at B$3.50 per stick. At Sunset Crest, across the road from Inn on the Beach and directly across from the 99 Convenience Store, is a small farmer's market featuring homegrown fruits and vegetables. There are also a number of small markets in the prefecture's towns.

ST. THOMAS PARISH

Along with neighboring St. George, St. Thomas is one of only two island parishes which are unexposed to the sea. Three highways (Highway 1A from St. James, which runs into 2A, Highway 2, and Highway 2A) intersect the parish. Its features include the island's only cave, a nature preserve, and some classic architecture.

ALONG HIGHWAY 2A

Warrens: Once the center of a working plantation, this magnificent great house has been encroached upon by residential housing and commercial structures and no longer serves as a plantation house. Built in 1686, it has been preserved by its owners, the C. O. Williams Construction Company. To the E lies one of the island's most venerable baobab trees—approximately 250 years old and smaller than the one in Queen's Park, it was planted in 1735.

Sharon: Oldest Moravian church on the island, Sharon stands on the side of a hill on the main road between Bathsheba and Bridgetown. Constructed in 1799, it is one of the few 18th C. structures on the island which have been preserved unaltered; it was restored to all its glory in 1989. Its Low Country architectural influences betray the spiritual roots of the faith.

Bagatelle: Situated off Highway 2A and owned by Richard and Val Richings, Bagatelle greathouse originally was the property of Lord Willoughby and named Parham Park House.

ST. THOMAS

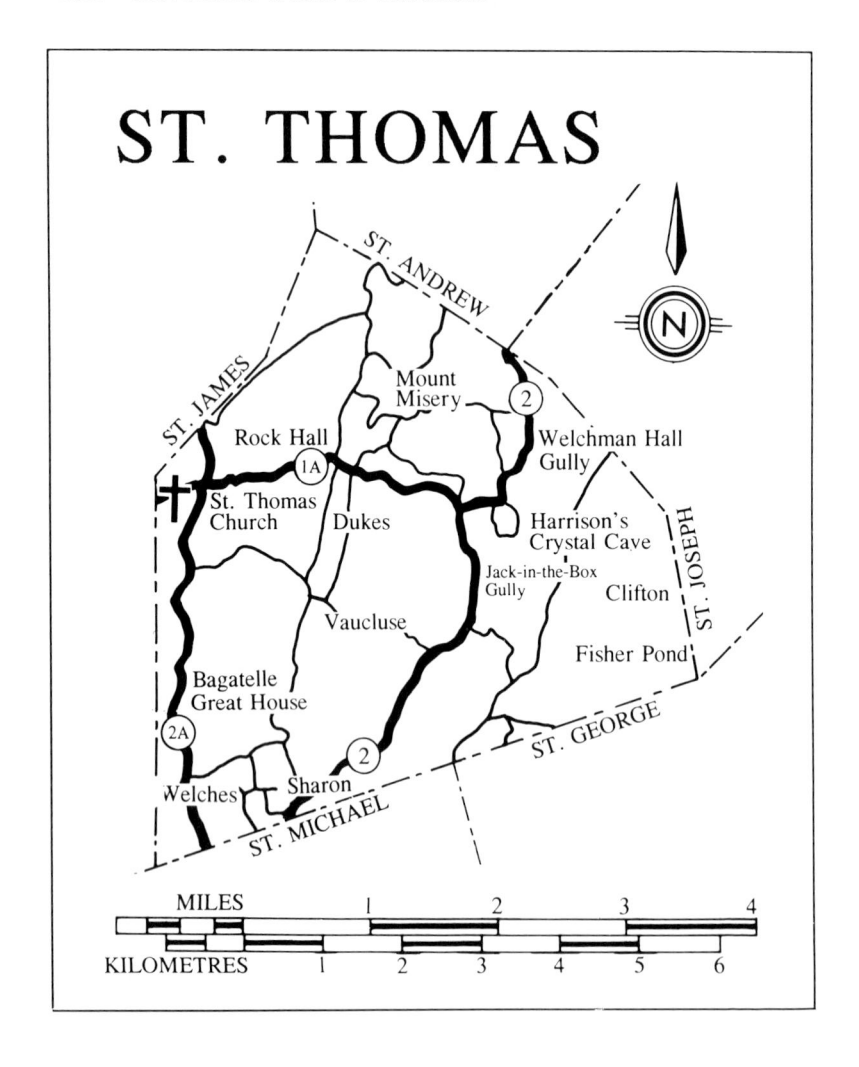

In 1877, its name was changed once more to Bagatelle by its new owners who took it over in partial repayment for a gambling debt. The story goes that after the property was lost the former owner shrugged and said it was just "a bagatelle," which is French for a "trifle." It was converted into a restaurant in 1970 and Lord Willoughby's bust graces the souvenir menus supplied with the meals served here. Several miles farther on is the St. Thomas Parish Church which has been destroyed by hurricanes in 1675, 1780, and 1831; it was damaged by the storm of 1731.

Welchman's Hall Gully: Open to the public since 1961, this windy, cool, and damp deep ravine has been developed as a national park. It is named after former landholder General Williams, a Welshman and one of the earliest colonists. Around 1860, one of his descendants cleared some acreage and planted fruit and spice trees here before wilderness again overtook it. Enter via an orange grove and a flower garden with blooms such as bougainvillea, frangipani, and begonias. The legendary Elephant Stalactite—a four-foot-high and wide stalactite which has merged with a stalagmite to form a large pillar—marks the entrance to the cave. Other vegetation includes tree ferns as well as nutmeg and clove trees. The nutmegs came from Grenada while the cloves were imported from Zanzibar. There's also a 25-foot-tall specimen of the traveller's tree which originates in Madagascar; the thirsty visitor could gouge the tree with a knife and drink the water collected in the interstices. Meet the chattering monkeys which abound on the grounds. A large variety of fruit trees grow in the village of Carrington nearby.

Harrison's Cave: On Highway 2 just near Welchman Hall, this is one of the largest caves in the Caribbean. The Visitor's Center has a handicraft shop along with an exhibit of Indian artifacts. A slide show provides an introduction, and visitors then set out on a 45-minute underground electric bus tour passing by waterfalls, streams, cascades, and pools. Tours are given every hour from 9–4. At the cavern's lowest point, visitors dismount and traverse the side of a waterfall that plunges 40 feet (12 m.) into a blue green pool. One of the cave's more remarkable features are the large number of virgin white, pear-shaped stalactites which hang suspended from the ceiling. Although they had been common knowledge among locals for hundreds of years, these caves were first explored in 1970 by Ole Sorenson, a Danish speleologist. Heavy flooding in that year had opened up the entrance to what came to be known as crystal caverns; exploring the cave, he discovered a number of large chambers. In 1981, the government decided to open the caves to the public.

Harrison's Cave

Fisher Pond: Antedating the 1831 hurricane, two-storied Fisher Pond house stands near the junction to Bathsheba. Two millwalls stand here; the second, the Olive Branch millwall, is 200 yards (183 m) away. Marked by vertical coral cliffs running along both sides, Russia or Rusher Gully is nearby.

ST. JOSEPH PARISH AND BATHSHEBA

St. Joseph may be the island's smallest parish, but it is not without its delights. In addition to Bathsheba, one of the island's most famous fishing villages, it contains a portion of Hackleton's Cliff, and a remarkable set of gardens in addition to a splendid coastline. The arriving African air here is said to be incredibly fresh and brisk as it hasn't been exposed to land for thousands of miles. Saharan dust has even been known to blow in on occasion. Highway 3A and the East Coast Road, which enter the parish from St. Joseph, are two of the major transportation arteries. Coming from St. George, Highway 3 descends steep Horse Hill to Joe's River Plantation and onward.

Bathsheba: Lying 14 miles from Bridgetown, this fishing village is a world apart. Its rocky terrain—one of the most photographed spots on the island—overlooks one of the island's most spectacular beaches. Named the "Soup Bowl," owing to its foamy surf, this shady beach plays host to an annual surfing competition. From Bathsheba the East Coast Road follows along the old railway route to Belleplaine, heading up into St. Andrew.

Flower Forest: Reached via Highway 3A which runs past the villages of Sugar Hill, Chimbarazo, Spa Hill, Fruitful Hill, and Cane Garden. Set in the heart of the Scotland District in Richmond, St. Joseph, this touristic attraction consists of an expertly landscaped forest which still retains much of its original wild ambience. A paved path runs through it bringing into view mango, golden apple, breadfruit, cocoa, avocado and bamboo. Just pick up a leaflet and follow it along: the 50 acres are

Bathsheba

divided into eight sections, each marked on ceramic stones. Monkeys may be seen at dawn or dusk here. In addition to a drink and concession restaurant, there's also a Best of Barbados shop here. Open daily 9 to dusk, B$8 admission, children B$4.

Cotton Tower: Near the top of Horse Hill, a byway leads here. Named after Miss Dorothy Cotton daughter of Lord Combermere, Gov. of Barbados, this three-storey four-layer structure served as a message relay post. Construction was begun in 1819. One window points in the direction of Gun Hill and another towards Grenade Hill. In the plantation era, messages originating from the Governor's residence in Queen's Park were relayed to St. Anne's Fort and on to Gun Hill, Moncrieffe (on the border between St. John and St. Philip), and then on to Cotton Tower. Hoisting the appropriate flags, Cotton Tower's soldiers would relay the message to Grenade Hall (on the site of Farley Hill). Although the tower is currently closed, from the top the view takes in Parks Road Saddle Back to the N and Buckden Gully to the S. Rising from atop the hill in the distance is St. Joseph's Anglican Church. From Cotton Tower, passing through a break in the cliff wall, hike down to Dacres Hill through the woods.

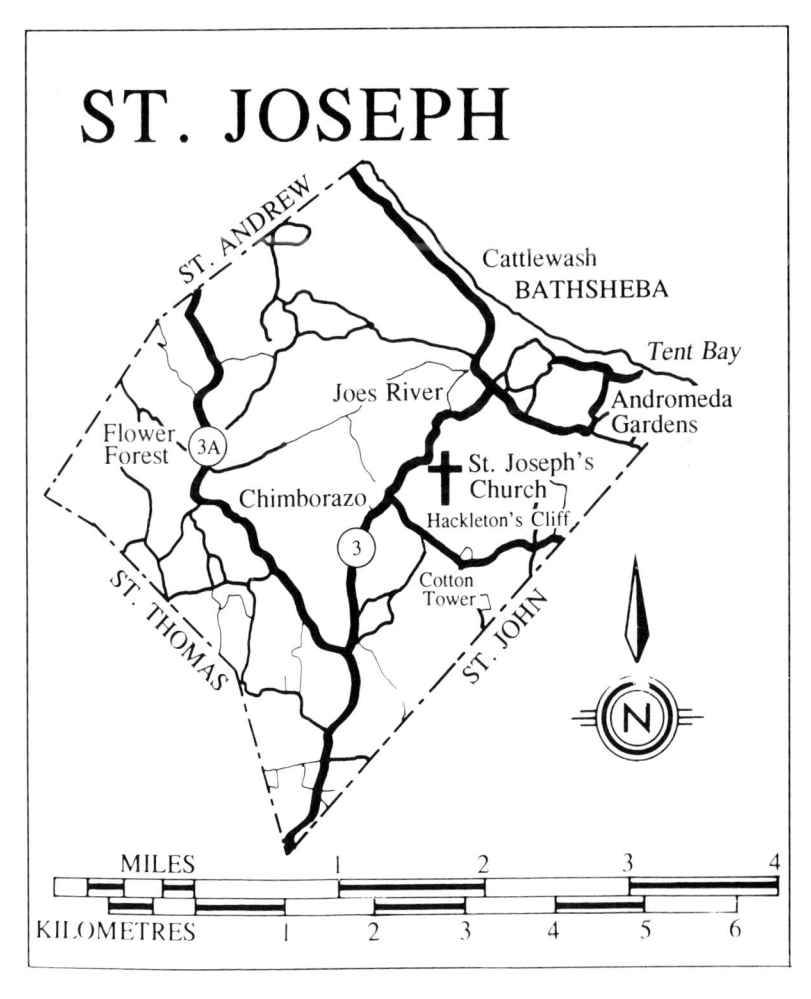

Andromeda Gardens: Begun by the late Iris Bannochie in 1954, this is the island's most famous garden, a visit to which might be the perfect prelude or climax to a leisurely lunch at the Atlantis Hotel. Named after the mythical Greek maiden who was tied to a rock as a sacrifice for a sea monster, the flowers in these gardens are also "tied" to rocks. Originally

Lilly pond, Andromeda Gardens

toppled by torrential flooding, the boulders are as wide as 27 feet (nine meters) in width. Trees here include the fustic, bearded fig, whitewood, pop-a-gun, and maypole. Bridged by a causeway, the lily pond has night blooming and day blooming lilies on opposite sides; this separation allows both types to flourish because, if they were to be planted together, the day bloomers would soon crowd the nighties out. Ingeniously-designed bridges and paths criss-cross the gardens. Some are made of local sandstone, others of brick; some have grass, others are concrete slabs decorated with leaf imprints. Flowers include begonias, hibiscus, red ginger lilies, and bougainvilleas. In one special section, part of the international collection of orchids, tied to halved logs, juts straight up. There's also one of the immense fig trees for which the island may have been named. A swimming pool was built in 1956 and the soil extracted was used to construct a terraced garden. There are also large palm and orchid gardens which, as with the entire grounds, you are free to explore at will. Singing birds complete the picture in this serene, reverentially peaceful setting—one which appears to incorporate a British sense of orderly restraint combined with an East Asian sense of arrangement and a tinge of Caribbean mysticism. Open 8 AM to dusk, B$8 admission. B$4 for children.

near Andromeda: Tent Bay, where the Atlantis Hotel is located, is the only place along the parish's coast where fishing boats operate. At 1–3 PM daily, view the unloading of the fish catch during the season. Also in the vicinity, Foster Hall Woods is second only to Turner's Hall Woods as an ecological preserve.

other sights: Atop Spa Hill, the ruins of Spa House command one of the island's most magnificent panoramas—over the wild and rugged territory to the E. The name Spa spawned the name "spawgee" for the "redlegs" who lived here. At the time it was christened, Chimborazo Hill was believed to be the island's highest point and was therefore named after Ecuador's Mt. Chimborazo, believed to be the world's highest peak at the time. A small chapel atop Gagg's Hill is built of coral stone and features four tombstones set into the floor.

PARISH PRACTICALITIES

accommodations: At Cattlewash at the southern base of the magnificent stretch of beach that runs along the East Coast, Kingsley Club is the perfect get-away-from-it-all location. With the exception of a few houses for rent, it is the sole accommodation in this area. All white and blue and wood, it has a classic West Indian guesthouse feel to it. While the guesthouse is of postwar construction, the restaurant is more than a century old. Its rooms are equipped with one or two double beds, overhead fan, and private bath with shower. The corridor has a large selection of books and magazines for guests' reading pleasure. Of Armenian parentage, owner Loris Arevian was born in Alexandria, Egypt and emigrated to Canada. He has made Barbados his home for more than two decades. In the works for the hotel are a series of condo additions as well as pool. Although Loris and his wife Sherry theoretically run the place, their dog Susie, a Jack Russell (a breed traditionally used in fox hunting), really rules the roost. The other hotel in the area is the Atlantis over in Bathsheba.

food and dining: Immaculately done up with blue-cushioned white wicker chairs and matching tablecloths and napkins, Kingsley Club is the exclusive venue for the Cattlewash area. Heading N along the East Coast Road in St. Andrew are the snackette on the beach across from Barclay's Park, the East Coast Cafe, and a snackette or so in Belleplaine. The Atlantis Hotel is best known for its buffet lunches which are a celebration of local cuisine. It can be crowded—especially on weekends—so be sure to reserve. The small Bonito Restaurant, on the main stretch in Bathsheba, features local seafood including crab. A small snackette is just down the road, and there are rum shops in the vicinity.

ST. ANDREW'S PARISH

One of the least populated parishes, St. Andrew (pop. 6,500) still retains an atmosphere and charm all its own. Containing part of the scenic Scotland District as well as a stretch of the East Coast Road, it also features the island's best preserved windmill, a nature reserve, pottery village, as well as other attractions. Other than the East Coast Road, the parish's major artery is Highway 2.

Cherry Tree Hill: Resplendent rows of wind-bent and gnarled-branched mahogany (not cherry!) trees line the avenue leading up to it. A great view from the top gazing southward to Chalky Mount and Hackleton's Cliff. There are also monkeys in the vicinity. A path at the base of the hill leads to the right which curves around E to a sheltered gully forested with casuarinas. A hundred-yard-long path leads to the flattened top of Mt. Stepney, known as "The Mount." In turn, a path from its top, heads along the escarpment's edge. One side is lined with sour grass and maypoles (century plants); the other is one wing of a dropoff. The result of a 1901 landslide, a jumble of huge boulders covering a one mile area—some of them house-sized—rests at the foot of Mt. Stepney. A winding path leads through them to Boscobelle Church. Paul's Point commands a magnificent view over Gay's Cove to Pico Teneriffe. From Cherry Tree Hill, the road continues on to St. Peter's Parish.

Morgan Lewis Mill: In line with its reputation as the best preserved sugar mill on the island, Morgan Lewis Mill is the only one with its arms and well house intact. Run by the Barbados National Trust, the organization has installed a permanent collection of sugar manufacturing accessories including ladles and yokes at the site. Typical of the Dutch-style mills

View of east coast from Cherry Tree Hill

which once dotted the island, it is the sole remainder of the era when around 500 ground cane; they lasted until the early 1900s when they were replaced by the more efficient steam-run mills. Three-roller Morgan Lewis is of the type introduced around 1798, and it was manufactured in Derby, England in 1908. Squeezing 50-65 percent of the sugar from the cane, these mills were a big improvement over the former cattle-powered mills which could extract only about 50 percent of the juice.

Morgan Lewis Beach: The territory lying to the S from Chandler Bay to Green Pond is some of the most remote area in the island. The view from here is of totally unexploited wilderness. Mount Gay gives its name to Barbados's foremost brand of rum. Also check out the view from Paul's Point.

St. Andrew's Anglican Church: Survivor of the disastrous 1780 and 1831 hurricanes, this church was condemned in 1842 and rebuilt from 1846-55. Near the church is the Walker's sand dune which has been threatened with ecological damage by extensive mining. While high quality clear glass cannot be produced from the island's sand, green and amber glass may.

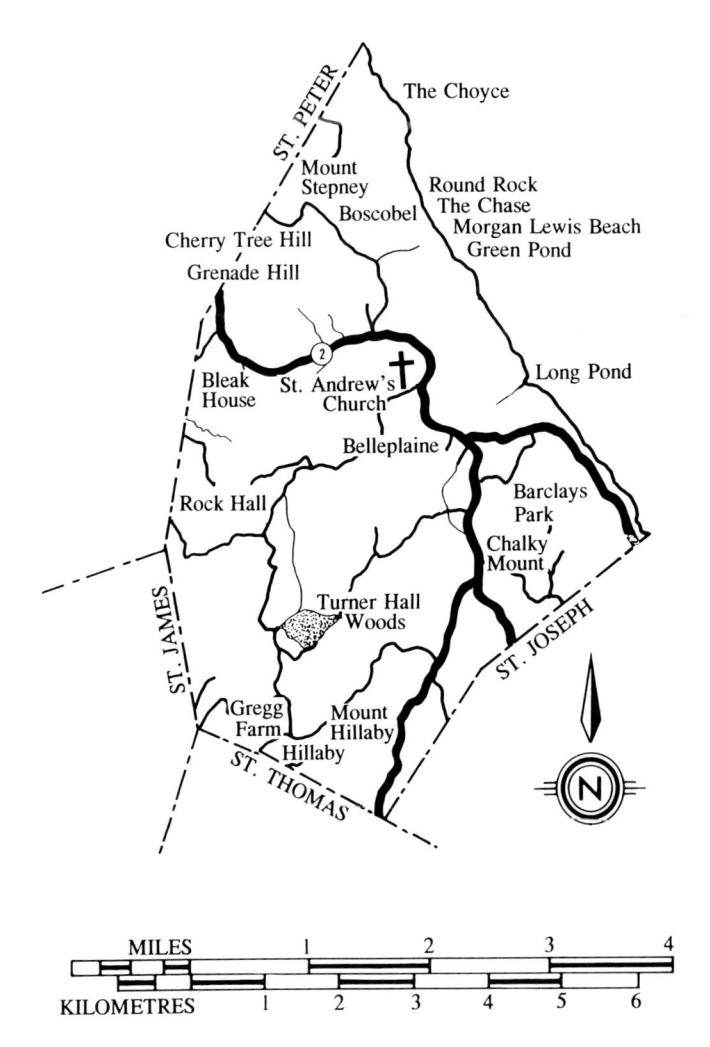

ST. ANDREW

Shorey Village nearby is of note for spawning legendary cricketeer Conrad Hunte.

Barclay's Park: Good picknicking but dangerous swimming at this 50-acre park which climbs up a hillside. A 1966 Independence gift from Barclay's Bank International, it lies off the East Coast Road near the border with St. Joseph.

Chalky Mount: Actually a rugged range of hills that rise 571 feet over the road, a few potters still linger on here, a reminder of the time when this community was *the* major supplier of household ceramic items. A great place to see the sunset. Reached from Highway 2. Take the road to the R toward Coggins Hill which leads up to it. A moderately difficult path takes you to the summit. Its brownish-red soil reflects its high clay content. Kickwheel-powered pottery produced here includes *conerees,* pots for pickling and cooking stews, and *monkeys,* water jugs which cool the water naturally.

Haggatts Agricultural Station: Home of the soil conservation plan for the Scotland District. Visitors can see the methods being implemented to improve the area. Because the clay foundation under the soil is impenetrable, the water slips away taking the topsoil with it. The station is working on developing various anti-erosion techniques. One method is to plant grass on hillsides to hold water; another is the use of *gaboins,* stone-filled wire baskets which are used to slow down the flooding after rains. The center also distributes fruit trees, including mango, Barbados cherry, and citrus.

Turner Hall Woods: One of the island's few remaining glades, these woods cover 46 acres of land on a spur running NE from Mt. Hillaby. Rising to 600–800 ft (180–240 m) above sea level, this preserve is half a mile in length and nearly a quarter-mile wide. It is similar to other semi-evergreen forests found elsewhere—in Antigua, Trinidad, Martinique, and other islands. Like them it receives 60–70 in. (150–175 cm) of rain per year. Present are at least 32 species of trees including such Bajan stalwarts as sand box, macaw palm, silk cotton, locust, fustic, red cedar, and cabbage palm. These are supplemented by 30 species of shrubs. One tree found only here is the jack-in-the-box. Its name comes from its small hollow, topless fruit which has a seed standing erect inside; it can be identified by its large, heart-shaped leaves. The woods are home to a few monkeys along with a four-foot-wide and-deep hole known as the Boiling Spring; the natural gas exuded from it may flicker if ignited.

up Mt. Hillaby: Perched on the back of a ridge, the road through Mount All and White Hill overlooks spectacular views. After reaching the top of White Hill, it passes into Hillaby. At the top of White Hill, turn L to reach the summit of Mt. Hillaby (1,116 feet) from which you can view the island from windward to leeward. To the S lie rolling fields of cane and other crops; to the N are the villages of White Hill and Gregg Farm with St. Peter's eastern ridge visible in the background. (*Pudding and souse* is for sale on Sun. at Gregg Farm village). But the best view is to the east—ravines, hills, and gullies. Actually a dirt-covered, chalk-configured hill, it's rather undramatic. To determine that you're in the right place, search for the metal-capped cement stump which reads: "Inter American Geodetic Survey. Do not Disturb. Hillaby. 1953."

Bleak House: A plantation commanding a great view of the entire Scotland District located at the parish's W end close to its border with St. Peter. Reached by following Highway 2; make the first left turn after Farley Hill Park. Constructed in 1886 by order of eccentric Charles Peddlar, its 160 acres are being used for farming and animal husbandry.

PARISH PRACTICALITIES

budget dining and market food: Belleplaine has Belleplaine Supermarket and Snackette and Likorish Bar & Grocery. Try the East Coast Cafe and the snack bar at Barclay's Park.

SAINT PETER'S PARISH AND SPEIGHTSTOWN

Facing both the W and the E coasts, Saint Peter is the only prefecture to cross the island W to E, although the eastern portion *is* mighty skinny. Easily accessible are twin contrasts: ultra-posh St. James to the S and ultra-rural St. Lucy to the N. The parish's charms include one of the island's architectural gems—a ruined greathouse transformed into a national park, the island's second major town, and a wildlife reserve. As an added feature, at least 20 millwalls stand in St. Peter, the most of any parish. Although the most popular route runs via Highway 1 from St. James, the approach from St. Peter is particularly scenic—either via Cherry Tree Hill or Farley Hill. If you enter this way, the first attraction you come to will be St. Nicholas Abbey. If you should enter from St. James on the other hand, you will doubtless be passing through Speightstown, the mainstay of the island's north.

SPEIGHTSTOWN

This is currently the second most important town, one which once played a close second fiddle to Bridgetown in terms of economic and cultural importance. It is all archetypal balconied houses and narrow streets, with the exception of a shopping mall. Virtually unchanged for over a hundred years, it is not so much the individual architecture in this town that gives it its unusual ambience but the total effect created by the

ST. PETER

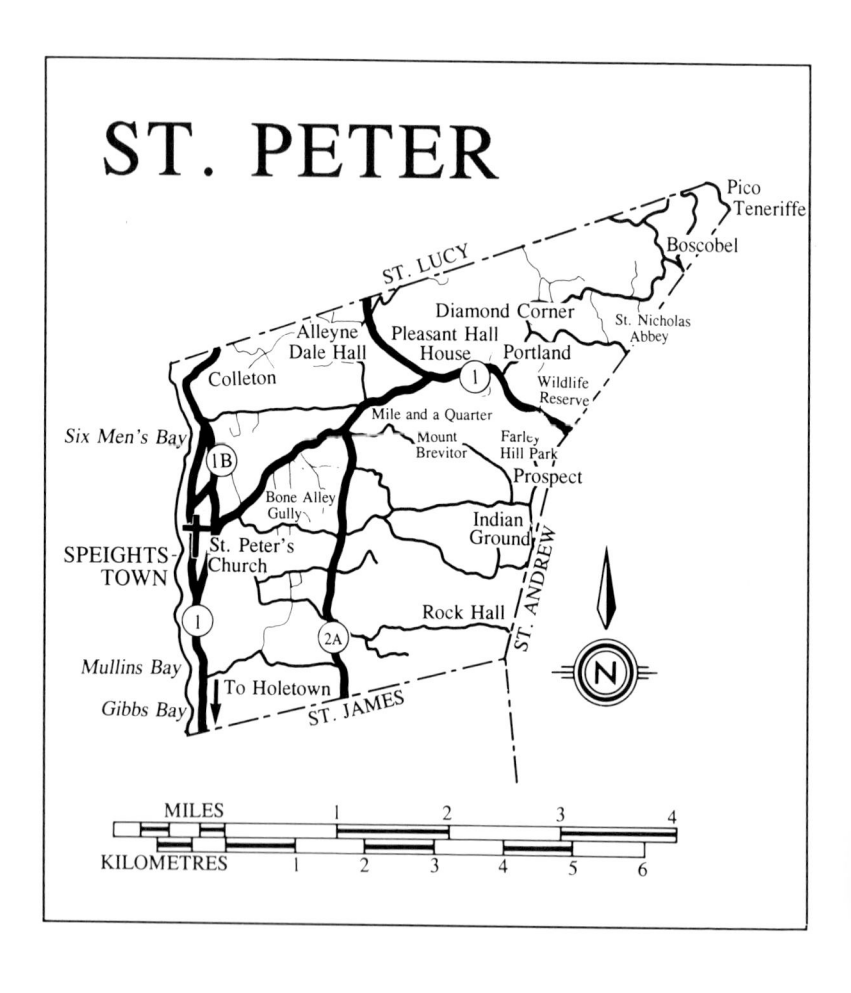

whole. Although it is currently somewhat shabby in appearance, the National Trust is planning restoration work here that could transform it into one of the most elegant towns of the Caribbean. Its bypass channels traffic out of the center of town thus retaining the town's serenity. Walk around here on a Saturday morning when the hucksters are out selling vegetables in full force.

history: The town's name (pronounced "Spikestown") comes from the land's previous owner one William Speight—who became a member of the first assembly. Becoming rapidly important, it was well known for its trade with Bristol and dubbed with the sobriquets "Little Bristol" and "New Bristol." Its importance derived from two sources: poor communications between the northern parishes and Bridgetown and from the distant financial connections of a few entrepreneurial expatriate merchants. As the merchants passed up, up, and away into the great marketplace in the sky, and as intra-island communications improved, the town's prominence faded. During the days of the *Speightstown Schooner,* passage could be made three times per week. Although the time to be consumed by the voyage was always an uncertainty, it generally required from 1–1.5 hours. Denmark Fort played a prominent role in the town's defense when Cromwellite Sir George Ayescue attacked. One of its less enviable features was the town's reputation for racism and upper class snobbery—a tradition which is thankfully receding. One island saying—"Speightstown hens don't lay home"—came out of the empirical observation that the town's women frequently married outsiders to the community. Another insightful designation is the "Speightstown Compliment"—a backhanded one.

sights: Escaping the 1780 hurricane, St. Peter's Church, at the corner of Church and Queen Streets, was destroyed by the whopper of 1831. A Georgian-styled structure stood from 1837 until 1980 when a fire destroyed all but its walls and steeple. The subsequent restoration (from 1980–83) cost B$750,000. The side of Church St. opposite St. Peter's Church retains some of the shops—with overhanging galleries supported by slender poles—once so characteristic of the streets of Barbados towns. The remnants of the Denmark and Orange forts stand

Beach near Cobbler's Cove, St. Peter

in the town's center. Be sure to see the building next to the Golden Crust Bakery with religious slogans painted on brown boards covering its walls and windows. The Esplanade along Sand St.—delineated by a row of cannon pointing seaward—is a good place to hang out. Here, seated on lime green benches set below mahoe and tamarind trees filled with singing birds, you may enjoy a respite. Everyone is staring off into the distance—as though they are characters in a play pausing before speaking their lines at the beginning of an act.

in and around town: Speightstown Mall, opened in 1980, offers a wide variety of shops, banks, and fast food. On the outskirts of Speightstown near Cobbler's Cove stand some magnificent estates. One is Claudette Colbert's mansion—to which Ronald Reagan was flown in daily by helicopter from Sandy Lane Hotel; if you're fortunate you might tread over one of the spots on the beach where he once basted his buns. Another is Leamington, the former residence of the US ambassador. Farther down the road, Mullin's beautiful beach is generally near-to-deserted. Located on six cliff-topped acres of landscaped gardens, Eastry House next door commands a great view.

Speightstown bus terminal: Speightstown's modern and comfortable bus terminal (tel. 422–2410) stands in the northern part of town near the bypass. Its mandarin-orange striped interior features benches, piped in music, and a TV set which shows estimated departure times. All buses departing from here originate in Bridgetown except for the Oistins and Speightstown buses. Ask at the information counter concerning departure times. Although it is a virtual certainty that the bus you want will be late, it is also dead certain that the one time you go out for a walk and are late in returning your bus will have departed on time! The Boscobel bus runs to Ashton Hall, Mile and a Quarter, Diamond Corner, the Castle, the Baltic, and Boscobel. The Indian Ground bus runs to Portand, Welchtown, Prospect, Indian Ground, and French Village. The Josey Hill bus runs to Checker Hall, Bourbon, Mt. Gay, and Josey Hill. The Connell Town bus runs to Heywood, Six Men's, Checker Hall, Harrison's, Crab Hill, Cluffs, Bright Hal, Flatfield, Connell Town, and River Bay. The Pie corner bus runs to Six Men's, Pickering's, Half Acre, Spring Hall, Spring Garden, Rockfield, Pie Corner, Graveyard, and The Baltic. The St. Lucy's Church runs to Litchfield, St. Joseph's Hospital, Mile and a Quarter, Alleynedale, St. Lucy's Church, Trents, Friendship, Crab Hill, and Samond (near Archer's Bay). The Archer's Bay bus runs a similar route. The Speightstown bus covers the same route as the Indian Ground bus, but instead of turning off it travels on to Welchtown, Greenland, Walker's, Belleplaine, and on to Cattlewash before climbing the hill past Andromeda Gardens to Bathsheba. The Oistins bus bypasses Bridgetown but still passes by the coast from the Garrison area on to the east. If you want to get to Farley Hill, take an Indian Ground or Bathsheba bus; for St. Nicholas Abbey, take a Boscobel, and for the magnificent stretch of coast surrounding Little Bay take the Pie Corner to the end of the line.

heading N: Opposite the Heywood tourist development—the island's largest resort—to the N of Speightstown, lies Heywood Beach. No one has ever satisfactorily explained why the small bay farther on, once a whaling center, is so oddly known as

"Six Men's," but one story has it that six Indians were found there by arriving settlers. Today, it features hauled up fishing boats resting on wood blocks and oil drums amidst the wrecks of cars. Turn L at the nearby junction where houses are named "Snugness" and "Snug Haven." Past Sherman's Bay, another fishing area, is a narrow but long sand beach. A frequent sight along this stretch during the fall months is boats being caulked prior to painting in preparation for the winter season. Here, you can see the loading ramp extension belonging to the economically ailing Arawak Cement Plant off in the distance. Next up the road is the Half Moon Bathing Facility, which has a rather small beach. To reach Maycock Bay, continue along the main road until the turnoff past the cement plant. Stretching for about a mile with a width of only 100–200 feet (60–90

Maycock's Bay, St. Peter

m), this bay is the most spectacular location before Harrison Point. Two steep trails lead down to the beach and the ruins of Maycock's Fort. At Harrison's Point nearby stands the compound of the Barbados Defence Force, formerly the US Naval Facility. Although the base itself is off limits, a track leads down to Harrison's Point Lighthouse, from which another path at its base leads to the ruggedly eroded coast. Hangman's Bay lies to the S nearby.

All Saints Church: Constructed in 1649, the oldest church on the island stands about 1.5 km away from the district of Mile and a Quarter. After braving the hurricanes of 1675 and 1780, it succumbed to the 1831 storm. A foundation stone was laid in 1839, and the newly-rebuilt church was consecrated in 1843, only to be demolished some 40 years later after structural problems were uncovered. The present version dates from 1884. To be found among its collection of 17th C. graveyard bones, the remains of William Arnold who was alleged to be the first Englishman to set foot on Barbados. Back on Highway 2A is monkey-inhabited Baker Woods; at its end Sion Hill Gully, populated with rubber trees, runs under the road. From Pleasant Hall off Highway 2A, a narrow and twisting road leads through the Second High Cliff. Immediately at the beginning of this to the right stands Arawak Cave, which has a small carved sculpture apparently in the shape of an Indian head.

Bone Alley Gully: Also known as Whim Gully, Bone Alley Gully lies in the vicinity of Speightstown off Highway 1. Despite the forbidding name, it is actually a wide-open natural area—a great place to go for a walk. Another attractive and impressive location, N of Speightstown, accessed by Highway 2A, is Sailor Gully and Rock Hall. The Rock—a set of 80-ft. (25 m) vertical white cliffs festooned with thick vines—overlooks 80-ft.-deep, 300-yard-long Sailor's Gully. Orange Hill offers a panoramic view of the surrounding area.

Mount Brevitor and vicinity: Caves containing Indian artifacts have been located in the area between Mount Brevitor and Portland, and in a large stalactite and stalacmite laden cave underneath the hill. The caves were used by the Indians for burial and possibly for religious ceremonies. Don't miss the spectacular view of the Leeward Coast. Another great view can be found from the road which connects Rock Hall to that leading from Mount Brevitor.

Alleyne Dale Hall: Built by the Terril family possibly around 1680-85, it was known as The Terrils until the nickname Cabbage Tree Hall—after the long avenue of majestic towering cabbage palms that once flanked the entrance road—stuck. Even after Sir John Alleyne purchased the plantation house in the 18th C., it was said that the ghost of the last Terril—who committed suicide and was interred in the cellar—still paced the hallways. Sweet lime hedges, more than a century old, surround the three-storey building. Built in 1861, the millwall on the grounds is the island's tallest. Washing Pond, also on the estate, has the reputation for never drying up—even under the severest drought.

Prospect: This relatively high (823 ft.) area near St. Peter's Parish is named for its view. It's off a side road down the highway just before Farley's coming from Speightstown. From here the sea is visible on both sides; it's a great place to plan a picnic. If you walk through Prospect Woods, you can find another fine viewpoint with Cleland downhill and Chalky Mount off in the distance.

Farley Hill: One of the island's top tourist attractions. Until the demon fire so rudely and thoughtlessly destroyed it some years back, this mansion commanded a view of the ocean on three sides. Today, it consists of several acres of verdant parkland containing carefully cultivated tropical vegetation. The grounds offer varieties of fruit trees; cross the bridge below the greathouse ruins near the parking lot to find a grove of casuarina, young mahogany, and whitewood. Don't miss sitting on the lime green benches which are sheltered by casuarina trees—cooled by the ocean breeze and set on the edge of the cliff; the bluff commands a dramatic view over the rugged Scotland District and the coast.

history: Standing 900 ft. (275 m) above sea level, the greathouse entrance was once lined with towering cabbage palms. A side mahogany staircase once led upstairs to the bed-

View from Farley Hill

rooms. Distinguished visitors over the years included Prince Alfred Duke of Edinburough (in 1861), Prince Albert Victor, and Prince George (later King George V). Camouflaged almost unrecognizably, the house starred in an incognito role as the mansion *Belle Fontaine* in the 1956, 20th Century Fox production of the classic flick "An Island in the Sun." The coral gates in front of the ruin were brought in during the film's production. It was declared a national park after its purchase by the Barrow Government in 1966 and Queen Elizabeth II unveiled a statue here during the opening ceremonies. Open daily, 9–6; $2 parking fee. From Farley Hill, Highway 1 leads down to the W toward the parish's more populated sector and on through to Speightstown; the E coast is in the other direction.

Barbados Wildlife Reserve: Termed a reserve but more accurately described as an open air zoo because the animals have all been imported, this is a project of the Barbados Primate Center; it gives you an opportunity to observe the island's green monkeys (see "fauna" in the "Introduction") and other indigenous and not-so-native fauna clase at hand. Located across the highway almost due N of Farley National

Farley Hill ruins

Park, a gravel road running through the sugar cane fields leads up to the entrance. Inside there's a small covered restaurant along a brick path that leads past aloe vera and clumps of cactus plants frequented by sportive sunbathing monkeys. As you walk you might see a gigantic solitary box turtle meandering by while munching on a plant. His head moves back and forth as though he's a mechanical windup toy. While the turtles and monkeys pop into continual view everywhere, it takes a bit more doing to spot the raccoons (now extinct elsewhere in the island), wallabies (from Australia), hares, otters, and deer that frequent the glade of young mahogany trees. The information center is beautifully constructed featuring circular brick flooring, picnic benches of polished wood, and hanging, plexiglass-encased charts and diagrams. Sneak a peak into the closed-off breeding center in its rear. Just past the center open the screen door to enter the aviary. At the top of the tall, cylindrical cage to the rear, multicolored parrots squawk, discursing no doubt on the subject of their visitors' frivolous finery. On the edge of the pond 'round the back, the four pelicans, a gift of Florida Sen. Birch Bayh, may be bedded down for a nap; after awakening they preen themselves fastidiously, never venturing a glance at the snoring cayman lying below. The reserve is not a place to be rushed through but must be savored slowly. Open daily 10–5, B$6 admission; B$3 children.

St. Nicholas Abbey: Located near Cherry Tree Hill and Farley National Park in St. Peter, this great house—the oldest on Barbados—may be the island's architectural highlight. Constructed during the 1650s, its formal garden, gables, and four fireplaces bring to mind an English country mansion. Its sash windows and interiors date from the 17th C. Despite its name, the house was never used by either Santa Claus or any member of the clergy as an abbey. Approached by a mahogany-lined avenue, it is one of only three greathouses of Jacobean design surviving in the Americas; the other two are Drax Hall on Barbados and Bacon's Castle in Virginia. Incredibly, the mansion weathered the severe hurricanes of 1675, 1780, and 1831. It is thought that Richard Beringer, who owned the 400-acre estate in the 1650s, had the house constructed. The two front rooms were paneled in 1898, utilizing the now nearly-extinct West Indian cedar. There's a display of old photos and journals, and a film presentation, shown twice daily, depicts Bajan life circa 1935. The former outhouse in the back—which once housed four unpartitioned seats—now encloses a generator. Farther to its rear is a monkey-populated gully. To the N just to the R side lie the ruins of the estates's sugar factory which has been closed since 1947. Some gnarled mahogany trees surround the tractors here, and green, waving tassels of cane stretch as far as the eye can see. Follow the narrow road behind which goes via Diamond Corner to Boscobel, where a large red-roofed Anglican church stands next to the ruins of a mill which is equipped with a shiny bright red mailbox. Or continue over to the L and climb and then descend Cherry Tree Hill.

St. Nicholas Abbey,
St. Peter

PARISH PRACTICALITIES

accommodations: St. Peter's preeminent resort is unquestionably Cobbler's Cove. The stately main building was originally known as Camelot and owned by the Haines family during the 1940s. When Aland Godsail, a descendant of the Colleton family, took over he instructed the architect to "design a hotel that we would enjoy staying at." The delightful result was this establishment: a series of two-storey black and white wooden suites grouped around an immaculately manicured lawn. The suites have a front room which, after the white-vented accordion doors are opened, face the patio and lawn. This design allows for the idea of "outdoor casual living" that is the resort's watchword. Off the kitchen is a small kitchenette with an honor bar; a kettle is available upon request. Sliding doors connect the front with the bedroom and adjacent bath. Said to be more country home than hotel, Cobbler's Cove, while an ideal honeymoon spot, is hardly suited for flashy yuppies. The summer crowd here tends to be more established and family oriented; the winter season draws a somewhat older, more established type of guest. People staying here are those who are comfortable with having wealth and have no need to flaunt it. The resort's atmosphere delightfully combines the British stiff upper lip with the Bajan welcoming smile and right hand extended in greeting—the atmosphere is neither too loose nor too formal. In addition to the tennis courts and swimming pool, the following watersports are available free of charge: water skiing, wind surfing, sunfish sailing, snorkeling, and use of the glass bottom boat. Prices range from a low of US$120 for one person during the summer to US$990 for the Camelot Suite during the Christmas season. For more information or reservations call 1-800-223-6510 in the US and 1-800-424-5500 in Canada. In Britain call 01-730-7144. With the exception of the government-owned and Wyndham-managed Heywood's Resort, all of the other hotels are grouped around Speightstown down the road from Cobbler's Cove. These include Sugar Cane Club, Eastry House Hotel, and the Sandridge Beach Hotel. The only guesthouse is Chrizel's Garden (tel. 422-2403).

dining out: Cobbler's Cove's restaurant is renowned for its cuisine. Sandridge and Kings Beach, both down the road, also feature restaurants. In Speightstown, local restaurants with tourist prices include L'il Ole Bristol, Shirley's, and Reddydun. Heywoods Resort, to the N of Speightstown, has four restaurants on the premises: Captain's Table, Carolines, Los Barbados, and Trawlers. Diners at Carolines are entertained by music most evenings. Located in Gibbs, Chrizel's Garden features low sodium and vegetarian dishes among its entrees.

budget dining: Best budget place in Speightstown is Fisherman's Pub. Offering a real local feel, it offers authentic, reasonably priced local food including stew, chicken, and (in season) fish. Their bar is one of the few that offers draft Banks beer. Open Mon. to Sat. 10-10, PIZZA MAN DOC sells Bajan-style pizza at bargain prices; a slice is just B$1.75. A small warmed bread and cheese sub sells for B$1.25. Also try

Children, Speightstown

Adriana's Ice Cream Shop just inside the mall and Colonel Sanders to its rear.

market food: Hucksters line the main road up just past the esplanade; they sell giant avocadoes, papaya, yams and the like. The fish market, farther up the road, is the place where the perpetual domino game is going on next to the wire grill windows. Back past the esplanade, Elmer's is the town's only supermarket. Sample prices: Pine Hill Dairy milk, B$2.82/litre; Pine Hill Dairy orange juice, B$3/litre; Sunflower margarine, B$2.85/lb; New Zealand cheese, $10.50/kg.; carrots, $7.99/kg.; aubergine (eggplant), $3.96/kg.; broccoli, B$11.60/kg.; local alfalfa sprouts, B$3.49/6oz; apples B$7.45/kg.; pineapples, B$4.12/kg; onions B$4.40/kg.; bran bread (16 oz.), B$2.20; two litre plastic Pepsi container, B$5.28; Cadbury's Fruit & Nut Bar (200g), B$6.85; Ivory soap (bath size), B$2.79; Cheerios (15oz.), B$8.50; Kellogg's Cornflakes (12 oz.), B$6.48; Canadian-made Skippy Peanut Butter (500g.), B$6.54; Rite Paper Towels, B$3.40/roll; *Weekly World News* ("UFO CAPTAIN IS SOVIET PRISONER"), and *Time,* B$5.

SAINT LUCY'S PARISH

Entering this semicircular parish, which caps the top of the island, rough and ragged scenery is presented at every turn. Its small and classic chattel houses—the best of which can be seen in the villages of Greenridge and Connell Town near Archer's Bay—are gradually being supplanted by bland stone bungalows. The parish's thin soil lowland with small hills and cliffs bear the brunt of the Atlantic storms. One of the best ways to tour this parish, its fine coastline speckled with dramatic viewpoints, is on foot. The lush countryside—with its black and white cattle grazing contentedly and fine fields of green and growing cane—is simply a pleasure to experience.

St. Lucy's Church: Constructed after the 1831 hurricane, this church, with its sweet lime hedges and Palladian windows, stands near Alleyndale greathouse. To get here from River Bay take the road heading toward the center of the parish.

Archer's Bay: This popular local spot is one of the island's most beautiful locations, one that is home to hordes of chirping birds, and butterflies which flit and hover over wildflowers. Above the bay, there's a large grassy area—populated by cud chewing cows and lazy goats, sheltered by giant casuarinas which blow in the light sea breeze. A path leads from the cliff down to the rock-strewn bay where jade water clashes against the eroded bluffs. Two stout, gigantic stone columns guard the entrance to the beach on the R. The Archer's Bay bus terminates at a mini mart where you can get last-minute provisions. A track from nearby Crab Bay through sugarcane fields leads to Duppies, a premier surfing spot. Cluff's millwall can be viewed off in the distance.

ST. LUCY

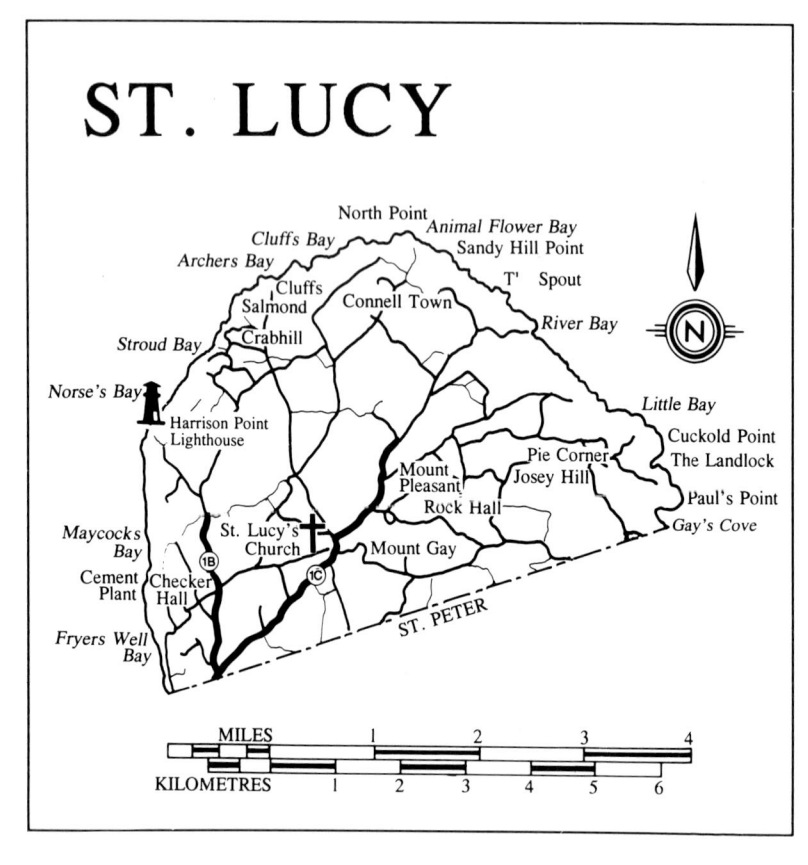

(Map of St. Lucy parish showing locations including North Point, Animal Flower Bay, Cluffs Bay, Sandy Hill Point, Archers Bay, T' Spout, Cluffs, Connell Town, Salmond, River Bay, Stroud Bay, Crabhill, Norse's Bay, Little Bay, Harrison Point Lighthouse, Cuckold Point, The Landlock, Mount Pleasant, Pie Corner, Josey Hill, Paul's Point, Rock Hall, Gay's Cove, Maycocks Bay, St. Lucy's Church, Mount Gay, Cement Plant, Checker Hall, Fryers Well Bay, and the border with ST. PETER. Scale in miles 0–4 and kilometres 0–6.)

Animal Flower Cave: Carpeted with "sea flowers" and adorned with rock formations this set of sea caves—set at the island's northernmost central point is justly famed for its yellow sea anenomes. These short, cylindrical marine animals feed with the tentacles attached to their tops. The tentacles contain nematocysts, stinging cells that paralyze prey then move it to the anemone's mouth. Fertilization occurs underwater. (It is not known whether they experience orgasm). Another feature of the cave, run by Winston and Manuel Ward, is their pet sheep, Pepita, who is fond of drinking 7-Up straight from the bottle. Try her if you don't believe it! Their cafe has namecards galore, thousands of them covering the walls and ceilings, tacked up with glue and then varnished on. They also have a collection of hanging banners including "Yorkshire," "Barbados Rum," and "Cornish Pastries." The Manuels serve drinks, sandwiches, and baked beans. Although currently barren, the surrounding land once produced cane under the name of Animal Flower Plantation. These days a perpetual domino game goes on in the nearby red shed selling corals from which a huckster also vends her goods. Out towards the sea, a forest of wooden signposts points the way to such destinations as Germany, the US, and Venezuela with the distance indicated in kilometers. Out on the rocky bluffs, waves crash against the sharply convoluted coral cliffs—sending salty sprays flying into the air with poetic violence. Check out the seaward view from the parking lot.

North Point: As you head S from the cave area, the nearly abandoned ruin you pass is North Point Resort. Once a top resort during the 60s, it contains the remains of what was once the island's sole Olympic-size swimming pool. These days, B$5 is charged for admission and another B$5 to use the pool when it's in operation. If you walk down across the coral-encrusted

St. Lucy's Parish

plain, littered with patches of cacti, to the sea and then across, you avoid the entrance fee and reach the beach. What appears to be a coral block fortification surrounds the sand; the ground below is continually pummeled by hyperactive waves. Proceeding back from there, the buildings have the look and feel of a bombed-out war zone. As you pass through to the front, however, instead of finding a waiting batallion of tanks or some newly dropped parachutists, you reach a shimmering blue mirage—the swimming pool with its somewhat makeshift bar. For the truly adventuresome, there are some rooms available here. Another interesting site right next door is a set of dried-up ponds which were formerly used as salt processing ponds until the 1940s. Sea water would be pumped into the ponds and, after its evaporation, the salt would be collected. From the North Point walk to the W following a path which passes a series of promontories alternating with coves.

The Spout: Although it can be viewed from the North Point, this attraction is located at Ladder Bay near River Bay. Here, the sea spurts geyser-like through the coral promontory, spouting as high as 100 ft.

River Bay: This bleak but scenic park is a famous and favorite spot for Barbadian picnics. Its name stems from a small stream flowing to the sea here. Cut into chalk and limestone, the bay features spectacular wind-blown coastal scenery. From River Bay, a mile-and-a-half track leads to Little Bay and Waits Bay.

Little Bay to Boscobel: This is one of the most spectacular stretches of coast on the island if not in the Caribbean. To get here, either drive or take a Pie Corner bus to the end. At Little Bay, waves pummel into an outlying coral outcrop and spray comes flying into the air; the overflow comes into a wide trough in which you can either lay back and let it roll on top of you or move towards the front to meet the surf head on. Climb up on top of the doughnut-shaped arch for a magnificent view. Continuing along the coast to the R, you pass a series of indentations along a bleak, windswept coral-encrusted plain until you come to another major bay. Then you reach a track sheltered by casuarina trees serving as a windbreak for the palm

Little Bay, St. Lucy's Parish

tree grove to the rear. Soon you will come to a magnificent view of Pico Teneriffe across the way. Rising to the S side of Cove Bay (Gay's Cove), it appears higher than its few hundred feet. On misty days, it is said to resemble a sorrowful and anxious Madonna gazing seaward in search of her wandering fishermen. This location, Paul's Point, is touted widely as the island's most attractive spot. Decide for yourself. Gay's Cove Beach below—which can be reached by a goat track—consists

Pico Teneriffe

of rounded stones. Continue along the side, following the pink splotches of paint that mark the way until you reach Boscobel, a nondescript jumble of houses along the road. From above the village, it is possible to walk on to Morgan Lewis Beach. However, the path is convoluted and can be difficult to find without guidance. Descending to the village, the local rum shop is straight up the road at the top of the hill on the R. Note the collection of beer can caps which have been pounded into the tarmac by passing vehicles. If taking a bus, this is a good place to wait because minibuses generally turn around up here.

Goat House Bay: Near the Rockfield corner 1800 feet E of St. Clement's Village, this beautiful spot lies smack in the middle of an unspoiled stretch reaching from River Bay to the twin bays of Chandler and Laycock.

THE SOUTHERN PARISHES

ST. GEORGE'S PARISH

Mostly flat and landlocked—as the Bajans say, "it has no sea"—this fertile parish's rolling fields of cane firmly remind one of its link with king sugar. It is home to large sugar estates such as Valley Plantation and Salters as well as to Bulkley Sugar Factory, the parish's sole remaining sugar refinery. An area of large scale population growth, the parish's western portion grew at an average annual rate of 23% during 1970–1980.

Drax Hall: One of the best places to explore the dynamics of cane growing in Barbados is in St. George Valley. And a great place to start is at this estate, one of the places where cultivation began. Another in the line of Jacobean-style plastered coral stone great houses which once dotted the island, Drax Hall is one of numerous plantation houses still standing today. Unlike the other survivors, however, it has the distinction of being the only one still in the possession of its original owners. Sir James Drax, the builder and family patriarch, was one of the movers and shakers behind the sugarcane industry who became the island's richest planter. He improved the manufacturing process by bringing a Dutch model of a sugar mill to his

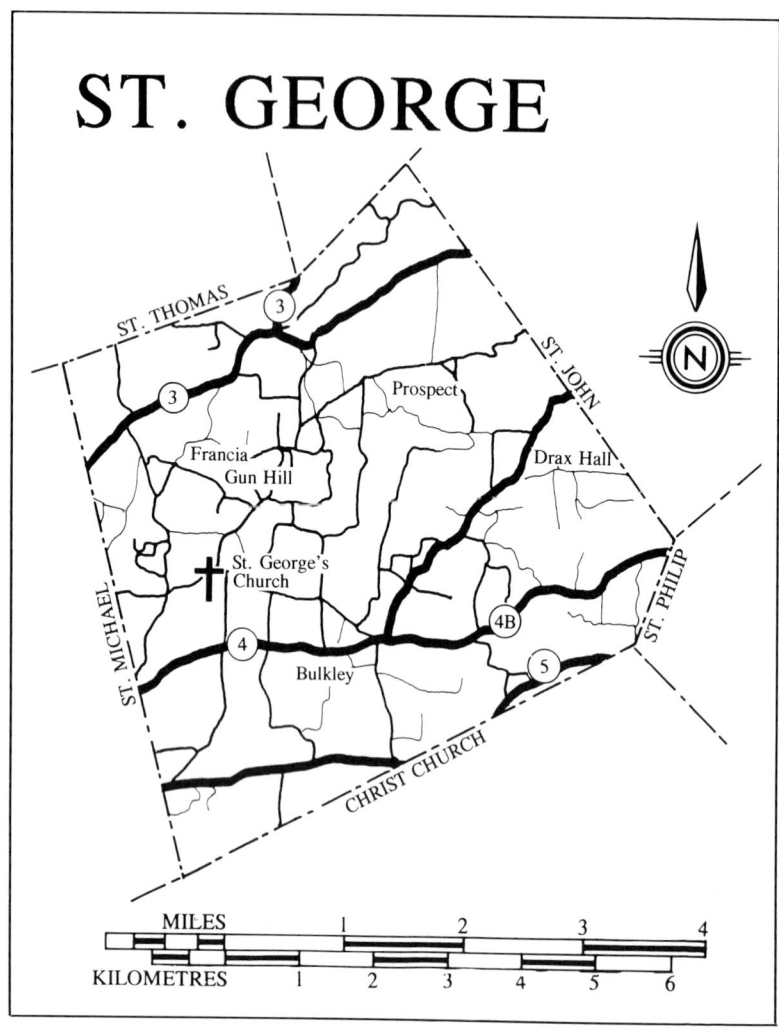

estate and experimenting with it, and with his success came
prosperity. Built during the mid-1600's, the house overlooks
one of the nation's largest sugar estates. The powerful influence of this estate on the area is reflected in nearby place
names such as Drax Hall Woods, Drax Hall Jump, and Drax
Hall Green. Off Highway 4, a 50-ft. high millwall stands to the
E. The white millwall and ruined boiling house of Redland
cottage stand off the main highway nearby.

Brighton Great House: One of the island's oldest greathouses, it has been under the control of the Pile family for over 100 years. A marble slab in the south wall reads "Wisheir" and is dated 1652. Thick columns of mastic wood support the roof with its 20-foot (6-m) beams; its walls were fabricated from a mix of corn husks and rubble.

Byde Mill: Set several miles farther E on Highway 4B in the parish's eastern tip near its borders with St. Philip and St. John, this home's age is a mystery. It is thought to have been built by a Joshua Steele who leased the estate in 1777.

St. George Parish Church: At the top of Rectory Hill, which runs off the crossroads at the end of Salters at Charles Rowe Bridge. While filled with monuments—some of which are by famous English sculptors, its most famous tomb is that of the Honorable Richard Salter (d. 1776) sculpted by Nollekens. Philadelphia-born and London-famed Benjamin West painted *The Rise To Power,* a depiction of the Resurrection which serves as the church's altarpiece. Because of a falling out be-

Gun Hill Signal Station

tween the donor and the rector at the time, the painting was relegated to an outhouse wall for years. The eye of the painting's centurion was poked out by the finger of an irate thief because he claimed it was staring at him too intently. A painting on copper entitled *The Descent from the Cross* hangs in the N porch. The church also has antique silverware. From here ascend to Gun Hill.

Gun Hill: This signal station served double duty: as a communications point and as a convalescent station for sick solidiery. A full-sized milkwhite limestone lion—a representation of the British Imperial Lion—was carved out of the rock by Henry Wilkinson of the "ninth Regiment of Foot—Adjuntant General" in 1868. Its Latin inscription translates as follows: "It shall rule from the river to the sea, and from the sea, to the end of the world." Also accessible by car and farther up, the towering Signal Station—with its panoramic view praised by visitors over the centuries—is definitely a not-to-be-missed sight. Open daily 9–5, B$2 entrance.

The lion at Gun Hill

Francia Plantation: Opened to the public for the first time in 1989, this small but stately greathouse stands on a wooded hillside at the heart of a still-operating plantation. It contains antique furniture along with a fine selection of old prints and maps. Be sure to see the charming fountain featuring a youth holding an umbrella. Open Mon. to Fri., 10–4, B$6 admission.

SAINT JOHN'S PARISH

Hillier than neighboring St. George, this sugar-plantation-rich parish has its entire NE dominated by the imposing Hackleton's Cliff. The major highways running through here are 4 and 3B. In addition to the nation's oldest college, it contains a number of greathouses, one of the nation's most intriguing and scenic churches, and a splendid coastline. Martin's Bay houses the parish's population of fisherman.

Hackleton's Cliff: Rising 12 miles from Bridgetown, this 997-ft. (305-m) cliff, topped by a line of casuarinas, commands a breathtaking view of the Scotland District. The cliff was carved several million years ago during the era in which powerful pummeling tidal waves pulverized the Scotland District, eroding its coral cap. Rising to 305 meters and dominating the area, it provides a view dominating the area from Pico Teneriffe in the N to Ragged Point in the E. Note the reforestation work going on here and at Joe's River.

St. John's Parish Church: Located off a feeder road which runs into Highway 3B approximately 14 miles from Bridgetown, this small church lies in the center of the island's most productive sugarcane acreage. It can be approached from Malvern via Edey's Village and Clifton Hall. Framed by frangipani, it overlooks the Atlantic coast where waves crash continuously, breaking on the reef 800 ft. below. It is the quintessential English church set in the tropics. Its interior features high-backed pews and a double staircase of light colored cedar extends up to the organ gallery. Its wooden pulpit allegedly contains six varieties of hardwood: ebony, locust, mahogany, machineel, oak, and pine. The original was built in 1676 and destroyed by a hurricane in 1831; the present structure

ST. JOHN

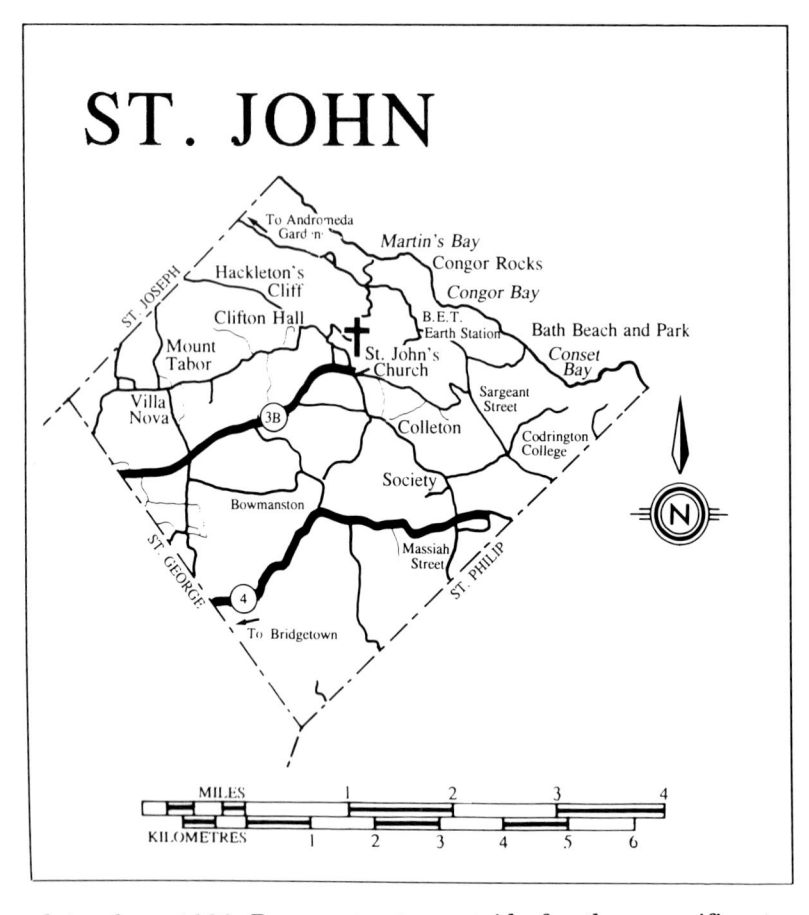

dates from 1836. Be sure to step outside for the magnificent view of Pico Teneriffe on the L and the lighthouse at Ragged Point on the R (off in the distance in neighboring St. Philip). Note "The Chair" carved out of the cliffs; it marks the beginning of the southward bend in the topography. By the sundial at the back you may view the dish antenna at Bath below. Also outside lie the tombs of 17th and 18th C. planters—so large they seem fit for emperors! Elizabeth Pinder's beautifully carved memorial was sculpted by Sir Richard Westmacott. Probably the most famous grave on the island is that of the Greek expatriate Ferdinando Paleologus. Churchwarden and surveyor Paleologus owned Clifton Hall, a nearby cotton plantation. When the church was razed by the 1831 hurricane, what remained of Ferdinand was discovered in a vault under the organ loft embedded in quicklime—his head facing west in line with Eastern Orthodox traditions. The faded pink tombstone in his memory, which stands to the side of a vault to the rear, was erected in 1906. From the church, a road swings left to the N, passing the Newcastle greathouse and heading towards Martin's Bay, a fishing village, which has a raised coral reef close to shore; search for shells here. Known as Glen Burnie, the surrounding semi-wild area has a path, following the old railroad line, which leads into Bath in neighboring St. Joseph's Parish.

Codrington College: Located 15 miles from Bridgetown, Barbados's first institution of higher learning was originally built in modified Italian Renaissance style. However, only the main building's open portico and the exterior of the Principal's home survive from the original. Be sure to check out the lines of poetry inscribed at the swimming pool. Approached by a row of stately cabbage palms—some of which are reputed to be more than a century old, this theological college for the training of West Indian clergy stands on one of Codrington's former plantations overlooking Conset Bay. The college was constructed, owned, and operated by the Society for the Propagation of the Gospel in Foreign Parts, an organization which during the 1700s propagated the radical and highly controversial concept that slaves had souls and should, therefore, be converted to Christianity. Although the local elite in general weren't too wild about this concept, Cristopher Codrington, a wealthy landowner and Oxford graduate, bequeathed his plantation to the society in 1710. Now part of the University of the West Indies, the college has some very interesting architecture. Check out the chapel which features a glass mosaic of the Good Shepherd hanging over the altar, enormous carved mahogany sanctuary rails and gates, and an altar composed of ebony, lignum vitae, and cordia pedestals. Standing next to the college and overlooking a lily pond and small park, Codrington's family home is constructed of coral with a roof-long balustrade, and a seven-pedimented window out front; it is now used as the Principal's lodge. Fire gutted its interior in 1887.

Codrington College

from Codrington College: Following the road from the college to the S which descends a steep hill, you'll find the entrance to Conset Bay to the L. See fishing boats here land in the afternoons; otherwise you may be entertained by troupes of bounding, mischievously playful green monkeys. Good walks in this area. Another route is to follow Sergeant Street and take a R down Bath Hill. The ruins of Bath Factory are nearby. The Bath Beach facility has a bathing area and a small forest. The large white dish antenna provides satellite communication. Overlooking Conset Bay and College Savannah, St. Mark's Church is worth visiting for its view alone. From there, a road leads through Fortescue Plantation to the picturesque fishing village at Skeete's Bay. View Conset Bay from Coach Hill. Also from Codrington College you may follow the abandoned railway tracks to the E coast at Tent Bay; take the Bridgetown-bound bus back from Bathsheba.

Villa Nova: Located N off Highway 3B to the L from Four Cross Roads, this beautiful great house is built on a ridge overlooking the St. John and St. Phillip tablelands; it rises 830 ft.

(256 m) amidst six acres of woods and gardens. Constructed in 1834 by Edmond Haynes, it has been a private residence—as opposed to a working plantation house—since 1907. It has passed from the Haynes family to the Avons to the Hunts on to its present owners, who have opened it to the public. The home's features include wide porches, a parapet roof, and latticed wooden arches and balustrades. Despite its light and airy ambience, its thick walls ensure that it will survive any hurricane. Its antiques include a Regency secretaire and a Chippendale "pie crust" table. Many claim it is the island's best surviving specimen of a 19th C. greathouse. Be sure to tour the beautiful garden where you will find a profusion of orchids, a multitude of ferns, and trees such as the bearded fig, breadfruit, frangipani, Barbados cherry, flamboyant, and citrus. Open Mon.-Fri., 10–4, B$5 admission, children B$2.50; tel. 433-1524.

Clifton Hall: Two miles (three km) away from Villa Nova, this privately owned Georgian-style greathouse is currently closed to the general public. It has a three-sided arcaded veranda and a double staircase leading to a central porch.

St. John crossroads

Mount Tabor: One of two remaining Moravian churches. Built around 1850, its hilltop height commands a view of the woods down to the sea in the distance.

Eastmont: Located off the road leading S into St. John from Clifton Hall, this 19th C. house is the ancestral home of Prime Minister H. Bree St. John. His ancestor, mulatto blacksmith Miller Austin, purchased the estate in 1895—thus setting a historical precedent.

ST. PHILIP'S PARISH

The island's largest parish, St. Philip (pop. 18,500) is also one of the most remote. It is the home of calypsonians such as Red Plastic Bag, and its clannish inhabitants have their own manner of speech. Its topography consists of thin soil lowland with small hills and caved cliffs which bear the brunt of the Atlantic storms. Aloes and cotton are grown in the parish, and tobacco is farmed in the Boscobel district. Warblers, known locally as grass canaries, flirt through the sourgrass lining the parish's eastern shore. Two of the main roads running through the parish are Highway 4B and 5. Entering from Christ Church to the S, Highway 6 runs through the oil fields. The parish's best known sight is Sam Lord's Castle which lies off Highway 5 on a cliff above Long Bay.

Sunbury House: Near Highway 4B, 5, and 6, this early 18th C. plantation house was refurbished in 1981. A small historical museum of Bajan life, its collection includes antique furniture, antique buggies, and agricultural vehicles. An exhibition center is in the old yam center. Hanging in the belfry, the bronze bell on the estate is dated 1766. It was originally known as Chapman's, but John Henry Barrow changed the name in 1816 to match his British estates. At the time of its purchase in 1838 by Thomas and John Daniel, its size had increased to 413 acres. Busom buddies with Sam Lord, Thomas Daniel installed chandeliers to match those of Sam Lord's home, and Lord's personal claret set can be found in the living room. The estate also features a courtyard restaurant which is open for lunch; dinner parties can be accommodated by special arrangement. In its vicinity are St. Philip's Parish Church and the nationalized Woodbourne oil fields. Open Mon.-Fri. 10–4, Sat. 10–2.

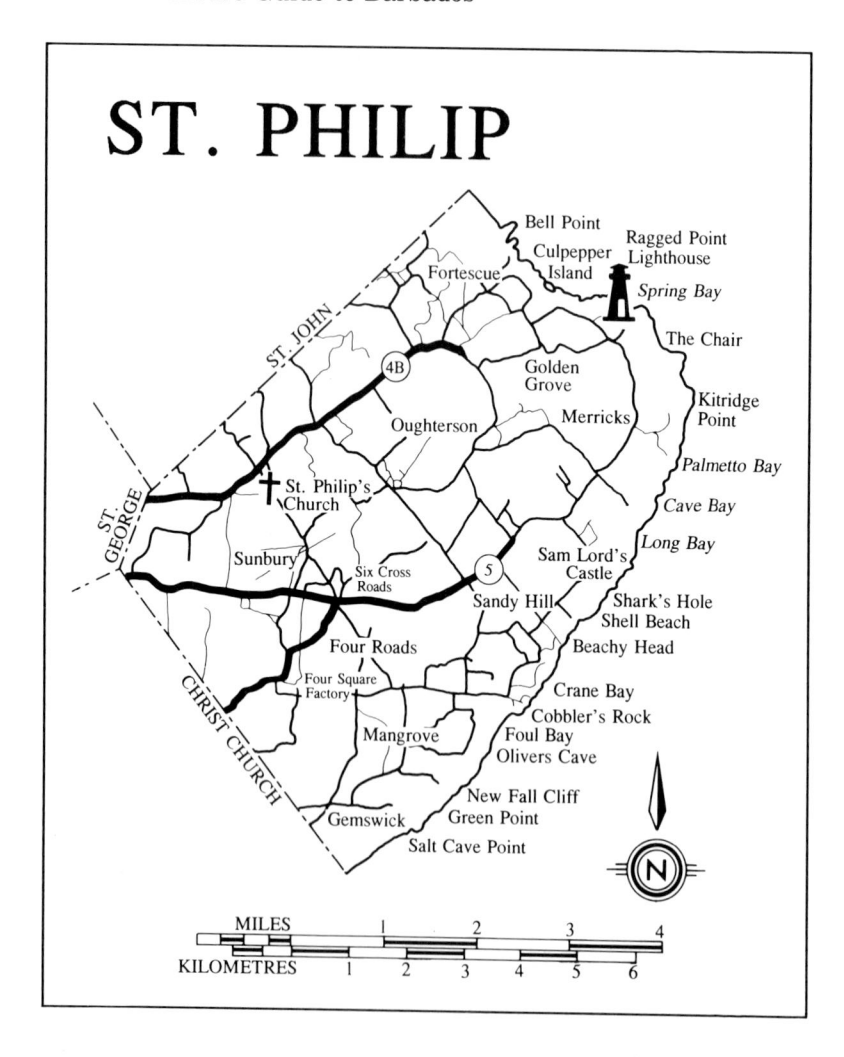

Oughterson Zoo Park: This St. Philip wildlife breeding and environmental education project has 22 acres containing a large variety of birds, plants, and animals. Visit the greathouse filled chock brim with oriental and Bajan antiques.

Foul Bay: Here, Chancery Lane Beach provides treacherous swimming amidst coconut palms felled as a result of the 1955 hurricane. A popular recreation spot, the bay received its unromantic name because it was a "foul" or unsuitable anchorage for ships in the 16th C. when small sailing ships of 150–250 tons made the journey to Barbados. Nearby, the cliffs running from Oliver's Cave S to Gemswick are the island's highest—rising over a hundred feet (35 m).

Crane Beach: Lying about 13 miles (21 km) from Bridgetown and 2.5 miles (4 km) to the SW of Sam Lord's Castle, Crane Beach is one of the island's most popular beaches; surrounded by towering cliffs, it's beautiful on moonlit nights. In coming here you are treading the paths of others who have been enjoying this spot since the 1700s. You cannot enter the beach from the hotel; you must walk around past it and then turn down. Exercise caution while swimming here. It's possible to traverse this beach to reach Shanty Beach, Beach Head, and Shell Beach, but you will have to climb up and then down again several times.

Harrismith sugar plantation ruins

Sam Lord's Castle

SAM LORD'S CASTLE

This "castle" is now a Marriot Hotel, but the main structure itself is still open for inspection. Originally built as a 19th C. country house, it stands on a rocky bluff, overlooking a coral beach graced with coconut palms and sea grapes. Its interior combines elegant plaster ceilings and fine woodwork with an elegant staircase. There is an adjoining finely crafted dining and drawing room. Some of the furniture adorning the hotel was owned by Sam Lord including the dining room table with brass lion's claw feet. The "dungeons" downstairs have been transformed into carpeted a/c offices.

history: Legend has it that in the 1800s one Samuel Hall Lord hung lanterns in the coconut trees facing Cobbler's Reef off the S Coast. When approaching sea captains—lured by lights they assumed to be those of the Carlisle Bay anchorage—neared shore, they capsized and were overtaken by Sam and scoundrels. Although, this story is likely apocryphal, there is no doubt that the man himself was a complete knave.

Truth or fiction, Sam somehow got the money to build the house—known also as Long Bay Castle—around 1820; it's called a "castle" because of its battlement-style notched roof; it combines Georgian symmetry and balance with Gothic details, as in the crenellated roof and the Tudor mouldings above the windows. The stucco interior was crafted by English and Italian workmen brought over to do the job. Its ceilings are wonders to behold; the one in the saloon is a replica of one in Windsor Castle. But getting back to the story: Sam died on 5 November 1845 in England leaving debts behind of £18,000—an astronomical sum at the time.

vicinity of Sam Lord's Castle: There's some great hiking in this area on the way to Ragged Point and then beyond to Culpepper's Island. To begin, go back out to the ticket window and then go around the corner following the narrow, unpaved road running along the side of the resort. At the end, a staircase leads down to a vendor-free beach facing an exposed coral formation just off the coast. If you keep walking along there's an abandoned house set on the cliff and, still farther, the ruins

Beach at Harrismith sugar plantation

Crane Beach Hotel

of Harrismith plantation house overlook a palm-tree-studded beach. Next is a villa perched above yet another beautiful beach at Bottom Bay. Take the road to the R and continue walking with the wall on your R and the small stonehenge-like ruined concrete and wire structure to your L. After passing another cove and beach, you will enter a windswept coral bluff, marked at its perimeter by a row of bent casuarina trees. Follow this along—peering periodically over the bluff at the knockout views of pounding surf—until the lighthouse comes into view. It sits atop Ragged Point, aptly named after its jagged limestone cliffs beseiged by surf. This bleak area gains some color only when the bright agave or Spanish needles are in bloom. Passing by some cows, turn where an abandoned bus stands next to a house. Turning up, follow—passing more goats and cows along the way—until you reach an asphalt road where there's a rum shop up on the R, just past the stand pipe to your L. From here you can take a bus back to Bridgetown, or within easy walking distance of Sam Lord's, or continue to Culpepper Island. In any case, it's a definite must to continue on the lighthouse. If you should meet the trickster near here who claims to sell "tickets" to the lighthouse, brush him off!

Culpepper Island: This, the nation's sole remaining island dependency, lies 35 yards offshore past the grounds of Whitehaven mansion. The 25-by-35-yard (25-by-35-m) coral-composed island rises to 20 feet (7 m) above sea level. The only way to get on the island is to swim.

PARISH PRACTICALITIES

accommodations: Crane Beach Hotel has the oldest history of any hotel on the island. Its name, as well as that of the beach, derives from the type of freight elevator which was installed behind its pier and eventually buried by sand drifts. Overlooking one of the island's most spectacular beaches, this hotel's deck juts out so far over the edge of the cliff that it resembles the prow of a cruise ship. The main building's design, shaped in large part by architect Oliver Messel in the early 1970s, can best be described as Mediterranean cool white. The pool, overlooking the beach, features two Roman columns and the bronze statues reflect a similar theme. Originally known as the Marine Villa, the main part of the 14-room hotel is some 180 years old. A typical one-bedroom suite features hardwood floors of pickled pine, antique mahogany furniture, tropical-patterned canopies hanging over the king size bed, and walls of white coral brick. Wooden doors open onto the chaise lounge equipped balconies or terrace; views vary, but the raging ocean is everpresent. A large living room has three tables and a couch; there's a gigantic closet with a full length mirror off the bedroom, and the bath features a gigantic stretch of mirror and a sunken tub. A kitchenette has a sink, kettle, and a pre-stocked refrigerator/honor bar. A major expansion of the resort is currently underway. Go Vacations, Canada's foremost mini-motorhome manufacturer and the world's leading rental company for recreational vehicles, is undertaking a US$70 million expansion, which will be completed in 1995. There will then be 200 rooms distributed over 38.5 acres. Facilities will include pools, artificial waterfalls, a

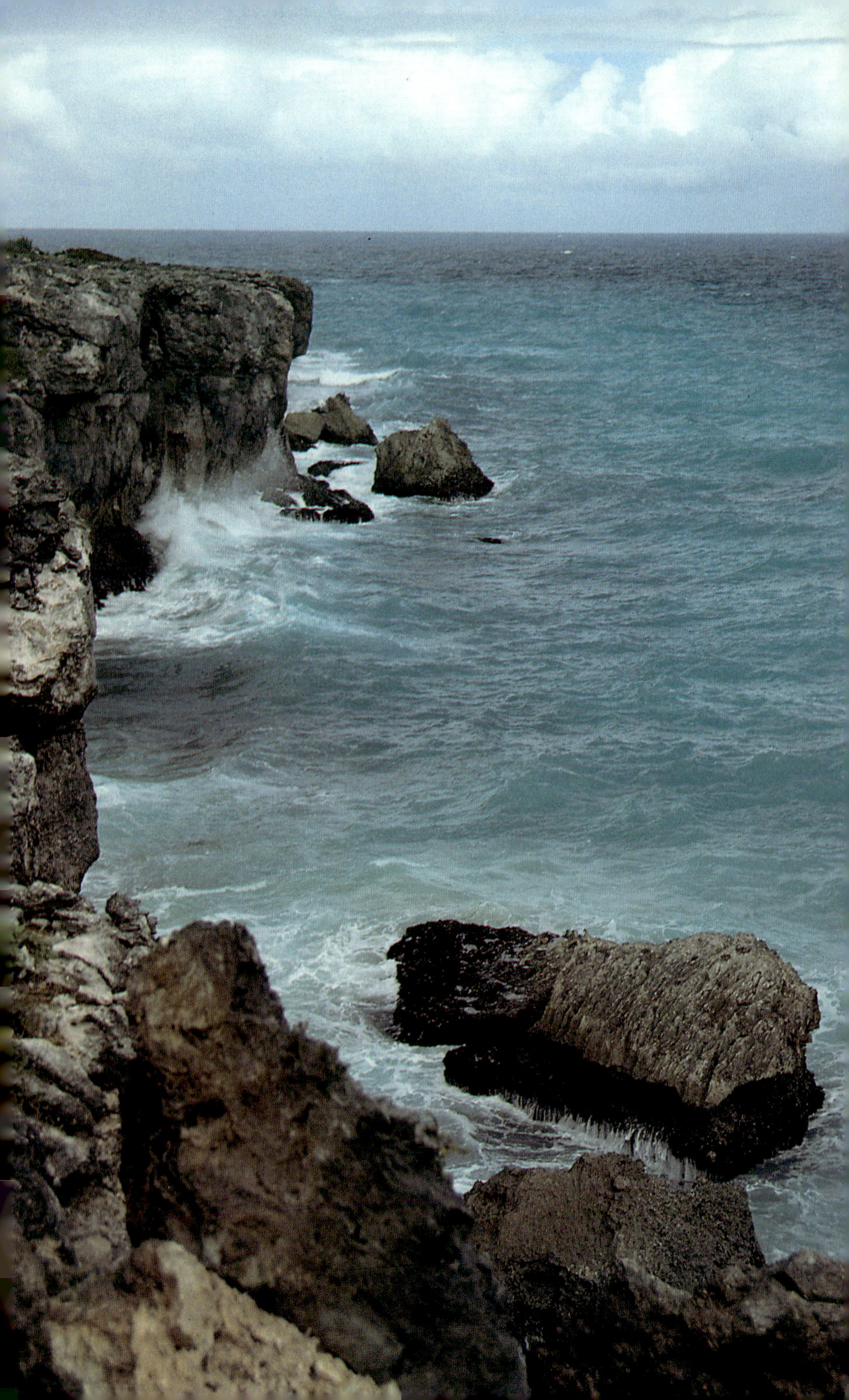

health spa, a wedding chapel, and a conference center. Currently, there are already two pools and four tennis courts. There's also a private locked stairway to the beach. Rates run from a low of US$110 for a standard room during the off season to a high of US$600 for a two-bedroom penthouse. For more information and reservations call 1-800-387-3998. But until completion of the Crane Hotel expansion, Sam Lord's Castle remains the parish's top resort. The grounds here begin with the ticket window where visitors (but not guests) must pay for admission. Bellhops ferry passengers to their rooms around the immaculately manicured grounds. Fountains and a variety of pools are in the rear of the plantation house. Upon check in you will be given a map of the grounds. The resort's features include three pools, a beach, tennis courts, two restaurants, and an activities center which features a small library, barber shop, beauty salon, game room, video theater, gym, and beach towel checkout. The beach is at the end of the property down a set of stairs. There's nary a dull moment at this resort and as you prepare for bed you'll find out why. The custom here is to turn down your sheets and lay a copy of the extensive list of events (tomorrow on one side, the next day on the reverse) on your sheet along with a small flower. The list tells you when the sun rises and sets, what band will be playing the next evening, what tours are scheduled, and various other miscellany. Every morning a copy of the *Nation* and the *International Herald Tribune* are delivered to your front door, providing literary fodder for your morning meal. Should you find yourself in want of reading material late at night you can open your bedside table to find copies of the Book of Mormon and Marriot's own autobiography—featuring photos of him with luminaries such as Nixon and Reagan. Room prices range from US$115 for a single or double during the summer to US$490 for a one-bedroom suite during the busiest portion of the winter season. For more information on the Marriott resort or to reserve call 800-223-6388 in the US, (01) 434-2299 in London. Other hotels in the parish include Ginger

Bay, and Robin's Nest. Budget travelers might try the Ragged Point Motel at Merricks (tel. 423-8021).

dining out: Sunbury Plantation House serves lunch in its courtyard restaurant; it also serves traditional English tea. One special feature is the three-course meals Sudbury serves on its antique mahogany table with silver service; reservations (tel. 423-6270) required. Another famous local restaurant is the Crane Beach Hotel's Pavilion Restaurant, which overlooks the magnificent beach. Sam Lord's Castle has the Wanderer and the Seagrille (open evenings only). They also serve tea in the drawing room above their activities center from 3–4:30 daily.

CHRIST CHURCH PARISH AND THE GOLD COAST

Dominating the prettiest portion of the island's southern coast, Christ Church paved the way for Barbados's tourist industry. The narrow coastal route through the parish runs through a gamut of hotels, inns, restaurants, fast food emporiums, and shopping malls—with the occasional splash of blue sea and golden sand coming into view. Its phenomenal population growth has made the parish a center of business activity as well. The parish's northern half is dominated by sugar estates such as Staple, Newton, Bentleys, and Grove. Sea Island Cotton grows at Spencers and Fairy Valley near the airport. The major roads are Highway 7, which parallels the sea from Hastings to Oistins before veering inland to run past the airport, and Highway 6, which cuts through its pastoral core. Highway 7 runs past the following areas from W to E: Hastings, Rockley, Worthing, St. Lawrence Gap, Dover, Maxwell, and Oistins.

Hastings: Bordering St. Anne's Fort in neighboring St. Michael's Parish, the former red painted barracks here have been converted to apartments. Lying off Highway 7 to the S, the now residential Marine Gardens and Navy Gardens were once a naval hospital and homes for the Admiral and his assistants respectively. From here to Oistins, the beaches are beautiful but development has killed the coral reefs, thus eroding the sand and speeding the decline of beaches such as Accra, Worthing, and Dover. At Dayrell's Road, to the N of Hastings and to the E of the Garrison Savannah, is the field belonging to the

CHRIST CHURCH

Wanderer's, Barbados's oldest cricket association. An unlikely but very interesting sight to put on your itinerary is the playground outside the gargantuan and heinously ugly McDonalds. Judging from their goofy expressions and wildly bulging eyeballs, all of the characters in the playground outside— including Ronald McDonald—appear to be under the influence of some drug or other. Pleasant beach bars in this area include the Wave Breaker. Keswick Windsor House and Hastings Plaza are the main shopping areas.

Rockley: The next stretch of tourist-oriented coastline, Rockley is chiefly noted for its medium-sized beach which is packed with tourists at virtually all times. Here you might see dreads braiding tourists' hair while others smear on applications of aloe. At the end of the beach to the R a small path continues on to an unfrequented cove. Nearby Accra Beach is named after the hotel; the visitor will soon discover the reason why its nickname is "Sin Beach".

Worthing: This area is best known for its small beach and profusion of inexpensive guesthouses. Among the more notable ones here are Rydal Waters, Summer Place on the Sea, Shells, and Crystal Waters. A good place to hang out is the Carib Beach Bar.

St. Lawrence Gap: The parish's main restaurant and entertainment district. You may recognize it by Harry's Oasis on the main road and the Yellowbird Apartment Hotel at the entrance to the gap. There's a small beach opposite Yellowbird where fishing boats dock. Even if you're not a club fan, this area is fun to walk around and have a gander at night. Coffee and Cream Gallery, near Divi Southwind, is the island's only cafe/art gallery. Maxwell Coast Road, lying off Highway 7, also features dining and entertainment.

Yarico's Pond: Located at Kendal off the Ashford-Kendal road. A local folk song tells of the legend attached to this pond. Yarico, an Indian woman, became infatuated with Inckle, a British sailor whom she had rescued while he was exploring a neighboring island. Taking care of him until a search party from Barbados discovered them, she returned to Barbados with him. Inckle, an ungrateful lout, found a new woman and sold Yarico into slavery. She either drowned herself here or bore her son by the side of this pond, depending upon which version of this story you hear.

Graeme Hall Swamp: Covering some 80 acres and situated off Highway 7, this is one of the few remaining swamps on the island. It features white as well as the few remaining red mangroves on the island. It is also the sole remaining habitat for sedge—a type of grass that grows more than a yard high. The snowy red seal coot breeds here when it puts down roots for the winter. Yellow warblers and cattle egrets are also numerous.

Oistins: Six miles from Bridgetown, this is the nation's premier fishing village. Originally named Austin's Bay after a rather outrageous drunken lout named, naturally enough,

The South Coast

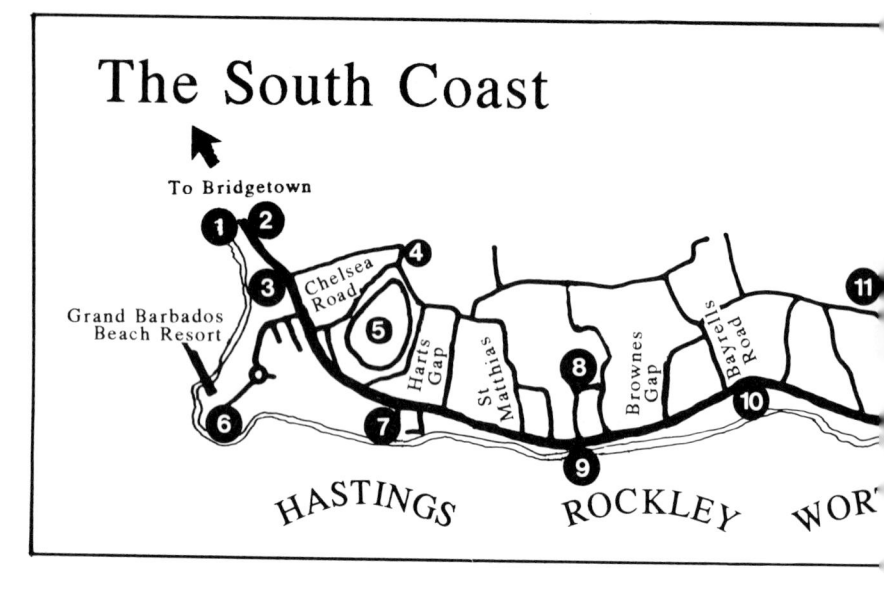

Austin. Here, the 1652 articles for the capitulation of the island—pledging obedience to Cromwell and his Commonwealth Parliament—were signed by the Royal Commissioners of Barbados after troops defending the island were defeated. During recent years this formerly primitive fishing entrepot has developed dramatically. Now a regional center, it has four acres of land which have been reclaimed from the sea. Much of the land is devoted to the fishery industry. Miami Beach, the town beach, was an accidental creation. The Coast Guard spent B$3 million to construct a barrier for mooring ships. No sooner had they finished than the sand, trapped by the new obstruction, came rolling in! Oistins now has two shopping centers: Oistins Shopping Plaza and Southern Plaza. **buying fish:** Oistins market is one of the best places in the island to buy fish if you are preparing your own. Expect to pay B$5/lb. for fish; flying fish vendors sell ten fish for $9. Fresh seasoning (B$5–10 per bottle) is also available. Just marinate the fish in it, then roll the fish in flour with breadcrumbs and deep fry.

Chase Vault: Set in Christ Church Parish Church's cemetery, seven miles from Bridgetown. Whenever the Eliot family tomb had been pried open during the 19th C. to inter a fresh corpse, it was found that the coffins were askew, some had rearranged themselves. Some were battered and splintered as

The South Coast -- East End

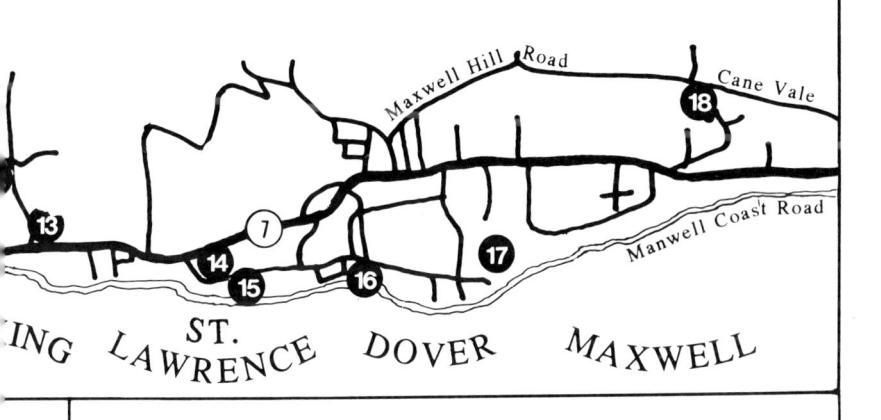

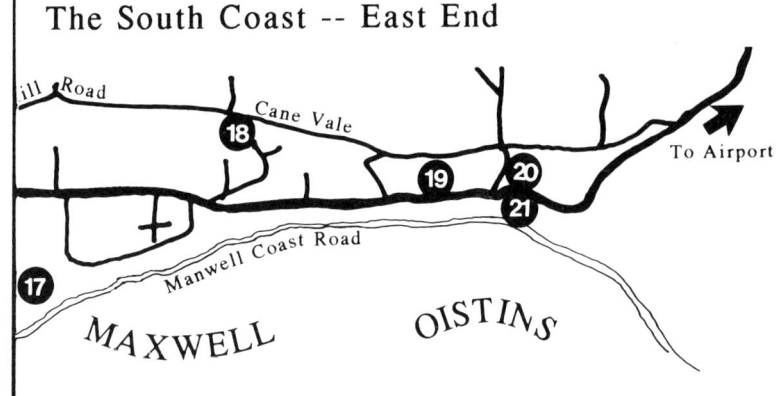

1. Harbour Lights
2. St. Paul's Church
3. Barbados Yacht Club
4. Barbados Museum
5. Garrison/Savannah
6. Hilton Hotel
7. Accra Hotel
8. Skyway Plaza
9. Ocean View/
   Caribee Hotel
10. Accra Hotel
11. Rockley Resort
12. Big B Plaza
13. Goddard's Plaza
14. St. Lawrence Gap/
    Yellowbird
    Apartment Hotel
15. The Backyard/
    After Dark/Ship Inn
16. Dover Centre
17. Half Moon Hotel
18. Fairholme Hotel
19. Southern Plaza
20. Basix
21. Miami Beach

though the occupant had been involved with levitating its boudoir. Other coffins were lying on end and yet others appeared to have engaged in post-mortem mate swapping with another box! This happened on four occasions, but only leaden coffins were affected. Vincent Combermere, Governor of Barbados, made impressions with his seal in the mortar when the vault was shut on 7 July 1819; he was again present on 20 April 1820 when the vault was once more unsealed. This time the door opened to mayhem and disorder. The coffin of an infant had been tossed into a corner, and the heavy coffin of Samuel Brewster, murdered the previous year in a slave rebellion, had shifted position. This being the last straw, the vault was subsequently emptied. Similar happenings have also occurred in Wiltshire and St. Michael's Cathedral—also with lead coffins, and it is now thought that gas exuded from decomposing corpses is responsible.

Newton Plantation: Set to the NE of Oistins, Newton Plantation can be reached by following Lodge Road E for 1.5 miles (2.5 km) to a four way crossing. Take a L on the road heading N and then turn R. This working sugar cane plantation has served as the setting for the ceremonial delivery of the last canes marking the beginning of the Crop Over Festival.

Enterprise Coast Road: Runs along the way to the South Point past coastal forests. Thorn scrubs and sweet briars populate this road along with machineel. Sand dunes—built of sand stabilized by seaside yam, splurge, and bean plants—have sprung up. The Arawak Inn and the Silver Sands Resort are in this area. Other dunes lie in the vicinity of Long Bay, Christ Church. At Paragon the three-mile (five km) coastline is bound by cliffs. From the N corner of Long Bay, a series of little rocky coves stretch out for a mile (1.5 km). A great view can be had from Penny Hole Rock and Salt Cove Point.

Long Beach: Located along the site of the former Inch Marlowe Swamp—drained in order to make way for tourist development—this mile-and-a-half (2.5 km) swamp stretches from Paragon (near the airport) to Inch Marlowe Point. Although big things were planned for the property, they failed to materialize. The Silver Sands Hotel is here as is the Long Beach Club and the Surf View Condominiums.

Sunset, St. Lawrence Gap, Christ Church

PARISH PRACTICALITIES

accommodations: With four storeys in height, Yellowbird Apartment Hotel has the altitude of a hotel but the attitude of an owner-operated guesthouse. Owned and operated by Milton and Pat Stills, they bring with them the six years of experience they had running a hotel in Britain along with the love they acquired for the Caribbean during their 12 years in Jamaica. The color theme here, naturally enough, is yellow, and everything that you would want to have in your own home is supplied here. Bring your own sponge, scrubber, and foodstuffs. The coffee funnel and filters, a welcome touch, came to be supplied because Scandinavians, having no direct experience with tea kettles and pots, would make tea and coffee directly in the pots. They charge US$50 summer, US$80 winter plus 5 percent tax; $10 per additional person. There's no service charge, but tips are appreciated. Among the major hotels in the parish are the Caribee, Coconut Court, Golden Beach, Ocean View, Regency Cove, and the Windsor Arms at Hastings; the Accra, Blue Horizon, Rockley Resort at Rockley; the Best Western Sandy Beach Sichris and Worthing Court at Worthing; Andrea on the Sea, Bresmay, Dover Beach, Half Moon, Southern Palms, Divi Southwinds, and Spinnakers in St. Lawrence Gap; and Barbados Windsurfing, Casuarina, Fairholme, Golden Sands, Rainbow Reef, San Remo, Sand Acres, and Welcome Inn in Maxwell.

budget accommodations: Perhaps the best deal going in the parish is at the Roman Beach Apartments in Oistins. Mrs. Francis Roman and family have been making themselves loved by their guests for decades. Rooms here are very simple but fan, sink, stove, cooking utensils, and shower are all supplied. Miami Beach is just across the road, and the library, a supermarket, bakery, restaurants, and the fish market are all within a few minutes walk. To get here when coming from Bridgetown, make a R by the police station and then turn L. They charge US$25–$35 summer and US$47.50–$55 winter, tax and service are added. At Hastings, Mr. Bryan Cheeseman, the owner of the Flamboyant Restaurant, charges US$25 for s or db, and US$35, s or db, for studios, one bd. with kitchen. He also charges US$45 for a two bd. Accommodation is spartan but functional, and prices include tax. Also try the Beaumont (no listed tel.) nearby. George De Mattos runs Summer Place on the Sea (tel. 435-7424) in Worthing. Other small guesthouses include Pegwell Manor (tel. 428-7955), Pegwell Inn (428-6150), Rio Guest House (tel. 428-1546), Rydal Waters (tel. 435-7433), Shells Inn (tel. 535-7253), and Woodbine Guest House (tel. 427-7627). Way out in the country all by itself at Silver Sands, Coral House (428-7620) caters to students who come to the area to windsurf. The apartment-style rooms have a bedroom, kitchenette, and living area. Full only during the winter months, it's deserted most of the year.

dining out: Right off the side of the road in back of a flamboyant tree, The Flamboyant, set in an old white house, serves up a wide selection of international and Bajan dishes in a romantic, candle-lit setting. Also set inside an old home, the Virginian features lobster and steaks. In a historical building, the Ocean View Restaurant specializes in old world cuisine. Ile de France is famous for its French cuisine. Also at Hastings are the Appleessence Restaurant, Tamarind Tree, Asta Restaurant, the Pirate's Inn, the Sandy Bank Beach Bar & Restaurant, and the well known Italian restaurant DaLuciano. In the Riviera Beach Hotel, the Crown Restaurant serves Chinese food. Located inside the Sichris in Worthing, the Sugar Shak specializes in seafood with four different varieties of creatively named lobster specials. Ditillini's, at Morcambe House in Worthing, is run by NY Italians. Also at Worthing are the Clubhouse Restaurant in Rockley Resort, and Ron's Green House in the Sandy Best Western. In St. Lawrence Gap, there are a number of restaurants. Bagshot House is at Sandy Beach on the main road just before reaching the intersection. Also nearby, David's, owned and operated by the Bajan and American couple who operate Coffee and Cream Gallery, serves formal Bajan cuisine. Other places to dine here include Spinnakers, Divi Southwinds, The Steak House, Josef's, Witch Doctor, Flanagan's II, the Chinese-style Jade Garden and Susie Yong, and The Pisces which specializes in seafood. The Captain's Carvery and the adjoining Ship Inn Pub serve food from lunch on becoming major nightspots after hours. While Le Petite Flambe and the Garden Restaurant are in the Southern Palms, the Dover Reef Restaurant is in the Casuarina Beach Club. Luigi's is the area's best known Italian restaurant. China Gardens is in Maxwell. The Silver Sands Hotel's restaurant is in Silver Sands to the SW of the airport.

fast food and informal dining: The Gourmet Cookie Shop, which features "edible works of art," is in Hastings; it offers a vegetarian lunch. There's also an unusually (for fast food) decorative and tasteful Shakey's which also has sit down service and vegetarian subs for B$7.50; a one-topping mini pizza is B$7.35. Farther down the road, the Quayside Mall has three places offering counter service: Callaloo with Caribbean

Mini mart, Christ Church

dishes; Bistro Italia serving Italian food including pizza; and Toppers for ice cream. After dinner entertainment here can be found in Rockies where you can get zombied out over video games. A Chefette is adjacent. Barbados Pizza House is inside the Windsor Arms across the street here. If you want to sample Trinidadian-style (i.e. East Indian) rotis, Scoops features these (try the one with chick peas and eggplant) as does the Roti Hut down the road. Two moderately priced local restaurants nearby are the Rosebud and the Carib. Another Barbados Pizza House is right on the beach at Accra in Worthing as is Chossels Beach Bar and Restaurant. Prominently placed and with very friendly personal service, the restaurant inside the Yellow Bird serves up a storm from breakfast on. Pizza Heaven is right next door. The St. Lawrence Pizza Hut is right on the beach at St. Lawrence Gap. Boomers is run by an American expat and his Bajan wife; they serve local and other dishes. Also try the Windsurfer down the road in Maxwell. Out in Oistins, Granny's—open every afternoon until late except Sun.—dishes out chicken gizzards fried in a special batter, macaroni pie, and curried stew among other delights. Nearby Skeete's Bakery is the place in the parish for baked goods; buy turnovers hot out of the oven from 3-5.

market food: Goddard's Supermarket is at Rendezvous, Worthing. 99 Convenience Stores are located at Maresol in Dover, Rockley Resort on Golf Club Rd., and at Quayside Centre on Rockley Beach. The Big B Supermarket is at Worthing View. An excellent minimart/rum shop is up the road from Divi Southwinds next to the roundabout. Southern Plaza Supermarket is out at Oistins as is Basix.

ISLAND WIDE ACCOMMODATION FINDER

Key: Inexpensive accommodation is less than $50/dbl. per night; moderate $50–$100; expensive $100–$200; luxury, $200 and over.

HOTELS

St. Michael's Parish

Broome's Vacation Home, Pine Gardens, tel. 426–4955/2937, 429–3937/4192. **rate bracket:** guesthouse; inexpensive.

Cunard Paradise Village, Black Rock, 424–0888. **rate bracket:** luxury. **no. of bedrooms:** 172. **location:** on beach; many vendors. **facilities:** air conditioning, swimming pool, tennis courts.

De Splash Inn Guest House, Passage Rd., 427–8287. **rate bracket:** guesthouse; inexpensive.

Fortitude, Wellington St., 426–4210. **rate bracket:** guesthouse; inexpensive. **no. of bedrooms:** 6.

Grand Barbados Beach Resort, Aquatic Gap, 426–0890. **rate bracket:** luxury. **no. of bedrooms:** 133. **location:** on beach. **facilities:** air conditioning, swimming pool, suites available.

Hilton International, Needham Point, 426-200. **rate bracket:** expensive/luxury. **no. of bedrooms:** 185. **location:** on beach. **facilities:** air conditioning, suites available, swimming pool, tennis courts.

The Great Escape, 1st Ave, Belleville, tel. 436-3554. **rate bracket:** guesthouse; inexpensive.

Superville Guest House, 2rd Ave., Pickwick Gap, Wilbury Rd, Belleville, 427-5668. **rate bracket:** guesthouse; inexpensive.

St. James Parish

Barbados Beach Village, Fitts Village, 425-1440. **rate bracket:** luxury. **no. of bedrooms:** 88. **location:** on beach. **facilities:** air conditioning, suites and kitchenettes available, swimming pool, tennis courts.

Bella Beach Tropicana, Lower Carlton, 422-2277. **rate bracket:** moderate. **no. of bedrooms:** 24. **location:** on beach. **facilities:** air conditioning, suites and kitchenettes available.

Buccaneer Bay, Paynes Bay, 432-1362. **rate bracket:** luxury. **no. of bedrooms:** 29. **location:** on beach. **facilities:** air conditioning, suites available, swimming pool.

Coconut Creek, Derricks, 432-0803. **rate bracket:** luxury. **no. of bedrooms:** 53. **location:** on beach. **facilities:** air conditioning, swimming pool.

Colony Club, Porters, 422-2741. **rate bracket:** luxury. **no. of bedrooms:** 75. **location:** on beach; many vendors. **facilities:** air conditioning, swimming pool.

Coral Reef Club, St. James Beach, 422-2372. **rate bracket:** luxury. **no. of bedrooms:** 75. **location:** on beach. **facilities:** air conditioning, suites and kitchenettes available, swimming pool, tennis courts. **note:** see review in travel section

Discovery Bay Beach Hotel, Holetown, 432-1301. **rate bracket:** luxury. **no. of bedrooms:** 84. **location:** on beach. **facili-**

ties: air conditioning, kitchenettes available, swimming pool, tennis courts.

Divi St. James Beach Resort, Vauxhall, 432–7840. **rate bracket:** luxury. **no. of bedrooms:** 131. **location:** on beach. **facilities:** air conditioning, suites available, swimming pool.

Glitter Bay Resort, Porters, 422–4111. **rate bracket:** luxury. **no. of bedrooms:** 83. **location:** on beach. **facilities:** air conditioning, suites and kitchenettes available, swimming pool, tennis courts.

Inn on the Beach, Holetown, 432–0385. **rate bracket:** luxury. **no. of bedrooms:** 21. **location:** on beach. **facilities:** air conditioning, suites and kitchenettes available, swimming pool.

Royal Pavilion Hotel, Porters, 422–4444. **rate bracket:** luxury. **no. of bedrooms:** 75. **location:** near St. James Beach. **facilities:** air conditioning, suites available, swimming pool, tennis courts.

Sandpiper Inn, St. James, 422–2251. **rate bracket:** luxury. **no. of bedrooms:** 46. **location:** on beach. **facilities:** air conditioning, suites available, swimming pool, tennis courts.

Sandy Lane Hotel, St. James, 432–1311. **rate bracket:** luxury. **no. of bedrooms:** 112. **location:** on beach. **facilities:** air conditioning, suites available, swimming pool, tennis courts, golf course. **note:** see mention in travel section.

Settler's Beach Hotel, St. James Beach, 422–3052/1372. **rate bracket:** luxury. **no. of bedrooms:** 22. **location:** on beach. **facilities:** air conditioning, suites and kitchenettes available, swimming pool.

Smuggler's Cove Hotel, Paynes Bay, 432–1741. **rate bracket:** luxury. **no. of bedrooms:** 21. **location:** on beach. **facilities:** air conditioning, kitchenettes available, swimming pool.

Tamarind Cove, Paynes Bay, 432–1332. **rate bracket:** luxury. **no. of bedrooms:** 88. **location:** on beach. **facilities:** air conditioning, suites and kitchenettes available, swimming pool.

Treasure Beach, Paynes Bay, 432-1346. **rate bracket:** luxury. **no. of bedrooms:** 25. **location:** on beach. **facilities:** air conditioning, suites and kitchenettes available, swimming pool.

St. Peter's Parish

Chrizel's Garden, Gibbs, 422-2403. **rate bracket:** guesthouse; moderate. **no. of bedrooms:** 7. **facilities:** suites and kitchenettes available.

Cobbler's Cove, Road View, 422-2291. **rate bracket:** luxury. **no. of suites:** 38. **location:** on beach. **facilities:** air conditioning, suites available, swimming pool, tennis courts. **note:** see review in travel section.

Heywoods, St. Peter, 422-4900. **rate bracket:** luxury. **no. of bedrooms:** 306. **location:** on beach. **facilities:** air conditioning, suites and kitchenettes available, swimming pool, tennis courts.

Sandridge Beach Hotel, Road View, 422-2361. **rate bracket:** expensive. **no. of bedrooms:** 52. **location:** on beach. **facilities:** air conditioning, suites and kitchenettes available, swimming pool, tennis courts.

Sugar Cane Club, Maynards, 422-5026. **rate bracket:** moderate. **no. of bedrooms:** 20. **facilities:** air conditioning, suites available, swimming pool.

St. Joseph's Parish

Atlantis Hotel, Bathsheba, 433-9445. **rate bracket:** moderate. **no. of bedrooms:** 16. **location:** overlooks beautiful view.

Kingsley Club, Cattlewash, 433-9422. **rate bracket:** moderate. **no. of bedrooms:** 7. **location:** across from non-swimmable but beautiful beach. **note:** see review in travel section.

St. Philip's Parish

Crane Beach Hotel, The Crane, 423-6220. **rate bracket:** luxury. **no. of bedrooms:** 25. **location:** overlooking beach. **facilities:** air conditioning, suites available, swimming pool, tennis courts. **note:** see review in travel section.

Ginger Bay Beach Club, 423-5810, The Crane. **rate bracket:** luxury. **no. of bedrooms:** 16. **location:** on beach. **facilities:** air conditioning, suites available, swimming pool, tennis courts.

Sam Lord's Castle, Long Bay, 423-7350. **rate bracket:** luxury. **no. of bedrooms:** 256. **location:** on beach; many vendors. **facilities:** air conditioning, suites available, swimming pools, tennis courts. **note:** see review in travel section.

Ragged Point Motel, Merricks, 423-8021. **rate bracket:** inexpensive.

Robin's Nest Hotel, Long Bay, 423-6008. **rate bracket:** expensive. **no. of bedrooms:** 30. **facilities:** air conditioning, suites and kitchenettes available, swimming pool.

Christ Church Parish

Abbeville Hotel, Rockley, 435-7294. **rate bracket:** expensive. **no. of bedrooms:** 21. **location:** near Rockley beach. **facilities:** air conditioning, swimming pool.

Accra Hotel, Rockley, 435-8920. **rate bracket:** expensive. **no. of bedrooms:** 52. **location:** on beach. **facilities:** air conditioning, suites and kitchenettes available, swimming pool.

Andrea-on-Sea Hotel, St. Lawrence Gap, 426-6021. **rate bracket:** luxury. **no. of bedrooms:** moderate. **location:** on beach; many vendors. **facilities:** air conditioning, suites and kitchenettes available, swimming pool, tennis courts.

Apple Experience, Hastings, 436-7604. **rate bracket:** moderate. **no. of bedrooms:** 15. **location:** on beach.

Asta Apartment Hotel, Hastings, 427-2541. **rate bracket:** expensive. **no. of bedrooms:** 60. **location:** on beach. **facilities:** air conditioning, suites and kitchenettes available, swimming pool.

Bagshot House Hotel, St. Lawrence Gap, 435-6956. **rate bracket:** expensive. **no. of bedrooms:** 16. **location:** on beach. **facilities:** suites and kitchenettes available.

Barbados Windsurfing Club, Maxwell, 428-9095. **rate bracket:** moderate. **no. of bedrooms:** 15. **location:** on beach. **facilities:** kitchenettes available.

Beaumont, Hastings (no listed tel.). **rate bracket:** guesthouse; inexpensive. **no. of bedrooms:** 4.

Bona Vista, Rose Garden Ave. (off Golf Club Rd.), Rockley, 435-6680. **rate bracket:** guesthouse; inexpensive. **no. of bedrooms:** 3.

Best Western Sandy Beach, Worthing, 435-6689. **rate bracket:** expensive/luxury. **no. of bedrooms:** 89. **location:** on beach; many vendors. **facilities:** air conditioning, suites and kitchenettes available, swimming pool.

Blue Horizon Beach Apartments, Rockley, 435-8916. **rate bracket:** moderate. **no. of bedrooms:** 188. **location:** on beach; many vendors. **facilities:** air conditioning, kitchenettes available, swimming pool.

Bresmay Apartment Hotel, St. Lawrence Gap, 428-6131. **rate bracket:** expensive. **no. of bedrooms:** 50. **location:** on beach; many vendors. **facilities:** air conditioning, suites and kitchenettes available, swimming pool.

Caribbee Beach Hotel, Hastings, 436-6232. **rate bracket:** moderate. **no. of bedrooms:** 55. **location:** on beach. **facilities:** air conditioning, kitchenettes available.

Casuarina Beach Club, Dover, 428-3600. **rate bracket:** luxury. **no. of bedrooms:** 100. **location:** on beach; many vendors. **facilities:** air conditioning, suites and kitchenettes available, swimming pool, tennis courts.

Island Wide Accommodation Finder 239

Coconut Court Beach Apartments, Hastings, 427–1655/6. **rate bracket:** luxury. **no. of bedrooms:** 61. **location:** on beach; many vendors. **facilities:** air conditioning, suites and kitchenettes available, swimming pool, tennis courts.

Divi Southwinds Hotel and Beach Club, St. Lawrence Gap, 428–1457. **rate bracket:** luxury. **no. of bedrooms:** 160. **location:** on beach; many vendors. **facilities:** air conditioning, suites and kitchenettes available, swimming pool, tennis courts.

Dover Beach Apartment Hotel, St. Lawrence Gap, 428–8076. **rate bracket:** moderate. **no. of bedrooms:** 27. **location:** on beach. **facilities:** air conditioning, swimming pool, tennis court.

Fairholme Hotel and Apartments, Maxwell, 428–9425. **rate bracket:** inexpensive/moderate. **no. of bedrooms:** 31. **facilities:** air conditioning, suites and kitchenette available, swimming pool, tennis courts.

Flamboyant, Hastings, 427–5588. **rate bracket:** guesthouse; inexpensive. **location:** near beach. **facilities:** kitchenettes available.

Golden Beach Apartment Hotel, Hastings, 426–6784. **rate bracket:** moderate/expensive. **no. of bedrooms:** 25. **location:** on beach. **facilities:** air conditioning, swimming pool.

Golden Sands Apartment Hotel, Maxwell. **rate bracket:** moderate/expensive. **no. of bedrooms:** 27. **facilities:** air conditioning, swimming pool.

Half Moon Beach Hotel, St. Lawrence Gap, 428–7131. **rate bracket:** expensive. **no. of bedrooms:** 29. **location:** on beach. **facilities:** air conditioning, suites available, swimming pool.

Indramar Beach Hotel, Worthing, 435–7457. **rate bracket:** guesthouse; inexpensive. **no. of bedrooms:** 13.

Ocean View Hotel, Hastings, 427–7821–6. **rate bracket:** moderate/expensive. **no. of bedrooms:** 35. **location:** on beach; many vendors. **facilities:** air conditioning, suites available.

Pegwell Inn, Welches, 428–6150. **rate bracket:** guesthouse; inexpensive. **no. of bedrooms:** 9.

Rainbow Reef Hotel, Dover, 428–5510. **rate bracket:** moderate/expensive. **no. of bedrooms:** 43. **location:** on beach; many vendors. **facilities:** air conditioning, suites and kitchenettes available, swimming pool.

Regency Cove Hotel, Hastings, 435–8924. **rate bracket:** moderate/expensive. **no. of bedrooms:** 30. **facilities:** air conditioning, suites and kitchenettes available, swimming pool.

Rio Guest House, St. Lawrence Gap, 428–1546. **rate bracket:** guesthouse; inexpensive. **no. of bedrooms:** 7.

Rockley Resort and Beach Club, Rockley, 435–7880. **rate bracket:** expensive/luxury. **no. of bedrooms:** 111. **location:** off beach; shuttle available. **facilities:** air conditioning, suites and kitchenettes available, swimming pools, tennis courts, golf course.

Roman Beach Apartments, Miami Beach, Oistins, 428–7635. **rate bracket:** guesthouse; inexpensive. **location:** across road from beach. **facilities:** kitchenettes available. **note:** see review in text.

Rydal Waters Guest House, Worthing, 435–7433. **rate bracket:** guesthouse; inexpensive.

San Remo Hotel, Maxwell, 428–2822/2816. **rate bracket:** moderate. **no. of bedrooms:** 23. **location:** on beach. **facilities:** air conditioning, suites and kitchenettes available.

Sand Acres Beach Club, Maxwell, 428–7141/7234. **rate bracket:** expensive. **no. of bedrooms:** 37. **location:** on beach. **facilities:** air conditioning, suites available, swimming pool, tennis courts.

Shells Inn, 535–7253, Worthing. **rate bracket:** guesthouse; inexpensive.

Island Wide Accommodation Finder 241

Shonlan Apartments, 8 Coverly Terrace, 428-1722. **rate bracket:** guesthouse; inexpensive.

Sichris Hotel, Worthing, 435-7930. **rate bracket:** expensive. **no. of bedrooms:** 24. **facilities:** air conditioning, suites and kitchenettes available, swimming pool.

Silver Sands Resort, Silver Sands, 428-5936. **rate bracket:** expensive. **no. of bedrooms:** 106. **location:** on beach. **facilities:** air conditioning, suites and kitchenettes available, swimming pool, tennis courts.

Southern Palms Beach Club, 428-7171, St. Lawrence Gap. **rate bracket:** expensive/luxury. **no. of bedrooms:** 93. **location:** on beach. **facilities:** air conditioning, suites and kitchenettes available, swimming pool, tennis courts.

Spinnaker's Hotel, St. Lawrence Gap, 435-6569. **rate bracket:** moderate. **no. of bedrooms:** 6. **location:** on beach. **facilities:** air conditioning, suites available, kitchenettes, swimming pool, tennis courts.

Summer Place Home on the Sea Guest House, Worthing, 435-7424. **rate bracket:** guesthouse; inexpensive. **no. of bedrooms:** 7. **location:** on beach.

Sunhaven Beach Apartment and Hotel, Rockley, 427-3550. **rate bracket:** expensive. **no. of bedrooms:** 35. **location:** on beach. **facilities:** air conditioning, suites available, swimming pool.

Welcome Inn Apartment Hotel, Maxwell Coast Rd., 428-9900. **rate bracket:** expensive. **no. of bedrooms:** 110. **location:** on beach. **facilities:** air conditioning, suites and kitchenettes available, swimming pool.

Woodbine Guest House, Rockley, 427-7627. **rate bracket:** guesthouse; inexpensive.

Worthing Court Apartment Hotel, Worthing, 435-7910. **rate bracket:** moderate/expensive. **no. of bedrooms:** 24. **facilities:** air conditioning, suites available, swimming pool.

APARTMENTS AND COTTAGES

St. Michael's Parish

Nautilus Beach, Bay St., 426–3541. **rate bracket:** moderate. **no. of units:** 14. **location:** on beach. **facilities:** studios and one-bedrooms, maid service, air conditioning.

Paradise Villas, Black Rock, 424–4581. **rate bracket:** moderate/expensive. **no. of units:** 15. **location:** on beach. **facilities:** one- and two-bedrooms, maid service, air conditioning.

Tower Hotel, Black Rock, 424–3256. **rate bracket:** expensive. **no. of units:** 14. **location:** on beach. **facilities:** one-bedrooms maid service, air conditioning, swimming pool, tennis courts.

Walmer Lodge Apartments, Black Rock, 425–1026. **rate bracket:** inexpensive/expensive. **no. of units:** 10. **facilities:** studios and one-bedrooms, maid service, air conditioning.

St. James Parish

Angler Apartments, Derricks, 432–0817. **rate bracket:** moderate. **no. of units:** 7. **location:** on beach. **facilities:** studios one-bedrooms and two-bedrooms available, maid service, air conditioning, swimming pool, tennis courts.

Beachcomber Apartments, Paynes Bay, 432–0489. **rate bracket:** expensive. **no. of units:** 9. **location:** on beach. **facilities:** studios, one-bedrooms and two-bedrooms available, maid service, air conditioning, swimming pool, tennis courts.

Caribbean House Apartments, Paynes Bay, 432–1375. **rate bracket:** moderate. **no. of units:** 31. **facilities:** studios, one-bedrooms and two-bedrooms available, maid service, air conditioning, swimming pool.

Golden Palm Hotel, Sunset Crest, 432–6666. **rate bracket:** expensive. **no. of units:** 71. **location:** on beach. **facilities:** one-bedrooms available, maid service, air conditioning, swimming pool.

Homar Rentals, Sunset Crest, 432–6750. **rate bracket:** moderate. **no. of units:** 104. **facilities:** one-bedrooms available, maid service, air conditioning, swimming pool, tennis courts.

Na-Diesie Apartments, Holetown, 432–0469. **rate bracket:** moderate. **no. of units:** 20. **location:** on beach. **facilities:** studios available, maid service, air conditioning, swimming pool, tennis courts.

Palm Beach Hotel, Second St., Holetown, 432–1384. **rate bracket:** expensive. **no. of units:** 30. **location:** on beach. **facilities:** studios and one-bedrooms, maid service, air conditioning, swimming pool.

Sun Rentals, Sunset Crest (no listed phone). **rate bracket:** moderate. **no. of units:** 65. **facilities:** one-bedrooms, maid service, air conditioning, swimming pool, tennis courts.

Traveller's Palm, 266 Sunset Crest, 432–7722. **rate bracket:** moderate. **no. of units:** 16. **location:** on beach. **facilities:** one-bedrooms, maid service, air conditioning, swimming pool.

St. Peter's Parish

Gibbs Gardens Apartments, Gibbs, 422–4211/4234/4251. **rate bracket:** expensive. **no. of units:** 3. **facilities:** one-bedrooms, maid service.

New Haven Mansions, Suite 1, Gibbs, 422–4124/2537/1828. **rate bracket:** expensive. **no. of units:** 6. **facilities:** two-bedrooms, three-bedrooms, four-bedrooms, maid service, air conditioning, swimming pool.

Christ Church Parish

Adulo Apartments, Rockley, 427-2686. **rate bracket:** moderate. **no. of units:** 12. **facilities:** two-bedrooms, maid service, air conditioning, swimming pool, tennis courts.

Bernita Apartments, Maxwell Hill, 428-9115. **rate bracket:** moderate/expensive. **no. of units:** 12. **facilities:** maid service.

Blythwood Beach Apartments, Worthing, 435-7712. **rate bracket:** expensive. **no. of units:** 14. **location:** on beach. **facilities:** one- and two-bedrooms, maid service, air conditioning, swimming pool.

Cacrabank Beach Apartment Hotel, Worthing, 435-8059. **rate bracket:** moderate. **no. of units:** 21. **location:** on beach. **facilities:** studios and one-bedrooms, maid service, air conditioning, swimming pool.

Carib Blue Apartments, 60 Dover Terrace, 428-2290. **rate bracket:** inexpensive/moderate. **no. of units:** 15. **facilities:** studios available, maid service, air conditioning.

Chateau Blanc Apartments, Worthing, 435-7518. **rate bracket:** inexpensive/moderate. **no. of units:** 9. **location:** on beach. **facilities:** studios and two-bedrooms, maid service, air conditioning.

Coral Sands Apartments, Worthing, 435-7495. **rate bracket:** inexpensive/moderate. **no. of units:** 9. **location:** on beach. **facilities:** two- and three-bedrooms, maid service.

Dorisville Apartments/Goldwater Flats, Dover, 428-8686. **rate bracket:** inexpensive/moderate. **no. of units:** 20. **facilities:** one-, two- and three-bedrooms, maid service, air conditioning.

Fedey, Dover, 428-4051. **rate bracket:** expensive. **no. of units:** 12. **location:** on beach. **facilities:** studios, maid service, air conditioning.

Four Aces Cottages and Apartments, St. Lawrence Gap, 428–9441. **rate bracket:** inexpensive/moderate. **no. of units:** 14. **location:** on beach. **facilities:** one- and two-bedrooms, maid service, air conditioning.

Fred-La-Rose Bonanza Apartments, Dover, 428–9097. **rate bracket:** moderate/expensive. **no. of units:** 20. **location:** on beach. **facilities:** studios, one-bedrooms and two-bedrooms, maid service, air conditioning.

Inchcape, Silver Sands, 428–9476. **rate bracket:** moderate/expensive. **no. of units:** 6. **location:** on beach. **facilities:** studios, one-bedrooms, two-bedrooms, maid service, air conditioning.

Kingsway Apartments, Maxwell, 428–8202. **rate bracket:** moderate/expensive. **no. of units:** 8. **location:** on beach. **facilities:** studios, one-bedrooms, two-bedrooms, maid service, air conditioning, swimming pool, tennis courts.

Leeton-On-Sea Apartments, Maxwell, 428–4500. **rate bracket:** inexpensive. **no. of units:** 3. **location:** on beach. **facilities:** studios, maid service.

Maresol Beach Apartments, St. Lawrence Gap, 428–9300. **rate bracket:** moderate/expensive. **no. of units:** 12. **location:** on beach. **facilities:** one-bedrooms, two-bedrooms, maid service.

Melrose Beach Apartments, Worthing, 435–7984. **rate bracket:** inexpensive. **no. of units:** 15. **facilities:** one-bedrooms, maid service, air conditioning.

Monteray Apartment Hotel, Dover, 428–9152. **rate bracket:** moderate/expensive. **no. of units:** 22. **location:** on beach. **facilities:** studios, one-bedrooms, two-bedrooms, maid service, air conditioning, swimming pool.

Mysotis Apartments, Dover, 428–6484. **rate bracket:** moderate. **no. of units:** 11. **facilities:** studios, two-bedrooms, maid service, air conditioning.

Na-Diesie Apartments, Holetown, 432–0469. **rate bracket:** moderate. **no. of units:** 20. **location:** on beach. **facilities:** studios, maid service, air conditioning.

The Nook Apartments, Rockley, 429-6570. **rate bracket:** inexpensive. **no. of units:** 4. **location:** on beach. **facilities:** two-bedrooms, maid service, air conditioning, swimming pool.

Pirate's Inn Hotel, Hastings, 435-6633, **rate bracket:** moderate. **no. of units:** 25. **location:** on beach. **facilities:** studios, maid service, air conditioning, swimming pool.

Rostrevor Apartments. St. Lawrence Gap, 428-9298. **rate bracket:** moderate/expensive. **no. of units:** 44. **location:** on beach. **facilities:** studio available, one-, two-, three-bedrooms, maid service, air conditioning, swimming pool.

Round Rock Apartments On Sea, Silver Sands, 428-7500. **rate bracket:** moderate. **no. of units:** 7. **facilities:** studios and two-bedrooms, maid service, air conditioning.

St. Lawrence Apartments, St. Lawrence Gap, 435-6950. **rate bracket:** moderate. **no. of units:** 75. **location:** on beach. **facilities:** studios, one-bedrooms, maid service, air conditioning, swimming pool.

Salt Ash Apartment Hotel, St. Lawrence Gap, 428-8753. **rate bracket:** moderate. **no. of units:** 8. **location:** on beach. **facilities:** studios, maid service, air conditioning.

Sandy Cove Apartments, Landsdowne-On-Sea, Enterprise, 428-4358. **rate bracket:** moderate/expensive. **no. of units:** 4. **location:** on beach. **facilities:** two-bedrooms, three-bedrooms, maid service.

Sea Foam Haciendas, Worthing, 435-7380, 12. **rate bracket:** moderate/expensive. **no. of units:** 12. **facilities:** two-bedrooms, maid service, air conditioning.

Shangri-La Apartment Hotel, 428-9112. **rate bracket:** expensive. **no. of units:** 43. **facilities:** studios, one-bedrooms, maid service, air conditioning, swimming pool.

Sheringham Beach Apartments, Maxwell, 428-9339. **rate bracket:** moderate/expensive. **no. of units:** 25. **location:** on beach. **facilities:** studios, maid service, air conditioning.

Sierra Beach Apartment Hotel, Hastings, 429–5620. **rate bracket:** moderate. **no. of units:** 22. **location:** on beach. **facilities:** studios, one-bedrooms, two-bedrooms, maid service, air conditioning, swimming pool.

Southern Surf Beach Apartment Hotel, Rockley, 435–6672. **rate bracket:** moderate. **no. of units:** 12. **facilities:** studios, maid service, air conditioning, swimming pool.

Summerset Apartments, Dover, 428–7936. **rate bracket:** moderate. **no. of units:** 7. **facilities:** one-bedrooms, two-bedrooms, maid service, air conditioning.

Sunshine Beach Apartments, Hastings, 427–1234. **rate bracket:** moderate. **no. of units:** 8. **location:** on beach. **facilities:** studios, one-bedrooms, maid service.

Woodville Beach Apartments, Worthing, 435–6693. **rate bracket:** moderate. **no. of units:** 28. **location:** on beach. **facilities:** studios, maid service, air conditioning, swimming pool.

Yellow Bird Apartment Hotel, St. Lawrence Gap, 428–3110. **rate bracket:** moderate. **no. of units:** 28. **location:** on beach. **facilities:** studios, maid service, air conditioning, swimming pool. **note:** see review in travel section.

GLOSSARY

Backra, Buckra—nickname for poor white. Its name likely originates from the 'back row' of the church to which the less prosperous Bajans were relegated. Other names for these much maligned folk include "redlegs" and "ecky-becky."

BWU—Barbados Worker's Union

Big Six—the group of large companies said to dominate the island's commerce.

Bim—nickname for islanders. Apparently derives from Major Byam who defended the royalist cause (1650–52). His followers became known as 'Bims.' Although the term may be applied to all Barbadians, it is sometimes used only to mean white Bajans. The island is also sometimes referred to as Bimshire.

calabash—small tree native to the Caribbean whose fruit, a gourd, has multiple uses when dried.

callaloo—Caribbean soup made with callaloo greens.

Caribs—original people who colonized the islands of the Caribbean, giving the region its name.

cassava—staple crop indigenous to the Americas. Bitter and sweet are the two varieties. Bitter must be washed, grated, and baked in order to remove the poisonous prussic acid. A spongy cake is made from the bitter variety as is cassareep, a preservative which is the foundation of West Indian pepperpot stew.

cays—Indian-originated name which refers to islets in the Caribbean.

century plant—also known as karato, coratoe, and maypole. Flowers only once in its lifetime before it dies.

cerro—hill or mountain.

chattel house—basic Bajan dwelling. Chattel is an old legal term denoting "moveable property." As most Bajans own their home but not the land it is built on, the name seemed suitable. Built on very basic foundations—such as a layer of rocks—the houses are typically built with uninsulated wood frame construction with lapboard siding and corrugated metal peak red roofs. These box-like structures have traditionally been expanded as the family (and its wealth) grows.

conch—large edible mollusk pounded into salads or chowders.

corn'n'oil—falernum with dark rum added to mix.

cou-cou—stirred corn meal mixed with okra. When served with flying fish, it forms the national dish.

cutlass—the Caribbean equivalent of the machete. Originally used by buccaneers and pirates.

duppy—ghost or spirit of the dead which is feared throughout the Caribbean. Derives from the African religious belief that a man has two souls. One ascends to heaven while the other stays around for a while or permanently. May be harnessed for good or evil through obeah. Some plants and birds are also associated with duppies.

falernum—A sweet liquor consisting of white rum matured with lime and almond.

guava—indigenous Caribbean fruit, extremely rich in vitamin C, which is eaten raw or used in making jelly.

Johnny—descendant of Scottish or Irish indentured servants.

jug jug—a thick puree made from guinea corn, flour, peas, and a minced mix of meat, onions and herbs. Served with ham slices at Christmas.

Landship—a friendly society serving as a form of lower class insurance against sickness, unemployment, and death. Run by an 'admiral' who has members 'assigned' to his 'ship.' Its naval imagery and attire are often prominent at funerals and at Crop Over festivities.

Leeward—Caribbean sea side of Barbados.

love vine—orange colored parasitic vine, found on Jamaica, St. John, Barbados, and other islands. Resembles nothing so much as the contents of a can of spaghetti.

machineel—small toxic tree native to the Caribbean. Its fruit, which resembles an apple, and milky sap are lethal.

mauby—a bitter sweet, frothy beverage made with dried mauby bark, cinnamon, orange peel, mace, cloves, sugar, and water.

meeting turn—informal financial cooperative for mutual savings. Each person would take a turn receiving the kitty's contents at the sessions.

millwalls—ruins of windmills used in sugar production.

Mr. Harding—effigy of the cruel slave driver of yore. Usually constructed from sugarcane trash and dressed in an old black coat and top hat and burned at the Crop Over festivities.

obeah—Caribbean "magic" imported from Africa. Although it is virtually extinct on Barbados, an 1806 law making its practice a felony punishable by death is still on the books.

parish—unit of local administration.

poinciana—beautiful tropical tree which blooms with clusters of red blossoms during the summer months. Originates in Madagascar.

red legs—nickname for poor white Bajans who are descendants of indentured servants. Refers to the sun's effect on their skins. Other similar terms include: backras, backra johnies, ecky bekkies, poor whites, spawgees, or white niggers. Predominately found today in St. John, St. Joseph, and St. Andrew.

Scotland district—a hilly, eroded area of NE Barbados.

sea grape—West Indian tree, commonly found along beaches, which produces green, fleshy, inedible grapes.

sensitive plant—also known as mimosa, shame lady, and other names. It will snap shut at the slightest touch.

star apple—large tree producing segmented pods, brown in color and sour in taste, which are a popular fresh fruit.

taro—tuber also known as sasheen, tannia, malanga, elephant's ear, and yautia.

tuk band—strolling musicians playing calypso-type music. Often joined by spontaneous dancers.

BOOKLIST

TRAVEL AND DESCRIPTION

Arciniegas, German. *Caribbean: Sea of the New World.* New York: Alfred A. Knopf, 1946.

Blume, Helmut. (trans. Johannes Maczewski and Ann Norton) *The Caribbean Islands.* London: Longman, 1976.

Bonsal, Stephen. *The American Mediterranean.* New York: Moffat, Yard and Co., 1912.

Caimite. *Don't Get Hit by a Coconut.* Hicksville, NY: Exposition Press, 1979. The memoirs of an Ohio painter who escaped to the Caribbean.

Doucet, Louis. *The Caribbean Today.* Paris: editions j.a., 1977.

Forde, G. Addington, Sean Carrington, Henry Fraser, and John Gilmore. *The A-Z of Barbadian Heritage.* Bridgetown, Heinemann Caribbean: 1990. The definitive encyclopedia by the island's top experts.

Hart, Jeremy C. and William T. Stone. *A Cruising Guide to the Caribbean and the Bahamas.* New York: Dodd, Mead and Company, 1982. Description of planning and plying for yachties. Includes nautical maps.

Morrison, Samuel E. *The Caribbean as Columbus Saw It.* Boston: Little, Brown and Co.: 1964. Photographs and text by a leading American historian.

Naipaul, V.S. *The Middle Passage: The Caribbean Revisited.* New York: Macmillan, 1963. Another view of the West Indies by a Trinidad native.

Radcliffe, Virginia. *The Caribbean Heritage.* New York: Walker & Co., 1976.

Rodman, Selden. *The Caribbean.* New York: Hawthorn, 1968. Traveler's description of the Caribbean by a leading art critic.

Ward, Fred. *Golden Islands of the Caribbean.* New York: Crown Publishers, 1967. A picture book for your coffee table. Beautiful historical plates.

Wood, Peter. *Caribbean Isles.* New York: Time Life Books, 1975. Includes descriptions of such places as Pico Duarte in the Dominican Republic and the Blue Mountain region of Jamaica.

FLORA AND FAUNA

Kaplan, Eugene. *A Field Guide to the Coral Reefs of the Caribbean and Florida.* Princeton, N.J.: Peterson's Guides, 1984

de Oviedo, Gonzalo Fernandez. (trans. and ed. S.A. Stroudemire). *Natural History of the West Indies.* Chapel Hill: University of North Carolina Press, 1959.

HISTORY

Campbell, P.F. *The Church in Barbados in the 17th Century.* St. Michael: Barbados Museum and Historical Society, 1982.

Comitas, Lambros. *The Aftermath of Sovereignty: West Indian Perspectives.* New York, 1973.

Deer, Noel. *The History of Sugar.* London: Chapman, 1950.

Handler, Jerome S. *Plantation Slavery in Barbados.* Cambridge: Harvard University Press, 1976.

Harlow, Vincent T. *History of Barbados, 1625–1685,* Negro University Press: 1926.

Hoyos, F.A. *Barbados: A History from Amerindians to Independence.* London: Macmillan Caribbean, 1978.

Hoyos, F.A. *Grantley Adams and the Social Revolution.* London: Macmillan Caribbean.

Hovey, Graham and Gene Brown, eds. *Central America and the Caribbean.* New York: Arno Press, 1980. This volume of clippings from *The New York Times,* one of a series in its Great Contemporary Issues books, graphically displays American activities and attitudes toward the area. A goldmine of information.

Hunte, George. *The West Indian Islands.* New York: The Viking Press, 1972. Historical overview from the Western viewpoint with information added for tourists.

Kortright, Davis. *Cross and Crown in Barbados: Caribbean Political Religion in the late 19th Century.* P. Lang Publishers, 1983.

Knight, Franklin W. *The Caribbean.* Oxford: Oxford University Press, 1978. Thematic, anti-imperialist view of Caribbean history.

Levy, Claude. *Emancipation, Sugar, and Federalism.* Gainesville: University Press, 1980.

Lignon, Richard. *A True and Exact History of the Island of Barbados* (1647). London: Frank Cass & Co. Ltd., 1970.

Mannix, Daniel P. and Malcolm Cooley. *Black Cargoes.* New York: Viking Press, 1982. Details the saga of the slave trade.

Schomburgh, Sir Robert, *The History of Barbados,* 1971.

Watson, K. *The Civilized Island of Barbados. A Social History 1750–1860.* Bridgetown: Caribbean Graphics.

POLITICS AND ECONOMICS

Barry, Tom, Beth Wood, and Deb Freusch. *The Other Side of Paradise: Foreign Control in the Caribbean.* New York: Grove Press, 1984. A brilliantly and thoughtfully written analysis of Caribbean economics.

Blanshard, Paul. *Democracy and Empire in the Caribbean.* New York: The Macmillan Co., 1947.

Duncan, Neville C. *Women and Politics in Barbados, 1948–81.* Cave Hill: Institute of Social and Economic Research, University of the West Indies, Barbados, 1983.

Gooding, Bailey W. and Justine Whitfield. *The West Indies at the Crossroads.* Cambridge, Ma.: Schenkmann Publishing Co., Inc., 1981. A political history of the British Caribbean during the 1970s.

Matthews, Thomas G. and F.M. Andic, eds. *Politics and Economics in the Caribbean.* Rio Piedras: Institute of Caribbean Studies, University of Puerto Rico, 1971.

Mitchell, Sir Harold. *Caribbean Patterns.* New York: John Wiley and Sons., 1972. Dated but still a masterpiece. The best reference guide for gaining an understanding of the history and current political status of nearly every island group in the Caribbean.

SOCIOLOGY AND ANTHROPOLOGY

Abrahams, Roger D. *After Africa.* New Haven: Yale University Press, 1983. Fascinating accounts of slaves and slave life in the West Indies.

Callender, Jean H. *Barbadian Society, Past and Present.* Cave Hill: Main Library, University of the West Indies (Barbados), 1981.

Dann, Graham. *The Barbadian Male: Sexual Attitudes and Practices.* London: Macmillan Caribbean, 1987. A survey, built into book form, which tackles the male, his role in society, socialization, etc.

Dann, Graham. *Everyday Life in Barbados.* The Hague: Smits Drukkers-Uitgevers B.V., 1976. A fascinating compilation of studies dealing with topics as diverse as picnics and the rum shop.

Forde, G. Addington *Folk Beliefs of Barbados.* Barbados: National Cultural Foundation, 1987.

Horowitz, Michael H. (ed.) *People and Cultures of the Caribbean.* Garden City, New York: Natural History Press for the Museum of Natural History, 1971. Sweeping compilation of social anthropological essays.

ART, ARCHITECTURE, AND ARCHAEOLOGY

Alleyne, Warren. *Historic Houses of Barbados.* Bridgetown: Barbados National Trust.

Buissert, David. *Historic Architecture of the Caribbean.* London: Heinemann Educational Books, 1980.

Gosner, Pamela. *Caribbean Georgian.* Washington D.C.: Three Continents Press, 1982. A beautifully illustrated guide to the "Great and Small Houses of the West Indies."

Hill, Barbara (Henry Fraser. ed.) *Historic Churches of Barbados.* Bridgetown: Art Heritage Publishers, 1984.

Lewisohm, Florence. *The Living Arts & Crafts of the West Indies.* Christiansted, St. Croix: The Virgin Islands Council on the Arts, 1973. Local crafts illustrated.

MUSIC

Bergman, Billy. *Hot Sauces: Latin and Caribbean Pop.* New York: Quill, 1984.

Marshall, Trevor. *Folk Songs of Barbados.* Barbados: Cedar Press, 1981.

LANGUAGE

Collymore, Frank A. *Notes for a Glossary of Words and Phrases of Barbadian Dialect.* Bridgetown: Barbados National Trust, 1955.

Forde, G. Addington *De Mortar Pestle: A Collection of Barbadian Proverbs.* Barbados: National Cultural Foundation, 1987. A fascinating book which not only lists Barbadian proverbs but gives their near equivalents in the Caribbean and Africa.

LITERATURE

Braithwaithe, Edward. *Mother Poem.* Oxford and New York: Oxford University Press, 1977.

Braithwaithe, Edward. *Sun Poem.* Oxford and New York: Oxford University Press, 1982.

Callender, Timothy. *How Music Came to the Ainchan People.* St. Michale, Barbados: 1979.

Drayton, Geoffrey. *Christopher.* London: Secker and Warburg, Collins, 1961.

Fowler, Robert. *Spoils of Eden.* New York: Dodd Mead, 1985.

Hutchinson, Lionel. *Man from the People.* London: Collins, 1969.

Kellman, Tony. *Black Madonna Poems.* Bridgetown, 1975.

Jackman, Oliver. *Saw the House in Half.* Washington, D.C.: Howard University Press, 1974. The classic expatriate novel set in London and Lagos.

Jackson, Carl. *East Wind in Paradise.* London: New Beacon Books Ltd., 1981.

Lamming, George. *The Emigrants.* London: Allison & Busby, 1980.

Lamming, George. *Of Age and Innocence.* London: Allison & Busby, 1981.

Lamming, George. *In the Castle of My Skin.* London: Schocken, 1983. His most famous novel.

Lamming, George. *The Pleasure of Exile.* London: Allison & Busby, 1984.

Small, Jonathan. *The Pig Sticking Season. Jamaica Poems, 1985.* Bridgetown: 1966.

INDEX

Accommodations: 95–96, 158–160, 171–172, 190–191, 217–220, 227–228, 233–247
Adams, Grantley: 27, 28
Adams, J. M. G. M. (Tom): 28, 32–33
Agriculture: 35–38
Airfares: 85–86
Andromeda Gardens: 169–171
Anglicans: 59–60
Animal Flower Cave: 194–195
Animals: 12–14
Antiques: 121
Apartment rentals: 96
Archer's Bay: 193
Art galleries: 73–74
Art: 72–73
Banks: 109
Barbados Labour Party (BLP): 25, 26, 28, 32–33
Barbados Wildlife Reserve: 187–188
Barbados Workers Union (BWU): 25, 27, 28
Barrow, Errol Walton: 27, 28, 32–33, 35
Bathsheba: 167
Belleville District: 141
Boscobel: 196–198
Bridgetown: 124–147
Broad Street: 127–134
Broadcasting: 110–111
Buses: 88–89
Calalu: 78
Calypso: 67–71
Car Rental: 91–92
Careenage: 132–133
Caribbean Basin Initiative: 34
Catholicism: 60
Chalky Mount: 176
Chase Vault: 224–226
Cherry Tree Hill: 173
Christ Church: 221–231
Christianity: 59–61
Climate: 5–7
Codrington College: 207–208
Cohobblopot: 78
Columbus: 16
Concerts: 101
Conduct: 111–112
Conkies: 78
Coral reefs: 16
Cotton Tower: 168
Cou cou: 78
Courteen, Sir William: 19
Crafts: 120
Crane Beach: 218–219, 220
Cricket: 106–109
Crop Over Festival: 76
Culpepper Island: 217
Currency: 109
Customs: 122–123
Dance: 72
Democratic Labour Party (DLP): 27, 32–33
Democratic League: 24
Dining: 77–84, 117–118, 148–149, 160–161, 172, 179, 191–192, 211, 220, 229–231
Drama: 71–72
Drax Hall: 199–200
Drinks: 81–84
Driving: 92–93

Duty free shopping: 122
Earl of Carlisle: 19
Economy: 33–35
Entertainment: 96–101
European discovery: 17–18
Events: 75–77
Falernum: 83–84
Families: 45–46
Farley Hill: 186
Fauna: 12–14
Female travelers: 113
Festivals: 75–77
Fishing: 102
Flora: 7–12
Flower Forest: 167–168
Flying fish: 79
Folkestone Park: 156–157
Food: 77–84, 117–118, 148–149, 160–161, 172, 179, 191–192, 211, 220, 229–231
Foul Bay: 212–213
Francia Plantation: 203
Friendly Societies: 47
Fruit: 81
Gabby, the Mighty: 69–70
Ganja: 62–63
Garrison: 144–145
Garvey, Marcus: 61
Golf: 104
Government: 30–33, 131–132
Gun Hill: 202
Hackleton's Cliff: 205
Harbour: 140
Harrison's Cave: 165
Hastings: 221–222
Health: 111
Hiking: 104
History: 17–29, 125–126, 146–147, 153, 181
Holetown Festival: 75
Holetown: 155–157
Horseback riding: 104
Hotels: 95–96, 158–160, 171–172, 190–191, 217–220, 227–228, 233–247
House of Assembly: 19, 30, 131–132
Hurricanes: 5–7

Indians: 17–18
Insects: 14
Jug-jug: 78
Land, the: 2–5
Language: 43, 51–56
Libraries: 117
Literature: 74–75
Little Bay: 196–197
Lord, Sam: 214–215
Machineel: 10
Male and female relationships: 44
Manley, Norman Washington: 27
Manufacturing: 34–35
Marine life: 14–15
Markets: 121, 149–150, 161, 224
Marley, Robert Nesta (Bob): 65–66
Mauby: 81
Measurements: 109
Media: 110–111
Methodism: 60
Money: 109
Monkey, the Barbados green: 12
Moravians: 60–61
Morgan Lewis Mill: 173–174
Mt. Hillaby: 179
Museum: 146–147
Music: 64–71
National Independence Festival of the Creative Arts: 77
North Point: 195–196
O'Neal, Charles Duncan: 24–25
Obeah: 58
Oistins Fish Festival: 76
Oistins: 223–224
Oughterson Zoo Park: 212
Package tours: 87
Painters: 73
Parish system: 31
Parliament: 30, 131–132
Pelican Village: 139–140
Photography: 114

Index

Pico Teneriffe: 197, 198, 206
Platinum Coast: 153–161
Political parties: 32
Politics: 30–33
Population: 41–42
Prescod, Samuel Jackman: 23
Pudding and souse: 79–80
Queen's Park: 135–136
Rastafarians: 61–63
Redlegs: 43
Reggae: 65–66
Reptiles: 14
River Bay: 196
Rockley: 222–223
Roti: 79
Rum: 82–84
Sailing: 104
Saint Lucy: 193–198
Saint Peter: 179–183
Sam Lord's Castle: 214–216, 219
Sandy Lane Hotel: 153–154
Scuba: 101–102
Sea eggs: 79
Sealife: 14–16
Selassie, Haile: 61
Senate: 30, 131–132
Shopping: 119–122, 150
Snorkeling: 101–102
Speightstown: 179–192
Sports: 101–109
St. Nicholas Abbey: 189
St. Andrew: 173–177
St. George: 199–203
St. John, H. Bernard "Bree": 32
St. John: 205–210
St. Joseph: 167–172
St. Lawrence Gap: 223
St. Michael's Cathedral: 134–135
St. Philip: 211–220
St. Thomas: 163–165
Steel band: 66
Stew food: 80
Sugarcane: 36–37
Sunbury House: 211, 220
Surfing: 102
Swimming: 101
Taxis: 89–90
Temple Yard: 138
Tennis: 104
The Landship: 47–48
Theater: 71–72
Theft: 116
Tie Heads: 63–64
Tourism: 35
Tourist offices: 116, 123
Tours: 93–95
Trafalgar Square: 127–128
Transportation: 86–95
Trees: 8–9, 10
Tuk bands: 66
Turner Hall Woods: 176
University of the West Indies: 140
Vegetables: 80–81
Vegetarian dining: 118–119
Villa Nova: 208–209
Visas: 109–110
Wailers, the: 65
Welchman's Hall Gully: 165
West Indian National Party: 26
West Indies Federation: 27–28
What to take: 114–115
Worthing: 223

ADDITIONAL READING

Additional Adventure Travel Books and Tour Guides from Hunter Publishing

THE OTHER PUERTO RICO
by Kathryn Robinson
Escaping the tourists and the crowds, this guide shows you where to find the secret beaches, unspoiled valleys, jungles and mountains of the island. Aimed at the traveller interested in outdoor adventures, each chapter explores a separate route: down the Espiritu Santo River; the Long Trails of El Yunque; beaches and birds in Guanica; tramping on Mona; scrambling through San Cristobal; on the track of history; the heart of coffee country; Vieques by bike; and many others. Photos throughout, plus a fold-out map.
6" x 9" paperback / 160 pp. / $11.95

THE ADVENTURE GUIDE TO PUERTO RICO
by Harry S. Pariser
The best all-around guide to the island. History, people & culture, plus what to see, where to stay, where to dine. All color, with maps.
5³/₈" x 8" paperback / 224 pp. / $13.95

JAMAICA: A VISITOR'S GUIDE
by Harry S. Pariser
Newest guide to the island. History, culture and politics of Jamaica as backdrop to what you will find today. Complete what-to-see information, plus hotels and the best eating places. All color, with maps.
5³/₈" x 8" paperback / 320 pp. / $15.95

THE ADVENTURE GUIDE TO THE VIRGIN ISLANDS
by Harry S. Pariser
The most up-to-date, comprehensive, and colorful guide to both the American and British Virgins—celebrated for their incredible beauty since Columbus first discovered and named the islands in 1493. From St. Croix, St. John, and St. Thomas, to Tortola, Virgin Gorda, and Anegada, all of the islands are covered in depth. Maps of every island and town are included, with historical sections, complete sightseeing details, where to find the best food, and extensive information about hotels in all price ranges—from posh resorts to intimate guesthouses. Whether you are seeking the best walking trails at Cinnamon Bay, a good drugstore in Frederiksted, or a pay telephone on Tortola, this guide will show you the way.
5³/₈" x 8" paperback / 224 pp. / maps and color photos throughout / $13.95

MACMILLAN CARIBBEAN GUIDES
  ANTIGUA/BARBUDA $11.95
  BAHAMAS $13.95
  CUBA $17.95
  CURACAO $6.95
  GRANADA $11.95
  BERMUDA $12.95
  SINT MAARTEN/SAINT MARTIN, SAINT-BARTHELEMY, ANGUILLA, SABA, SINT EUSTATIUS $10.95
  TRINIDAD & TOBAGO $12.95
  NEVIS $10.95
  SAINT LUCIA $6.95
  ST. KITTS $11.95
  BRITISH VIRGIN ISLANDS $11.95
  These are comprehensive full-color guides, with practical information, walking tours, history, culture, flora & fauna, even the cuisine of each island detailed.
  5 1/2" x 8 1/2" paperbacks / 96–288 pp.

VIDEO VISITS
  BAHAMAS
  PUERTO RICO/VIRGIN ISLANDS
  JAMAICA
  THE CARIBBEAN
  These 50-minute video guides take you there in a way no guidebook can. Each is a complete sight-seeing tour. Programs have won top honors for excellence and educational value. *$24.95 each*

The above books and maps can be found at the best bookstores or you can order directly. Send your check (add $2.50 to cover postage and handling) to:
HUNTER PUBLISHING, INC.
300 RARITAN CENTER PARKWAY
EDISON NJ 08818

Write or call (201) 225-1900 for our free color catalog describing these and many other travel guides and maps to virtually every destination on earth.